CW00725326

THE GOLDEN JUNCTION

THE GOLDEN JUNCTION

Episodes in Alexandra's History

John McCraw

Square One Press

P. O. Box 2143, Dunedin, New Zealand
www.book.co.nz

THE GOLDEN JUNCTION . . . Copyright © John McCraw, 2002. All rights reserved. No part of this book may be used or reproduced in any manner whatsoever by any person or in any publication, or by any educational or instructive institution, by means of photocopy, stencilling, printing, magnetic or digital reproduction; audio and/or visual; or on the Internet without written permission except in the case of quotations embodied in critical articles and reviews. For further information address Square One Press, P. O. Box 2143, Dunedin, New Zealand.

Books by the same author
The Siren's Call
Mine Fire
Dunedin Holocaust
Coastmaster
Mountain Water and River Gold
Harbour Horror

Published by Square One Press, P. O. Box 2143, Dunedin, New Zealand. Phone 03 455-3117, Fax: 03 456 1053
Email: treeves@es.co.nz

ISBN 0 908562 38 1

Internet catalogue:
The Book Company of New Zealand:
http://www.book.co.nz

Book Design, Trevor Reeves.
Cover Ilustration, Judith Wolfe. (arts site: www.arts.org.nz)

Produced by Mediaprint Services Limited,
P. O. Box 2143, Dunedin, New Zealand.
Printed by Otago University Print, Dunedin.

CONTENTS

Comparison of Currency

Sums of money mentioned throughout this book have little relevance to modern values. One method of comparison is to convert the old value to the equivalent weight in gold. As gold was worth £3 17s. 6d. (£3.875) an ounce for much of the latter half of the Nineteenth Century, division of the sum of money by 3.875 will give its worth in ounces of gold. Multiplying the result by 600 (the value of an ounce of gold at present is $NZ600) gives some indication of the equivalent in today's currency. Using this method comparative values are:

Old Currency	Modern Currency ($NZ)
1s. (one shilling)	$8
2s. 6d (half a crown)	$20
£1 (one pound= 20 shillings)	$160
£3 17s. 6d. (value of one ounce of gold)	$600
£100	$16,000
£1,000	£160,000

Comparison of Weights

The **Troy** system of weight was used for weighing gold and the **Avoirdupois** system for weighing general goods.

Troy   **Metric**

1 grain		=	0.064 grams
24 grains (gr)	= 1 pennyweight (dwt) =		1.5 grams
20 pennyweights	= 1 ounce (oz)	=	31.1 grams
12 ounces	= 1 pound (lb)	=	373.2 grams

Avoirdupois

1 ounce (oz)		=	28.35 grams
16 ounces	= 1 pound (lb)	=	453.6 grams
112 lbs	= 1 hundredweight (cwt)	=	50.8 kilograms

PREFACE

The Golden Junction is a collection of essays about significant episodes in the history of the Central Otago town of Alexandra over its first 100 years. The book is the second in a three-part series dealing with the history of the Alexandra district. *Mountain Water and River Gold*, the first in the series, dealt with the history of gold mining activities, and the battles to obtain the necessary water, in various localities close to Alexandra. The third, as yet unnamed, will look at the gold mining activities in the outlying districts such as Campbells Creek, Fraser River, Fruitlands, Little Valley, Waikerikeri Valley and 'The West Bank of the Molyneux. It will also have essays on coal mining at Dairy Creek, dredging, Clyde water supply and Feraud's battle to obtain irrigation water for his farm and market garden.

Alexandra is a busy modern town. With a population of about 5,000, it is not yet very large, but with its low rainfall, crisp winters and hot summers, it offers a pleasant life-style especially attractive to those seeking an alternative to city life. The towns serves, thanks to irrigation, a district of flourishing orchards and fat-lamb farms, with an increasing number of vineyards. In spite of recent temporary set-backs owing to flooding, Alexandra enjoys continuing prosperity. But it was not always so.

Founded during the Gold Rush of 1862, the settlement became established and grew because of its location at the junction of two large rivers. Roads from several directions converged on the settlement, where from the earliest days, boats, then punts, and finally bridges, allowed the rivers to be crossed. As the more readily obtained gold became exhausted, however, the town declined and almost joined the other ghost towns of the goldfields whose locations are now barely recognisable. It was saved in the nick of time by the enterprise of several local citizens who bought second-hand steam gold dredges, and set them up on the Clutha River between Alexandra and Clyde. Others followed, and Alexandra became the centre of gold dredging, not only for Central Otago, but for New Zealand, and, indeed, for the world.

Alexandra became a boom town. At the beginning of the twentieth century there were not only large numbers of men manning the 30 or 40 dredges within a 15 kilometre radius of the town, but there were scores of others supplying logistical support. Among these were coal miners; those carting the coal to the dredges; those supplying accommodation and entertainment, and those working in a large engineering works which repaired and made parts for the dredges. The population attained a level that was not to be reached again until after the Second World War.

Just as the gold dredging began to decline, the railway reached the town, giving a tremendous boost to a promising fruitgrowing industry that had been struggling through lack of markets. With the railway providing easy transport to the cities, fruitgrowing expanded rapidly. For a time, it seemed that the industry might be dominated by large orchard schemes set up by city businessmen looking for fresh investment opportunities to replace those which had been offered by gold dredging. By and large, these large corporate enterprises were unsuccessful and the strength of the fruitgrowing industry remained with moderate-sized family orchards.

Mining did not die without a struggle and the period before the First World War was marked by battles between mining and fruitgrowing interests, not only over the use of land, but also the use of the all-important water. Gradually, however, people came to realise that the future of the district, and the town, lay not with one-crop gold mining, but with sustainable agriculture and horticulture. Step by step the rules were changed to allow more water to be shared between mining and irrigation, until finally, irrigation became the dominant use of water.

It was during, and immediately after, the Second World War that Alexandra became popular as a holiday and retirement venue. With the increasing population, Government Departments and branches of city firms moved in, and the town became the administrative centre of inland Otago.

Interest in the fascinating history of Central Otago is growing apace and many people have traced their ancestry to gold-mining forebears. Newcomers are increasingly curious about the unique landscape, the scars of early gold mining that are readily visible and the old buildings and structures connected with the early days of the town.

ACKNOWLEDGEMENTS

Thanks are due to the University of Waikato, particularly the Department of Earth Sciences and Campus Photography, for steady support over the years. I am especially grateful to the staff of the Interloan Department of the University Library for their patience over many years in arranging a constant supply of reels of microfilm of the early Central Otago newspapers.

Many of the older issues of goldfields newspapers, not yet microfilmed, were consulted in the Hocken library. The knowledge and cooperation, far beyond the call of duty, of the then Reference Librarian, the late David McDonald, is gratefully acknowledged. His death is a grievous loss to all those interested in the history of Otago.

Some of the Minute books of the Alexandra Borough Council are, unfortunately, missing, as is much of the Borough Council correspondence, including the documents and drawings associated with various engineering works. Marie Waldron, one-time assistant in the Borough Council office and latterly Librarian of the Alexandra Public Library, has been most helpful in searching for missing material.

Many Alexandra and Clyde people who contributed material are no longer with us — the late Glad. McArthur, Geoff. and Alex. Taylor, George Govan and Rowland Lopdell. Others were recorded on early tapes, thanks to the New Zealand Broadcasting Service and to Les Thomson of Alexandra. Others who have provided information or logistical support include Ernie King, David Blewett, Graeme Anderson, Jerry Sanders, John and Betty Wilson, Les Mathias, George Elder and Mrs Noel Watts.

Former managers of Alexandra's William Bodkin Museum, Helena Heydelaar and Cheryl Grubb, and the present Manager, Elaine Gough, have been very generous with information and in allowing photographs from the extensive Museum collection to be copied. The members of the Alexandra Historical Society have been most helpful and in particular Joan Stevens has spent much time in obtaining information and in trying to find answers to difficult questions.

Finally grateful acknowledgment is made to Dr David McCraw for field companionship, field assistance and editing and to Jean King for skilled proof reading.

ILLUSTRATIONS

Most of the photographs are from the author's collection and have been taken over many years, some from the mid-1940s. Almost all of the historic photographs are from the extensive and well-catalogued collections of the William Bodkin Museum at Alexandra. Some figures are from other sources:-

Alexandra Turnbull Library—2.1, 3.1; *New Zealand Mines Record:*—9.1, 9.4, 9.5, 9.7, 9.8. 9.10, 17.4; *Hocken Library*— 10.2, 10.3, 10.4, 10.5; 14.9; Mrs K. Croy—13.3, 18.5; *Otago Witness*—11.10, 15.1; Mrs Betty Wilson— 11.11; Clyde Museum—8.7; 15.4; *Cyclopedia of New Zealand*—12.6; Alexandra Public Library—17.2; J. Shepherd— 9.12.

Several people provided material for photographs. These include:-

Mrs Chapman of Earnscleugh (Theyers & Beck bottle) Figure 8.4

Winston Sorenson of Hamilton. (Merryweather catalogue) Figures 6.1, 6.3

Mrs Noel Watts of Cambridge. (Lord Lock's locket) Figure 7.3

Most of the air photographs were taken from a plane ably piloted by Norman McPherson of Clyde.

1.

RUSH TO

THE DUNSTAN

" Listen to this, will you!" Bearded men jumped up on wagons to read out the startling news. Two prospectors, they read, Horatio Hartley and Christopher Reilly, had last Friday, dumped 87 pounds weight of gold on the counter of Dunedin's Gold Receiver. With the promise of a £2,000 reward, they had disclosed that it came from a gorge where the Molyneux River[1] cut through the Dunstan Mountains.

The usual crowd had gathered for the arrival of the evening coach at the mining settlement of Gabriels Gully,[2] to meet newcomers and to hear the latest news. Now the excited miners quickly dispersed, and lights were soon flickering in tents throughout the Gully as men began to pack up their gear ready for leaving at first light. The report had said that the discovery was far away in the interior, but where precisely, no one at Gabriels Gully knew.

What the miners of Gabriels Gully did know, however, was that they were more than 100 kilometres closer to the discovery than was Dunedin, and so had perhaps two days' advantage over the hordes of gold seekers who would be already on their way from the town. The early morning of August 19, 1862 saw the greater portion of the population of Gabriels Gully taking part in that peculiarity of human behaviour, a Gold Rush. Undeterred by newspaper warnings that miners would have to be self-contained, as provisions were scarce or non-existent in the hinterland, the horde set out for the new El Dorado in the interior. Within days the Gully was virtually deserted.[3]

They started out as an enthusiastic crowd of perhaps 2,000. Almost all were men, as this was not regarded as a journey suitable for women. An exception was Mrs Sarah Cameron who, with her three young children, accompanied her husband, Lewis, on the Rush. Two toddlers were carried in boxes, one on each side of their horse, while the five-year-old walked. They were helped greatly on the journey by other miners, particularly the Holt brothers. Mrs Cameron, almost certainly the first woman on the Dunstan Goldfield, later became the well-known and highly respected owner of the Caledonian Hotel in Alexandra.

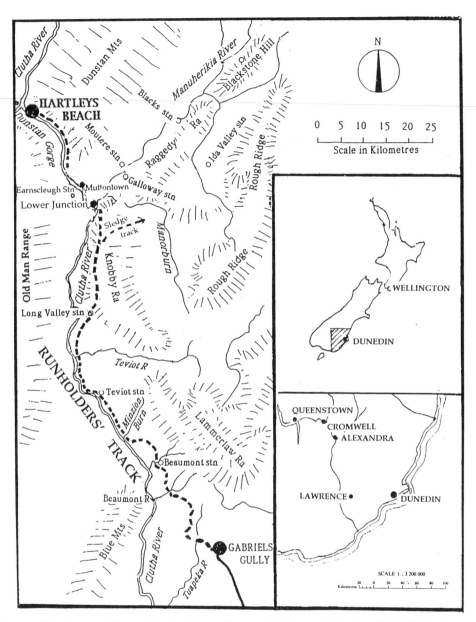

Figure 1.1. Route followed by foot travellers and riders during the Gold Rush from Gabriels Gully to Hartleys Beach in the Dunstan Gorge.

The gold-seekers were all young men, mainly in their 20s and early 30s, who looked older because of the universal beards. They were dressed in the mining 'uniform' of moleskin trousers, often with bowyangs tied below the knees, woollen jacket and peaked hat. A few fortunate ones had horses but most had to carry their worldly goods on their backs. Perhaps a small tent or at the very least a bedroll, shovel, axe, mining dish and billy dangling

13

behind or carried by hand, were the essentials. Any spare space was taken up with food. Food was a major problem. With the weight of mining tools, little food could be carried. Many miners arrived at the Dunstan Gorge with their food exhausted, and had to immediately turn round and force-march back to the nearest source of supplies.

Figure 1.2. At Evans Flat traces of the old track from Gabriels to the Dunstan can be seen below and to the right of the prominent trees on the hillside.

The Runholders' Track

A track of sorts already led up the Molyneux (Clutha) Valley. It had been marked out by the sledges of the runholders taking in supplies to their interior sheep stations, and by mobs of sheep going in the same direction. It was this track that the miners intended to follow. From Gabriels Gully they crossed over the ridge to Munros Gully and followed down the Tuapeka River to Evans Flat. Here they joined the runholders' track as it left the valley and climbed steeply to reach the leading ridge, which it followed for about 12 kilometres to the Beaumont River.

After crossing on a sapling bridge, the travellers were immediately faced with an hour or more of very steep climbing up the slippery, narrow ridge appropriately named 'Devils Backbone.' Once this was negotiated, easier ridges were followed to Gardiner's Beaumont Station on the Talla Burn. A natural bridge, formed by large boulders which had collapsed into a narrow defile, made this stream crossing easy, but the exhausted miners were glad to camp, or shelter as best they could, around the station. Next morning they crossed the Frind Burn and then turned down a long spur to the junction of the Minzion Burn with the Clutha River.

14

Figure 1.3. The so-called 'Devils Backbone,' The track up the steep, slippery ridge was a difficult section for those with horses.

Now the going was easier. For a long distance the track was along reasonably level river terraces. It passed Miller's Oven Hill Station on what was later to be called Millers Flat. At the top end of this flat, an awkward kilometre or so along a very narrow shelf above the river brought the track to Cargill and Anderson's big Teviot Station, another camping spot.

Upstream from this station, the path, squeezed between the river and a rock face, had to find its way through a maze of huge rocks that had fallen from the overhanging cliff. Progress involved some hand as well as foot work, and at one place meant squeezing into and out of a rock hollowed out like an inverted bowl. Those with horses, or those not prepared to face the acrobatics required to make use of the route along the river bank, had to bypass this stretch by climbing up the hillside for several hundred metres and then following down the Teviot River to its mouth. On the final stages of this section the track zigzagged down an almost vertical rock face.

Figure 1.4. Just below the junction of the Teviot River the track followed a narrow ledge between a rocky bluff (centre) and the river.

The going was made even more dangerous by the strong and erratic gusts of wind which blew up the face from the gorge below.

Crossing the Teviot River

Whichever route was followed, the already-weary traveller was now faced with the prospect of crossing the Teviot River which came boiling out of its gorge and crashing over large boulders on its way to join the Clutha River a few metres below.

Before its headwaters were dammed and its water drawn off for hydroelectric and irrigation requirements, this stream was a broad and rapid torrent, dangerous to cross on horseback, let alone on foot. Various stratagems were adopted. Some miners worked their way over clinging to a rope that had been flung across and anchored on the far side by some brave soul. Several were swept away and counted themselves fortunate to be washed ashore with the loss of only their gear. Others went further upstream and managed to find convenient rocks that would allow them to jump across. After rain the river was an impassable 40 metres in width and travellers had to wait on the banks, sometimes for days, until the flood abated.[4]

Once across the Teviot River the track led across the broad flats of Roxburgh East, and then up into the hills to Captain Baldwin's Long Valley Station (now known as Baldwyn Station). By this time food was running short and pleas and demands were made on the station for supplies. Kinross, the manager, sold what flour and other stores he had, but he had no hope of satisfying the hungry mob. There was a report[5] that an attempt was made by the miners to 'rush' the house and take whatever they wanted but this was discouraged by Kinross, who dealt out the remaining flour by the pannikin-full with one hand while holding a double-barrelled shotgun with the other. It wasn't until sheep were slaughtered and the meat boiled in a large-scale cooking operation that he was able to quieten the clamour.

Figure 1.5. The Teviot River, with much water diverted for irrigation, is no longer the large, swift stream that the miners found dangerous to cross.

Over the Knobby Range
A long climb, following a fairly well defined track through open tussock land, brought the miners to the summit of the Knobby Range some 1,000 metres above sea level.

There were still large patches of snow on the dark faces and a bitter wind swept down from the 'Snowy Mountains,' later to be called the Old Man Range. Those forced to camp out on this stretch were miserably cold in their small tents or lying under some overhanging rock. Nevertheless, the going was fairly easy along the broad summit ridge, although the wet peaty soils around the head of Shanty Creek were soon cut up into quagmire. In other places it was hard to pick up the track amongst the tall tussocks.

Figure 1.6. It was a long climb to the 900 metre summit of the Knobby Range. The patch of trees, (centre, extreme right edge) marks the former Long Valley Station.

Near Cairnhill the crowd left the run-holders' track, which bore away to the right towards the Manor Burn. They then made their own way straight along the leading ridge until they were brought up short by a precipitous slope which fell away towards a picturesque river junction far below. Obsessed though they were with pushing on with all speed, even the most dedicated gold seekers could hardly fail to notice the vast panorama that had opened out in front of them.

The Lie of the Land
They were looking out over the Manuherikia Valley, one of a number of large parallel valleys that are a feature of Central Otago. This roughly rectangular valley, some 60 kilometres long and 10 kilometres wide, is enclosed on all sides by mountain ranges. The rocky promontory on which the miners were standing is part of the line of hills which includes the Knobby Range, the Raggedy Range and Blackstone Hill, which make up the south-eastern side of the valley. Opposite the miners' viewpoint the Dunstan Mountains, with the distinctive Leaning Rock on the skyline, forms the north-western side of the valley. Far away to the north-east, the

long even wall of the snow-capped Hawkdun Range cuts right across the head of the valley, and the 1,800 metre high Old Man Range,[6] named from the tall rock monolith standing out conspicuously on the snowy summit, closes off the lower end .

It would be the Clutha River itself, though, that would attract most attention. Emerging from a gap in the Dunstan Mountains, it flows southwards across the valley floor in a series of sinuous curves, entrenched some 30 metres below the surface of an extensive alluvial plain. Directly below the viewpoint of our resting miners, the Clutha is joined by the Manuherikia River just before leaving the valley by way of a spectacular, narrow rocky gorge.

No doubt much of this impressive view was taken in at a glance by those eager to push on, and all eyes quickly turned to the great gap in the Dunstan Mountains just to the left of the Leaning Rock. It was the gorge of the Clutha River — the Dunstan Gorge they had come so far to reach. Somewhere in that gorge was Hartley's beach where the partners had garnered a fortune a few weeks before. But first the tired miners had to face the very steep descent to the Manuherikia River. Especially for those with horses, this was a difficult section of the journey. Once this obstacle was overcome, a few more metres saw the weary men emerge on to the sandy flat at the junction of the rivers.

Figure 1.7. There was still much snow on the bleak summit ridge of the Knobby Range when the Dunstan Rush passed this way in August 1862.

The miners no doubt noted a number of shallow pits here and there on the flat, but they would not know of the excitement and subsequent disappointment represented by these excavations. Henry Stebbing and his party had been sent out by the Provincial Government on an official gold-prospecting expedition, and they had found payable gold in these holes only a week or so before the arrival of the Rush.

Excitedly they had packed up and set off down the river intending to convey the good news to Major Croker, the Commissioner at Gabriels Gully, and claim a reward for the discovery of a new goldfield. They were not to know that while they were struggling down the rough gorges, two other prospectors were explaining to Vincent Pyke, the Secretary of the Goldfields Department in Dunedin, details of the location of another momentous gold strike. The same day that the bedraggled Stebbing and his men arrived at the Commissioner's Office, the newspapers brought the stunning news of Hartley and Reilly's success. Stebbing and his disappointed lads received a 'Prospectors claim' (double the usual size) on the flat where they had made their discovery. It is still known as Prospectors Point.

Some of our travellers chose to camp for the night at Prospectors Point before attempting the river crossing, but others preferred to cross at once. At its mouth the depth of the Manuherikia River is largely controlled by the level of the much larger Clutha River, and would normally be too deep to cross without swimming. However, at the end of winter 1862 the big river was abnormally low and it was just possible to wade across the tributary.

Some of those who scrambled across the river camped on a narrow, low terrace[7] at the fork between the two rivers but others, impatient to peg out claims in the gorge, scrambled up the high bank behind the terrace and

Figure 1.8. The Dunstan (Cromwell), seen from the Knobby Range, lies between the Dunstan Mountains on the right and Cairnmuir Hill on the left. Fog blankets the Clutha River in this early morning photograph. The snow-covered Pisa Range is visible through the gorge.

rushed off into the gathering darkness towards the scene of the gold strike some 30 kilometres away.

The narrow terrace, which was part of the flood plain that lay along both sides of the Clutha River, was a good camp site. There was ample scrub for warming fires, and river water for the billy was only two or three metres down the bank. For most, the camp was just a brief resting place before beginning the last stage of their journey to the diggings, but some who had already found gold in the nearby beach sands, decided to stay on.

It was soon very obvious that the total area of the beaches in the Dunstan Gorge was insufficient to provide claims for the several thousands of miners who arrived over the next few days. Many were forced to try their luck elsewhere. A number came back to the junction of the Manuherikia and Clutha Rivers. Here they began working the sands of the wide beaches exposed by the very low level of the rivers. Soon the little terrace was once more dotted with tents.

A report,[8] written on 11 September 1862 for the *Otago Daily Times* by 'Our Special Correspondent' mentioned that two small townships had grown. One was at Coal Point (the site of Clyde) and the other 3 kilometres lower down the river at Muttontown,[9] where Moutere and Earnscleugh Stations were slaughtering sheep for the miners. Apparently the collections of tents at the junction was not yet regarded as a township.

In mid-September, barely a month after the arrival of the Rush, the Clutha River began to rise. A warm north-west wind was melting the snow on the mountains in the headwaters. The beach claims along the river were flooded and the miners forced to seek gold elsewhere. Fortunately the Manuherikia River did not flood, and as miners swarmed over its beaches, the population of the junction camp increased rapidly.

Once wagons arrived with supplies, a store and the inevitable grog-shop were set up, and a settlement took shape. Space was soon at a premium on the narrow riverside terrace, especially as more permanent businesses began to arrange themselves in an untidy gaggle along the muddy path which passed as a street. The calico structures on the low side practically overhung the water, whereas those on the inner side of the track were hard up against the high bank behind. Newcomers had to climb this bank and camp on the extensive higher plain that stretched between the two rivers — where the town of Alexandra would eventually be established. Here another rough street was soon formed at right angles to that on the lower terrace. So almost from the beginning the town was divided into two parts — one part on the low terrace close to the river and another part on the higher terrace.

On this higher level, canvas stores and hotels appeared and marked the transition from a camp to a township. It was at first referred to as the 'Lower Township' to distinguish it from the 'Upper Township' (now Clyde) established at the mouth of the Dunstan Gorge. Sometimes it was called the 'Lower Junction,' but newspaper dispatches sent to the Dunedin newspapers were invariably headed 'Manuherikia.' In mid-1863 the place was to be formally named 'Alexandra.'

It was the discovery of payable gold in the Manuherikia River, followed by

21

the fabulous riches of Conroys Gully in early October, that doubtless led to the establishment of a township at the junction. Almost immediately there was a demand for ferries across the Clutha and Manuherikia Rivers and when these were later provided, the junction became a very busy place. As more and more wagons came through and the population increased in the neighbouring diggings of Conroys Gully, Butchers Gully and Manorburn Flat, so also did the township grow.

NOTES

1. Now the Clutha River.
2. Gabriels Gully is close to the present town of Lawrence. Gold was discovered here in July 1861 by Gabriel Read and led to the establishment of the Tuapeka Goldfield — the first successful goldfield in Otago.
3. When Gabriel Read passed through. *Otago Daily Times* 18 September 1862.
4. By mid-1863 the Provincial Government had constructed a rough causeway of large, slippery and unstable boulders across the river, and this was of considerable help although it took only a moderate rise in the river to put it 45 cm under water. *Otago Daily Times* 10 July 1863.
5. *Otago Daily Times* 6 September 1862.
6. This 25 metre high rock is a distinctive landmark in Central Otago and can be seen from great distances. It is officially called the 'Obelisk' but is almost always referred to in Central Otago as the 'Old Man Rock.' By extension the range became known locally as the 'Old Man' Range, but officially only the part south of the Obelisk was so named. Presumably to complement the Old Man Rock, a prominent high point on the Dunstan Mountains, Leaning Rock, is locally referred to as the 'Old Woman Rock' and the mountains as the 'Old Woman Range' — a confusing usage as there is an officially named Old Woman Range west of the Old Man Range.
7. The narrow terrace was a remnant of the flood plain of the river, a fact that was discovered the hard way. Buildings erected along the lower street were flooded each time the river rose and in 1866 the street was abandoned.
8. *Otago Daily Times* 18 September 1862. Although this report was headed 'Manuherikia' the correspondent was writing from Shennan's Moutere Station 10 kilometres up the Manuherikia River.
9. The name of this locality has been spelt in various ways but here the modern version for localities ending in 'town' is used. The exact location of this temporary township is uncertain. It is given (*Otago Daily Times* 18 September 1862) as 'two miles lower down the river' from Coal Point (Clyde). This would place it near the mouth of the entrenched course of Waikerikeri Creek which is still known as 'Muttontown Gully.' Infomap 260-G42 shows the locality as on Springvale Road. This is almost certainly an error.

2.

A TOUCH OF IRELAND

— Streets of the Town

Patrick Lysaght paused, as most travellers did when they came to the viewpoint on the Knobby Range track, and were confronted with the magnificent panorama of the Manuherikia Valley before them. But Lysaght did more than admire the view — he made a sketch of the scene below.[1] Drawn in December 1862, it gives us our first view of the bustling little township at the junction of the rivers. We can easily identify the main geographic features, including the various outcrops of rock which were a feature of the business area of the town. More importantly, we have a clear view of the two streets. One, already beginning to be regarded as the main street, runs almost due north and points towards the distant Leaning Rock. The other, at right angles, hugs the riverbank.

No one officially named these streets. The one along the river bank, was simply called 'Lower Street' or 'Low Street,' although there is one reference to it as 'Water Street.' The main thoroughfare on the higher terrace was called 'Broad Street,' or 'Broadway.' Later another street, running at right angles, connected Broad Street to the police camp, and as this was parallel with Lower Street, but at a much higher level, it was called 'Upper Street' or 'Victoria Street.' A short street in front of the police camp was, not unnaturally, called 'Camp Street.' Later a street was formed from Upper Street down to the ferry which was soon crossing the Clutha River, and it too, was easy to name as 'Ferry Street.'

Another traveller, pausing at the same spot as Lysaght on the Knobby Range track in March, 1863, has left us a description of the town:[2]

A very pretty sight is the Lower Dunstan township, when viewed from the overhanging crags. Perched on a high bank at the confluence of the Manuherikia and Molyneux Rivers, with rugged black rocks jutting out around and the open plain at the rear — rows of tents decorated with flaunting banners, forming a half square — a few vagrant stores straggling down to the water's edge, and some on the opposite side, where they seem to have wandered in a state of somnambulism, and to have settled down from sheer inability to get back again — the impromptu city looks like one of those stage scenes which cheat the senses by their unsubstantial

Figure 2.1. Manuherikia (Alexandra) township from the Teviot track, (Lysaght, December 1862). The wide street is Broad (later Tarbert) Street with the track to Dunstan (Clyde) leading off diagonally to the left. A crowd of tents marks Lower Street. Dunstan Gorge in the background.

mockery.

But this same traveller also made a prediction:

> The Junction will be a thriving township when some others, more legitimately ushered into existence, will only be heard of at the Crown Land Office.

The Site

What were the special factors that encouraged this confident prediction? They were surely to do with location. The confluence forms a Y-shape with the Manuherikia River flowing in from the east, represented by the right arm of the Y, and the Clutha River by the left arm and the stem. The area between the arms is the lower end of Dunstan Flat, and was to be the site of the future town of Alexandra. A gold mining township located at the junction of two rivers, becomes the provider of supplies and entertainment for the large number of miners working on the beaches of the two rivers. But the junction was also the point where the busy track from Gabriels Gully crossed the Manuherikia River and, within a short time, boats were available for crossing the Clutha River also. This meant that the township became the main starting point and supply base for miners working in the rich gullies along the Old Man Range.

The most striking feature of the area between the rivers was a high ridge

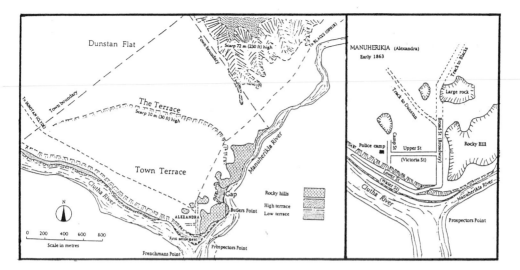

Figure 2.2. Early Alexandra and vicinity.
　　Left: The main township was quickly established on the 'Town Terrace'. A terrace scarp, cutting across the plain north of the township, separates a higher level. It is still referred to as 'The Terrace.' Further north, another much higher terrace (top right) forms a backdrop to the town. A discontinuous line of rocky hills runs along the north-western bank of the Manuherikia River.
　　Right: Manuherikia township in early 1863.

of schist rock lying along the eastern side. Isolated masses of rock, emerging through the otherwise fairly level surface of the gravel terrace, show where spurs, running down from the ridge, have been partly buried by river gravel. These large rock masses formed a rough curve that seemed to embrace the settlement, and confine it to a very restricted area between the rocky hill and the riverbank. In fact, 30 years later there were still fewer than a dozen houses out on the wide open flat plain beyond the rocks.

This plain stretched away northwards, but about a kilometre beyond the rocks it was broken by a terrace scarp, about 10 metres high, which curved across the flat from the banks of the Clutha River to the rocky ridge in the east. It became known as 'the terrace' and the name is perpetuated today in 'Royal Terrace,' a street which runs along the top of the scarp.

Beyond the terrace the alluvial plain, soon to be known as Dunstan Flat, lay between the banks of the Clutha River and the impressive 75 metre-high scarp of the even higher terrace which forms a backdrop to the town.

The Town Survey
It was only six months after the discovery of gold that the Provincial Government decided to survey and lay out the town. But the Survey Office was so pressed with work that the private firm of Connell and Moodie was hired to survey Manuherikia and other goldfields towns. The survey was

done in March 1863 by J. A. Connell and the resulting map published in August, by which time it had been decided that the township should be known as 'Alexandra.'[3]

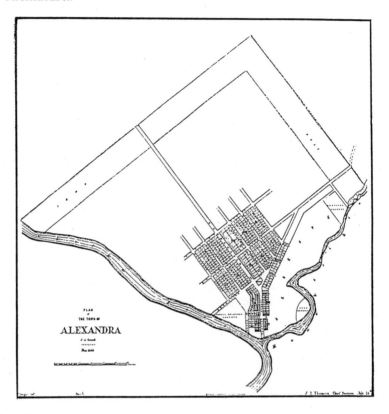

Figure 2.3. Connell's survey of March 1863. The boundaries of the town, with the Town Belt, were set out and part of the town was subdivided into blocks and sections.

Connell first defined the boundaries of his proposed town. From a point on the bank of the Clutha River 110 chains (2.22 km) above the junction he surveyed a line 119 chains (2.39 km) in a north-easterly direction until it reached the foot of the high terrace. He then struck off another line, at right angles to the first, 76 chains (1.53 km) long which met the Manuherikia River 88 chains (1.77 km) above the junction. He then designated a 10 chain (200 m) wide 'town belt' inside the two boundaries he had delineated. The area of the block of land within Connell's boundaries amounted to 840 acres (340 hectares).

Connell then proceeded to divide the part of his town nearest the river junction into 15 blocks. Most of these were subdivided into quarter acre (1,012 square metres) sections, except in the 'business area' where the sections were made smaller. In the 16 streets he set out, he preserved only three of those already existing. He dispensed with the local names for the existing streets and renamed them, along with the new streets he created, after localities in Ireland. The streets existing at the time of the survey were renamed as follows:

Broad St became **Tarbert St**
Camp St became **Ennis St**
Upper or Victoria St became **Limerick St**

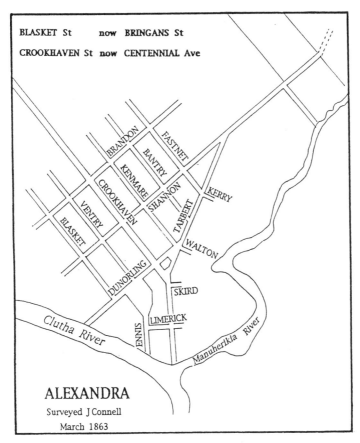

Figure 2.4. Streets set out and named by J. Connell during the first survey in 1863.

The full list of streets named by Connell, with some notes about the localities after which they were named, is:

Bantry St: Bantry is a market town in County Cork about 100 kilometres south-west of Cork. Population over 3,000.

Blasket St: (renamed Bringans St after a Mayor): The Blasket Islands lie off Slea Head, the north head of Dingle Bay. Great Blasket Island is separated from Slea Head by Blasket Sound.

Brandon St: Brandon is a village with a population of about 200 on Brandon Bay in County Kerry. Nearby are Brandon Mountain (938 m) and Brandon Point.

Crookhaven St: (renamed Centennial Avenue in 1940): A narrow inlet in Roaringwater Bay in County Cork. A small hamlet of the same name lies on the ocean side of the narrow peninsula separating the inlet from the bay.

Deel St: The Deel River flows north to the Shannon Estuary in County Limerick.

Dunorling St: No trace of this name can be found in Ireland. It may be the name of an estate or the word may be misspelt — a possibility is 'Dunirling ' which means 'beautiful fort.'

Ennis St: A town with a population of about 6,000 north of the Shannon River in County Clare. It is 40 kilometres north-west of Limerick and has a well-known Abbey.

Fastnet St: Fastnet Rock lies 6 kilometres off the south coast of Ireland near Cape Clear.

Limerick St: A city about 100 kilometres north of Cork.

Kenmare St: A small town in County Kerry with a population of just over 1,000, lying at the head of the estuary of the Kenmare River. It is known for its production of lace.

Kerry St: A county in the south-western part of Ireland.

Shannon St: Named after the longest river in Ireland which rises in the lakes of Northern Ireland and flows south-west for 370 kilometres to Shannon Bay .

Skird St: No trace of this name can be found in Ireland.

Tarbert St: A village (population 350) on the southern shore of the Shannon Estuary. The estuary narrows nearby to form the Tarbert Race.

Ventry St: A hamlet on Ventry Harbour on the north side of Dingle Bay 6 kilometres from Dingle. The combined parish and hamlet have a population of less than 1,000.

Walton St: No trace of this name can be found in Ireland.

All of these names, with the exception of 'Ennis' which is in nearby County Clare, are from **Counties Cork Kerry and Limerick** in the south-western part of Ireland. So we can be fairly sure than Mr Connell, the surveyor, came from Ireland and we can surmise that he lived in, or was familiar with, the south-west. But why he picked on mainly insignificant villages to supply his names is a matter for speculation.

Connell was wise to omit Lower St from the surveyed town. When the river rose more than six metres overnight on Sunday, July 27 1863, it swamped the lower street. Luckily the contents of most of the business premises were rescued before the rising waters claimed them. In some instances there was time to dismantle the entire building and remove it to higher ground.[4] James Rivers' store was one such. It was re-erected at the lower end of Broad Street where he continued his business as merchant for another 40 years.

A year after the flood a report[5] describes the town:

> Alexandra. . . consists of two streets, Broad and Lower Streets. The former contains most of the principal stores and hotels; is well formed and drained and is the main thoroughfare to the Dunstan and Dunedin roads. The lower street runs parallel with the Manuherikia River, and at right

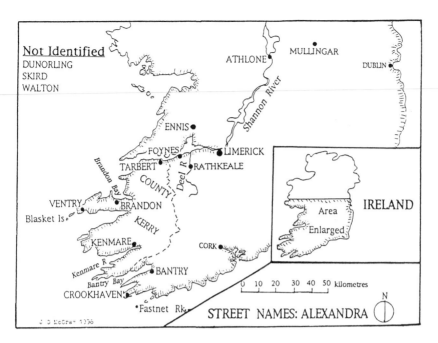

Figure 2.5. Map of southern Ireland with locations of places used by Connell in naming the streets of Alexandra.

angles with Broad Street. It is extremely narrow and inconvenient, and excessively muddy in wet weather, while many of the buildings are in danger of being washed away in the first high flood that occurs. Notwithstanding its disadvantages it contains some very respectable business places, and at the first of the rush was the principal resort of trade; but, through the vagaries of the river, its commercial importance has considerably dwindled, and the trade, like the diggers, has betaken itself further from the water's edge.

The Demise of Lower Street

A flood in mid-January 1866 sealed the fate of Lower Street. Remaining buildings were submerged to the eaves and after the flood they were gradually pulled down or shifted to higher ground. In fact one correspondent thought the flood was a good thing, as it had caused many vacant sections in the higher streets to be filled and this gave the town a much tidier appearance.

The 'Old Man Flood' of 1878 finally washed away the complete terrace on which the street and its buildings had stood, leaving a cliff at the foot of present-day Tarbert Street. Undoubtedly the hundreds of thousands of cubic metres of gravel washed into the river from the mining of Frenchmans Point on the south bank, diverted the current of the flooded river so it impinged on the north bank and eroded the low terrace there.

29

The Gully

Part of the block between Ennis, Limerick and Tarbert Streets was not included in the town survey because the ground was regarded as 'auriferous.'[6] In 1866 The Manuherikia Ground Sluicing Company announced that it intended to run a race down into the town and sluice this block. It is almost certain that the deep gully that existed in this locality right up until the 1960s, was the result of its activities.

Figure 2.6. The gully (right middle-ground), was sluiced by the Manuherikia Ground Sluicing Company in 1866. It later made a convenient landing place for the punt.

1865 Resurvey

In December 1865, only two years after the original survey had been completed and a map of the town published, the 'business area' was resurveyed, this time by G. Mackenzie, a surveyor of the Provincial Government Survey Department. If the map produced after this 1865 survey is compared with that of 1863, we see that the shape of lower Tarbert Street has been altered. From Deel Street southwards the sides are no longer parallel — the eastern side converges so that the street tapers. The taper was achieved by pivoting the whole of Block XV. Why was this done?

When Tarbert Street was first surveyed, the eastern boundary cut through most of the buildings at the lower end of the street which meant, of course, that parts of most of these building found themselves, illegally, on the new street. The reason for these buildings being where they were was obvious — they backed against a rock mass that came closer to the street as the river was approached. So the buildings, erected against the rock, protruded progressively further out on to the rough track that passed

30

for a street. This fact of topography was apparently not taken into account by the first surveyors who, in the interests of forming a neat and tidy street, simply made the eastern boundary parallel to the western. The crunch came when the Government decided to auction the sections in Block XV. A large crowd turned up but the Warden explained that, as the street line cut through the buildings and this would seriously inconvenience potential occupiers, the sections fronting Tarbert Street would be withdrawn from sale until a new survey was made. At this point almost everyone walked away, so when the sections in the back street (Mullingar Street, now McDonald Street) were put up for auction there was not a single bid.

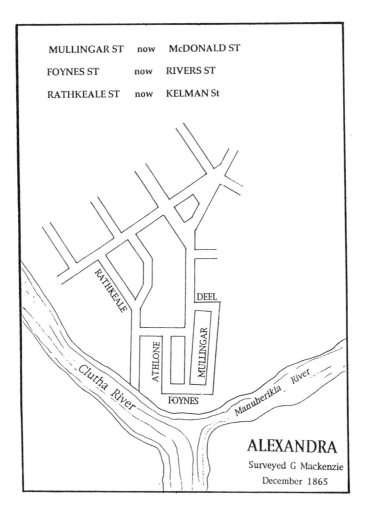

MULLINGAR ST	now	McDONALD ST
FOYNES ST	now	RIVERS ST
RATHKEALE ST	now	KELMAN St

ALEXANDRA

Surveyed G Mackenzie

December 1865

Figure 2.7. Additional streets surveyed and named by Mackenzie in 1865. He resurveyed the block between Deel and Foynes Streets and tapered the main street (Tarbert Street).

By pivoting the whole block to the west, most buildings found themselves, more or less, back on their own sections; but it was done at the expense of the street which, to this day, retains the taper. Although this may have seemed a sensible thing to do at the time, it gave rise to problems in the matter of traffic flow and parking that still persist. And whereas it may have provided space for the small buildings of the 1860s, modern builders are faced with either massive rock removal by blasting, or designing buildings with the rear portion at a higher level than the street frontage.

During this resurvey many more sections in the business area were surveyed off, and several new streets were created, including one to provide access to the ferry. Although Mackenzie was not part of Connell and Moodie's surveying firm, he continued the tradition of giving Irish names to the new streets. They were:

Athlone St: This replaced the original road to the river bank ferry. Athlone is a town 78 miles west of Dublin lying at the head of the Shannon estuary. The river, in fact, divides the town into two.

Foynes St: (renamed **Rivers St** after James Rivers, an early mayor). A village in County Limerick with a population of about 400 lying on the south shore of the Shannon River estuary. Nearby is Foynes House and Foynes Island is in the estuary.

Mullingar St: (renamed **Macdonald St** after an early mayor). A town with a population of over 5,000 in Westmeath County 80 kilometres north-west of Dublin.

Rathkeale St: (renamed **Kelman St** after an early mayor). A small town, population about 2,000, on the River Deel 30 kilometres south-west of Limerick. An interesting feature of this town is that a large party of Protestant Germans from Rhine-Palatinate settled there in the 1700s.

Why were the new names not used?

Townspeople were slow to adopt the new street names. Although the maps prepared by the first survey were published in late 1863 with the name 'Tarbert Street' for the main street, only 'Broad Street' and 'Camp Street' appear as addresses in the Electoral Rolls until 1867. It is only in the Roll for 1869-70 that a few examples of 'Tarbert Street' appear. As late as 1878, when the system was changed so that addresses were no longer given, the majority of businesses in the main street still gave 'Broad Street' as their address.

It is understandable that it would take some time for the new names to become known. There was no Borough Council Office (until 1867), let alone a Map Shop where maps of the town could be obtained. Anyway the locals would seldom use street names — they identified streets by the name of some well-known resident. Nevertheless it is strange that, in an official document such as the Electoral Roll, informal street names were accepted for nearly 20 years after formal names had been published.

It was not until the late 1890s, under pressure caused by rapidly increasing population through dredging activity, that a further area of 'the Flat' was surveyed and subdivided into sections. Many of the original streets, which had been left open-ended, were simply extended to meet a new major road running diagonally through the town. An appropriate gesture, perhaps suggested by an Irish councillor of the time, saw this street named 'Killarney' after the town and beautiful lake district of County Kerry. With the main streets retaining their Irish connections, new, minor cross streets were named after local gold dredges.

A request was put to the Borough Council in August 1920 by the Alexandra Women's Patriotic Association that the streets be renamed. Each street was to bear the name of a local man who had been killed in the Great War. After some consideration the Council 'could not see its way clear' to accede to the request.

NOTES

1. The original lithograph is in Turnbull Library. Apparently little is known about the artist.

2. *Otago Daily Times* 10 March 1863.

3. The name 'Alexandra' was adopted officially after the marriage of Edward, Prince of Wales to Alexandra, Princess of Denmark, in early 1863. Until then the settlement had been known by various names such as Lower Township, Lower Dunstan, Manuherikia and Manuherikia Junction. The Post Office retained the name 'Alexandra South' until 1914.

4. *Otago Daily Times* 18 August 1863.

5. *Otago Daily Times* 18 September 1863.

6. Meaning 'gold-bearing.' This word was much used in the early days and was generally applied to ground that had been proved to be gold-bearing by prospecting. It was the practice to reserve 'auriferous' ground for mining wherever possible.

3.

THE FERRY RACKET

Miners wanting to cross the Manuherikia River near its confluence with the Clutha had a choice. They could either wade through water perhaps up to their waists, or they could pay two shillings and six pence and be taken across on horseback. The two enterprising early arrivals who organised this service were reputed to have made £200 during the first two weeks of the rush.[1]

The Manuherikia River was not then the rather feeble stream we see today. Mining and irrigation had not yet siphoned off three-quarters of its water, nor had the great influx of mine tailings raised its bed. Near its mouth it flowed in a deep channel, but the depth of water depended largely on the level of the Clutha River.

Crossing the Clutha River was a different story. It was simply not possible other than by boat, and the only boats available were those belonging to Strode and Fraser of Earnscleugh Station. They were moored at the mouth of what was to become known as Muttontown Gully, some 3 kilometres downstream from Coal Point, the future Clyde.

Henry Hill

Only a fortnight[2] after the first miners reached the Dunstan Gorge, Henry Hill arrived armed with a letter from the Superintendent of the Province, allowing Hill to place two punts on the river. Hill was a man who would, these days, be regarded as an entrepreneur. According to George Hassing, who later worked for him, Hill had 'levanted'[3] (left without paying his bills) from a railway construction contract in Victoria, but now here he was on the banks of the Clutha River with two small boats and material for building punts. The boats were set to work immediately, and a couple of days later he had put together, and was operating, the two small punts — one at Coal Point (Clyde) and the other at Muttontown. The charge was six pence a head for passengers.

The punts were too small for such a large river. There was much criticism of the whole operation, especially when a party of miners who tried to use the punt at Coal Point after it had been closed down because of a flood, came to grief. Two of the men were thrown out and drowned, but a third was able to cling to the punt until he was rescued.

The episode was described in a letter[4] from 'a settler in the Manuherikia district' to a friend in Dunedin and was published in the newspaper:

> A pretty thing of the Government to allow Hill to come and turn off the only safe boats (Messrs Shennan and Fraser's whaleboats) from the river without stipulating that proper substitutes should replace them. Without having anyone to see to the public interest, a private speculator is allowed to come off [sic] with a letter in his pocket from the Superintendent, take possession of the settlers boating-places, drive their boats off the river, and then drown men and horses with impunity, I believe if Hill could be caught in the camp tonight, he would get a rating from the diggers he would remember for a time, and the Government are catching it for making the arrangement.
>
> The punts are perfectly useless, as at present wrought and constructed, too small and feeble and consequently highly dangerous. Shennan's boats have been kindly put on again to meet the difficulty, but it is merely done for the sake of humanity and to oblige the poor diggers.

The phrase about settlers' boats being driven off the river was obviously a reference to the rather extraordinary amendment that had been made to the Ferry Ordinance of 1854. It ruled that any person who crossed a creek, river or lake within 3 miles in a straight line from an established public ferry had to pay the appropriate ferry charge. The penalty for not doing so was to pay the ferry charge plus £5. This effectively stopped any competition near the ferries which, of course, was the intention of the legislation.

The *Otago Daily Times* investigated the criticism expressed in the letter and found that the writer did not have the full facts. Certainly, Mr Hill had received a letter from the Deputy Superintendent giving him permission to operate his punts for six months, but this did not mean they were 'public' or official ferries established by the Provincial Government. Therefore the restriction on competition did not apply. Once this was realised, a large number of punts and boats began to appear at favoured crossings, including Alexandra. Hill quickly sold out and went on to other fields of endeavour.[6]

Soon, at Alexandra, there were at least five boats on the Clutha River and four on the Manuherikia, with charges at six pence and three pence respectively, per person. Horses had to swim, towed behind the boats. Miners who crossed morning and evening to their work paid half fare or nothing at all if the ferryman thought they were particularly hard up. Notwithstanding this generosity, the boats were gold mines. There was talk of some boatmen making £12 a day, and the high prices at which boats were sold certainly indicated high returns. But the Provincial Council, hearing stories of accidents and near-accidents, was becoming increasingly alarmed about the safety of the operations.

Finally the council acted. Tenders were called for operating official ferries at nine river crossings[7] in Central Otago, including those across the Clutha River and the Manuherikia River at Alexandra. At the same time a schedule of charges was published. They ranged from two shillings for

Figure 3.1. Sketch of Manuherikia (Alexandra) (F. Nairn November 1862) showing ferry boats along the waterfront.

wagons, to one shilling for each person and two pence for each sheep. From one hour after sunset until sunrise the fares were increased by one half. Only the Mail and authorised employees of the Government were exempt from the charges.

The Contract

It was announced in July[8] that Henry Hill was the successful tenderer for all nine ferries. As these would now be official ferries,[9] the rules of the Ferry Ordinance applied and Hill would enjoy a monopoly. No one else would be able to operate punts or boats or even cross the rivers within 3 miles of a ferry without paying ferryage. By the end of July 1863, Hill's punts were the only ones on the river, and those who had been operating boats and punts at Alexandra had buried them in the sand of the river beaches to protect them from the weather.

As part of the contract, Hill had to supply punts whose design was approved by the Provincial Government, and until these were built he used only small punts. The one used to cross the Manuherikia River was described by the newspaper correspondent as:

> . . . a most disgraceful affair, being nothing more than a deal box, hauled across the river by a rope passing through upright standards fixed at

either end; in the bottom there is always a goodly supply of water swilling about, also the seats are constantly wet from the drippings off the rope which is for the most part immersed in the river, and as the punt is hauled across it drops a considerable amount of water aboard, so that to sit or stand is anything but agreeable especially on a cold frosty morning[10]

Although the list of new charges, which were double the previous going rate, had been published in *Otago Provincial Gazette* and in the newspapers at least six weeks previously, the implications of the monopoly and the high charges apparently did not immediately register with the miners. So they were stunned when they arrived at the punt on the morning of Friday 29 July to cross the river to their work, and read posters announcing the new arrangements and charges 'by order of the Superintendent.'

The Rumpus

There was nearly a riot. It was just as well that the two little punts were moored on the far bank of the river or they would have surely suffered severe injury. The newspapers interpreted[11] the thrust of the complaints as:

> The new charges would cost regular users 12 shillings a week to reach their daily work. Miners saw this as another tax.
>
> Lack of consultation. The Wardens had the facts and figures about the numbers crossing and could have supplied these to Council if they had been asked.
>
> The surprise involved. Certainly the new charges were advertised in the *Gazette* but who reads this obscure publication?
>
> Hill undertook to provide large safe punts some time in the future but meanwhile the high charges were being applied to his original small punts.

The business people were particularly upset and said that the town had been deprived of half of its trade. They threatened to put a boat on the river themselves and convey people free.

Numerous boatmen had already made small fortunes out of the three pence and six pence fares, so Hill stood to make a killing. The newspaper could do no more, it said, 'than reluctantly congratulate Mr Hill on being the most fortunate man in Otago.' But it also warned that the brawl that had recently occurred at the Cromwell toll bridge (owned by Hill) was 'only the beginning of evil.'

The reaction to the increased charges must have worried Hill, because he wrote to the Superintendent on 6 August informing him that he had reduced the charge on the Manuherikia ferry to 6 pence and asking for approval for this and, at the same time, for a reduction in his rent. But he also notified the Superintendent that he had formally taken possession of the official ferry reserves on 3 August, in spite of the opposition of occupiers of the land. Some of the required land was in possession of miners and business people who refused to give it up. Hill also accused the business people of the town of inciting the miners to violence about the new charges. He said too, that he had put boats on the Manuherikia River at three places within the 3-mile monopoly zone to save the miners walking to the ferry. Apparently Hill was in no hurry to put the proper punts on the rivers. As he pointed out, although he had cut the necessary timber, he would have to wait for it to season before the vessels were constructed.

The Superintendent gave Hill permission to reduce the charge at the Manuherikia ferry, but made it clear that only when Hill had reduced charges at all his ferries would a reduction in rent be negotiated. And he was told in no uncertain terms that he was not to interfere with people's property rights at ferry landings. Hill did not reduce the charges at the other ferries.

Public Meetings

There were 'indignation meetings' in Clyde and Alexandra, and a combined deputation from the two towns set off to Dunedin to present the Superintendent, Mr John Hyde Harris, with a Memorial signed by 850 people.

The Memorial[12] had seven clauses and summarised the points made at the public meetings. In brief they were:

1. Under private operators the crossings were made safely, economically and with dispatch.

2. Punts crossed at all hours at a uniform, but still profitable, charge rate.

3. Charge on the Clutha River was six pence and paid five men with five boats, but now there would be only two boats with two men so it should pay more than handsomely.

4. The Manuherikia crossing cost three pence and at that rate paid four boats and four men. Now one boat and one man would charge one shilling.

5. Public were upset and surprised at lack of publicity before the charges were levied.

6. Miners are a depressed class at present and cannot afford the new charges. Free passage for the poor would be a thing of the past.

7. Serious breaches of the peace were feared if the present situation continued.

At the interview with the Superintendent, the deputation began by getting a few things off its collective chest. It was suggested, as a starter, that not all of the tenders for the nine ferries had been passed on by the Wardens through whom they had been submitted. It was also disclosed that Hill had men patrolling the river taking the names of those who crossed within 3 miles of the ferries. Because Alexandra and Clyde were 8 miles apart, Hill had actually moved the Clyde ferry further down the river (at great inconvenience to the public) to ensure he had the whole stretch under control. Certainly there had been accidents with the punts, but they had been confined 'to Mr Hill's cockleshells.' The deputation ended their long list of complaints with a request that the contract with Hill be annulled and the previous situation reinstated.

The Superintendent was sympathetic. He was disappointed, he said, that a measure which was introduced to benefit the mining communities had obviously had the reverse effect. He pointed out that the Government had been concerned over a number of accidents at the ferries, and sought to exercise some control on the operations. It had thought that the monopoly and high charges were necessary to attract tenders under the stringent conditions imposed. The *Gazette*, with its list of new charges, had been sent to all Wardens and newspapers before they came into operation, so he was surprised to hear that the miners had had no warning. In response to the accusation that tenders had not been passed on, Mr Harris could only say that 21 tenders had been received by the Government. He pointed out that Hill's tender was more than double the next highest, but the arrangement with him was not yet complete. The punts that he was going to provide had to be approved by the Government, and so far there was no sign of plans for the new vessels. The Superintendent agreed that Hill had no right to be charging the high rates until the approved punts were in operation, nor could he interfere with the existing rights of people living near the ferries as he had done. Harris promised to put the whole matter before the Provincial Solicitor.

The members of the deputation[13] returned to their respective towns and received heroes' welcomes at the crowded public meetings that were quickly arranged to hear their news. Proceedings were often punctuated by cheers and applause, and after the delegates had pointed out that the Superintendent had promised to reduce the fares immediately and to look at the whole contract with Hill, three cheers were given, first for the Superintendent, and then for the deputation.

Fun in Court

Meanwhile the competition was trying out the legality of Hill's contract, and Hill complained to the Magistrate, Major Jackson Keddell. At first, Keddell wasn't particularly interested but Hill persisted, with the result that on 24 August a Mr Blakely[14] was charged with illegally crossing the river. The court case was a farce. Hill's ferryman, and main witness, could not swear it was Blakely's boat he saw (it was one and a half miles away); he had only *heard* that it was defendant's boat; no, he could not recognise the defendant as having been in the boat, and he could not even be sure which day he saw the boat.

Hill himself made an even worse botch of his evidence, and to the amusement (quickly suppressed by order of the Bench) of the crowded court room, he admitted that he was confused. The only thing that he was sure about was that he was the official lessee of the river ferries because he had signed certain documents. Magistrate Keddell agreed that he was the lessee, whether he had signed or not, but he dismissed the case.

Although this particular case failed on questions of identification, other cases brought by Hill failed because sharp-eyed magistrates spotted flaws in the legislation.

First, there was Anderson who had put on a boat to carry passengers, at three pence a head, across the Clutha River at Alexandra in direct opposition to Hill. He had lasted only one day before he was charged under the Ferry Ordinances. Magistrate Keddell fined him the mandatory £5 plus one shilling ferryage for each of the 40 crossings he had made. But why were the 153 passengers whom Anderson admitted carrying, not taken into account in setting the penalty?

All was made clear at the following week's Court at Teviot (Roxburgh), where Hill charged[15] Henry Tudor with illegally conveying passengers and stock across the river. The magistrate ruled that there was no doubt that the Teviot ferry was a public ferry and that Hill was the legal lessee, but the defendant was not guilty of the offence he was charged with for a reason that Tudor himself had not put forward. The magistrate quoted the relevant 1856 Amendment of the Ferry Ordinance which, because of its importance in this case, is worth reproducing in abbreviated form:-

> 1. Every person who shall cross or shall cause any cattle to cross, or who shall convey. . . for hire any cattle, cart, vehicle, or goods across any river . . . at, opposite to, or within three miles in a straight line from any point . . . at which a Public Ferry. . . is . . .established . . . without availing himself of the services of the Ferryman, or of the ferry-boat, shall be liable for, and shall pay to the Ferryman, the toll or rate that would have been demandable . . . if the Ferryman had been employed to convey such person, or such cattle, cart, vehicle, or goods across such ferry, in the ferry-boat.

As the magistrate pointed out, there is no mention of passengers!

In this case the illegal ferryman had stepped ashore only at the end of the day so had crossed only once and therefore Tudor was only liable for the toll for one crossing for himself each day and for the toll for six horses and nine sheep but not for the 593 passengers he had carried between 19 and 24 August. It is recorded that this decision appeared to give general satisfaction to the crowded courtroom.

Hill had consistently refused to lower his charges in spite of several requests from the Superintendent to do so, but on 3 September the Government had settled matters by publishing a new scale of charges which lowered the charge for persons to six pence. Hill had no option but to comply.

Hill now found himself stuck with a contract that would return a much lower income than he had anticipated when tendering. Nor, as a result of the various court rulings, could he enjoy the full monopoly he thought he had. So he was probably not unduly perturbed when, on 3 September, the Provincial Council resolved, on the motion of Mr George Brodie:[16]

> That a respectful address be presented to His Honour the Superintendent requesting that he would cancel the contract entered into by the Provincial Government with Mr Hill, for the conveyance of passengers and traffic across the Molyneux and its tributaries, as described in the *Gazette* dated May 6th, 1863.

Although the new, lower charges did not have the flexibility of the old system the miners seemed to accept them, and now that Hill was threatened with cancellation of his contract, sympathy, with the perversity of human nature, swung in his favour. Although there was an opposition punt running across the Manuherikia River alongside Hill's, and two unauthorised boats plying on the Clutha, passenger patronage for them was poor and almost all freight was carried on Hill's boats.

Finally at the end of September, Superintendent Hyde Harris sent his

'Message' to the Provincial Council giving his recommendation about the cancellation of the contract and compensation. He had been negotiating with Hill, who had asked for £4,500 which covered the cost of the bridge at Cromwell and its approaches, ferry-houses and eight punts totalling £3,288 together with £1,312 compensation for the loss of the remainder of the year's lease. Harris made it quite clear that he was not very happy with the idea of the ferries being left to the

> . . . speculation of individuals who cannot be brought under any efficient Government control.[17]

Nevertheless the contract was cancelled and Hill was paid, after the matter had gone to arbitration, the sum of £3,000.

Lessons Learned

The Provincial Government had learnt an expensive lesson about allowing important public services to be leased to one man. Within a month, on the instigation of Captain Baldwin, a Goldfields representative, legislation was introduced to require people to be licensed before operating boats on harbours, lakes and rivers. At the same time Captain Baldwin moved that a Select Committee be set up to investigate the controversial Amendment that forbade crossing a river within three miles on either side of an official ferry without paying ferryage.

The speed with which this committee reached its conclusions must constitute something of a record for such bodies. It met only twice, and in the middle of the second meeting, after hearing only three witnesses, it decided that it had sufficient evidence to report back to the council. It recommended that the Ferries Ordinance Amendment ordinance of 1856 should be repealed, and that boats and punts used as ferries should be licensed. It took until November of the following year before the Amendment was repealed.[18]

Later Punts

With Hill gone, a group of five local men calling themselves the Alert Company dug up their boats from the river beach where they had been buried to protect them against the elements during the Hill regime. Refurbished and placed back in service, they gave, according to a newspaper report,[19] a service that was every bit as safe and efficient as that provided by Hill. But whaleboats, while ideal for passengers, were less satisfactory for carrying horses and freight. So the company placed an order for a self-acting punt (ie. one driven across the river by the force of the current) for the Clutha River. It was constructed in Alexandra by Sweetman and McKenzie and consisted of two boats with a platform built across them. It was capable of carrying a six-horse wagon. At its launching early in May 1864 it was christened *Alexandra* by Miss Kennedy, daughter of the proprietor of Sportsmen's Arms Hotel. Charges were back to the original three pence per head for passengers.

Meanwhile the Manuherikia River crossing was still being made by boats pulled across by a rope. However, early in 1865 this changed with the

Figure 3.2. Punt men.
Left: John Mackersey and his wife Elizabeth.
Right: His partner, John Duley, was the punt operator.

launching of a self-acting punt built by Thomson and Co for Leslie Brothers. By 1868 this punt had been taken over by John Mackersey and was used until the Manuherikia Bridge, a kilometre upstream, was completed.

The Alert Company's punt on the Clutha River was too small to deal with the greatly increased traffic expected when the new road from Teviot, along the western side of the river, finally opened. So in October 1868 Mackersey and Duley commissioned Sparrow's Foundry of Dunedin to build what was described as one of the largest punts in New Zealand. It consisted of two iron boats each nine metres long and three metres wide, with a platform 11 metres by four metres built over them. It could carry 30 tons.[20]

This punt continued to give good service until 1878 when the huge flood in the Clutha River damaged the landing places and covered the access roads with deep silt. Mackersey was doubtful whether he would start again, but with some help from the Borough Council, the punt was recommissioned by September. However, the punt's days were numbered and it was decommissioned when the Alexandra Bridge was opened in 1882.

After serving for many years at Lowburn, the old Alexandra punt passed into private hands and is still in use by Mr Jack Mears, a farmer at Greenfield near Clydevale, to carry stock to and from the part of his farm

Figure 3.3. Mackersey and Duley's punt moored at Alexandra to the right of the new bridge which replaced it.

which is on an island in the Clutha River.[21]

Hill Levants Again

And what of Henry Hill? He went back to contracting, including the supply of poles for the telegraph line from Clyde to Queenstown. One of his subcontractors was George Hassing and his partner, who rafted poles down the Makarora River and Lake Wanaka to the outlet. But then news arrived that Hill had suddenly collected three quarters of the progress payments owing to him, declared himself bankrupt and disappeared. None of the workers on the telegraph line received any of the four months wages owing them, and Hassing himself lost £400. Once more Hill had 'levanted' — this time to Peru where, it was believed, he made a fortune on railway contracts.[22]

NOTES

1. *Otago Daily Times* 19 July 1864.
2. 16 September 1862 according to Parcel, 1951, but the *Otago Daily Times* correspondent at the goldfields wrote on 11 September that Hill had arrived on 9 September with two small boats and 'will have two punts working tomorrow' ie 12 September.
3. G. M. Hassing 1911, p.48. This means that Hill had absconded without paying his workmen — in today's vernacular he had 'shot through.' At the time of his appearance on the Clutha River he was a storekeeper at Waitahuna in partnership with James Lea Smithers. Smithers apparently did not appreciate being left to run the store as the partnership was dissolved the following year. *Otago Provincial*

Figure 3.4. The 130 year-old Alexandra punt in its present role as transport for stock. It is owned by Mr J. Mears of Greenfield near Clydevale.

Government Gazette 27 May 1863.

4. *Otago Daily Times* 1 October 1862. As both Shennan and Fraser are mentioned in the letter the only remaining settler who was likely to be the author of the letter was Low of Galloway Station.

5. Ferries Ordinance Amendment Ordinance, 1856. Otago Provincial Government.

6. Amongst other enterprises was a timber-rafting operation from the lakes and a wooden toll bridge across the Clutha River at Cromwell which Hill built in April, 1863. The raising of the toll on this led to a brawl in which the toll-keeper was seriously injured. *Otago Daily Times* 12 August 1863.

7. *Otago Provincial Government Gazette* 6 May 1863.

8. *Otago Provincial Government Gazette*: 22 July 1863. Hill's tender was accepted on 18 July but presumably he had been notified of his successful tender some time beforehand as he produced a letter dated 3 July in Teviot Court (*ODT* 7 September 1863) saying that the Government had no objection to Hill using the ferries at once. No clear statement of the amount of the tender can be found but the *ODT* reporter 'believed' that it was about £500 (*Otago Daily Times* 5 August 1863).

9. Proclaimed as such *Otago Provincial Government Gazette* 8 July 1863.

10. *Otago Daily Times* 15 September 1863.

11. *Otago Daily Times* 5 August 1863.

12. *Otago Daily Times* 12 August 1863.

13. The group consisted of J. C. Chapple, J. D. Wolfe (of Wolfe & Hart, Inglewood Store) from Alexandra, H. A. Gordon (of the firm of Gordon & Black) of Clyde and G. L. Brodie, a Member representing the Goldfields in both the Legislative Assembly and the Provincial Council. They were accompanied by Captain Baldwin, also a Representative of the Goldfields in the Provincial Council.

14. Almost certainly the John Blakely who had opened up a lignite pit on the western bank of the Clutha River midway between the mouth of the Fraser River and Alexandra. Blakely had already had difficulty with Hill over charging for conveying coal across the river but had reached a compromise of 12 shillings a week.

15. *Otago Daily Timos* 7 September 1863.
16. *Votes and Proceedings Session XVII* p.65.
17. *Votes and Proceedings Session XVII* p.134.
18. *Ordinances of the Province of Otago* Session XIX 1864 p.945.
19. *Otago Daily Times* 21 November 1863.
20. *Dunstan Times* 30 November 1868.
21. Tyrrell, A. R. 1996 p.63.
22. Hassing, G. M. 1911 p.48.

4.

BRIDGING THE RIVERS

Rivers were of huge importance to the goldfields towns whose prosperity, and indeed, very existence, depended on them. River levels were part of every conversation and it was said that a falling river, which would give access to the golden beaches, created more excitement than would a Government crisis.

Nevertheless, the rivers were also a great inconvenience. Without the Earnscleugh Station's boat, the first miners to arrive at the Dunstan could not have crossed the Clutha River, and the beaches on the western side with their wealth of gold, would have been inaccessible for some time. When boats and small punts did become available, miners, many of whom lived on one side of the river and worked on the other, were very much at the mercy of the ferry operators.[1] Until there was effective competition, ferrymen could not only charge almost what they wished, but could also keep people waiting until it suited them to answer the call to come across. It is little wonder that there was talk of bridges from the early days of the Rush, but for a long time it could only be talk.

MANUHERIKIA RIVER BRIDGES

The Manuherikia River was a substantial stream before its headwaters were dammed and diverted for irrigation. Certainly, at normal flows it was possible to wade across in many places, but for long periods of the year the river was high, if not actually in flood, so that crossing, even at the regular fords, became difficult if not dangerous.

Charlie Hensburgh, the proprietor of a little hotel on the southern bank of the Manuherikia River near the junction of the Manor Burn, had begun rowing people across the river even before the ridiculous clause in the Ferry Act had been rescinded.[2] Although his service, referred to as 'Charlie's Middle Ferry,' was satisfactory and cheap, agitation for a bridge began in early 1865.[2]

Simms Bridge

Thomas Simms, a successful miner of Manor Burn, was the energetic protagonist, and it was not long before it was announced[3] that a subscription bridge suitable for foot and packhorse traffic would be erected across the river.

Built by Edward Charnock, a local blacksmith and coal miner, it was opened on Easter Monday 1866 by Mrs J. C. Thomson,[4] who named it 'Simms Bridge' after its instigator. It put an end to Charlie's profitable ferry business, but for only a short period, as the new bridge was swept away in the big flood of November 1866 after only seven months of useful service.

Shaky Bridge

There was growing demand for a bridge for light wheeled traffic at Alexandra to replace the ferry across the Manuherikia River, and Vincent Pyke, Member for the district, was approached by a deputation while he was visiting the town in October 1876. He pointed out that such things were now to be the responsibility of the newly established County Councils.

Vincent County would agree only to call tenders for a bridge suitable for foot traffic and pack horses. There was a row at the council meeting in August 1877 when the Chairman, Vincent Pyke, disclosed that he had already opened the tenders, found them too high, and readvertised. In spite of this, the contract was awarded to Jeremiah Drummey. The Mayor of Alexandra promised a contribution of £100 and the County increased its allocation to £293 to cover Drummey's price of £393. But Alexandra wasn't satisfied. The townspeople wanted a traffic bridge rather than a foot bridge. As a result of a public meeting, at which Drummey said he was prepared to build a traffic bridge for an extra £300, a 'memorial' was sent to the County Council in September 1877, asking formally for a traffic bridge and promising to raise an extra £150 if the County Council would do the same.

The County Council saw some difficulties, and pointed out that it was unlawful for the present tenderer to be given a different contract — fresh tenders would have to be called. The County engineer estimated that a traffic bridge would cost £750 without the cost of cables. A problem arose when Drummey refused to relinquish his contract for the footbridge without compensation. He made another offer to build the traffic bridge for £250 over his original price.

In an attempt to resolve this stalemate, the Alexandra Borough Council appointed a high-powered delegation to meet Drummey and discuss his contract. The result was that Drummey agreed to having his contract for the footbridge rescinded, with £25 compensation to be paid by the Borough Council. Apparently the County Council took the view that, as it was Alexandra that wanted the traffic bridge and had caused the difficulty with the contract, it was up to the town to pacify Drummey.

With this difficulty out of the way, the County readvertised for tenders for a traffic bridge in early January 1878, and Grant and McKellar won the contract with their tender of £974 10s. The Alexandra Borough Council contributed £250, raised mainly by private subscription.

Work was started on 18 June, which the newspaper pointed out was the anniversary of the battle of Waterloo, so it would be appropriate to name the bridge 'Waterloo Bridge.' Fortunately this suggestion was not taken up,

Figure 4.1. The light traffic bridge across the Manuherikia River as originally built.

and the bridge was referred to for many years simply as the 'Manuherikia Light Traffic Bridge.'

Designed by County engineer, L. D. Macgeorge, the handsome suspension bridge spanned the narrow gorge about a kilometre upstream from the confluence with the Clutha River. It was supported by several wire ropes, bound into a bundle 120 mm in diameter, on each side. These ropes passed over pillars about eight metres high comprised of blocks of schist rock, and were attached to steel rods anchored deep into the country rock. The deck, some 60 metres long and three metres wide, was supported on heavy wooden stringers placed about three metres apart, which were in turn attached to the wire ropes by metal hangers.

The bridge itself was finished in April 1879 but was unusable by wheeled traffic, as the approaches had not been completed. A road was quickly formed from the bridge along the south-eastern side of the Manuherikia River towards the Manor Burn to link with the main road over the Knobby Range. However, it took the Borough Council another year to complete access through the difficult rocks on the north-western side.

Apart from the heaviest wagons, which still had to use Duncan Robertson's ford at Galloway, almost all of the Alexandra-bound traffic coming off the Knobby Range road and the Dunstan Road made use of the bridge. The rumble of wheels on the wooden decking became a familiar and characteristic sound in Alexandra.

Figure 4.2. The Manuherikia bridge in 1926 with Alexandra in the background and the Old Man Range on the horizon.

Upkeep, however, was quite expensive, and maintenance lagged so that the bridge became somewhat dilapidated. When the railway bridge, a few hundred metres upstream, was completed in 1906 and adapted to carry road traffic, it made the old bridge, in the County Council's view, redundant. It proposed that the bridge should be sold for demolition, and decided to call tenders for its removal as soon as the railway bridge was opened.

There were immediate howls of protest from those who lived across the bridge at Shag Point. A public meeting,[5] chaired by the venerable Billy Theyers, decided on the circulation of a petition to be presented to the County Council asking that the structure be preserved as a footbridge, a move supported editorially by the *Dunstan Times.* [6]

The December meeting of the Vincent County Council received a deputation from the settlers of Shag Point to present their petition and discuss the matter. What followed is one of the classic stories of Central Otago:

> After the deputation had explained the position fully the chairman [Mr John Butler was acting-chairman] suggested that the council should sell the bridge to the settlers for £1. On hearing this remark the genial spokesman for the deputation (Mr L. Cameron) promptly drew forth a sovereign and, taking the chairman at his word, laid the price asked for the bridge on the table, at the same time exclaiming "It's a bargain." The deal was soon settled, the council accepting the pound for the bridge on condition that it be closed for wheeled traffic, and the deputation accordingly withdrew rejoicing at so successful an ending to a fair and impartial request.

Figure 4.3. Lewis Cameron bought the Manuherikia bridge from Vincent County for £1.

With the ball at his toe, Lewis Cameron placed an advertisement in the paper:

> NOTICE IS HEREBY GIVEN that the Manuherikia Bridge will be CLOSED for TRAFFIC other than Foot passengers from SATURDAY, December 8th, 1906. No Wheeled or Horse Traffic will be allowed to Cross the Bridge and anyone thus trespassing will be prosecuted.
>
> For and on behalf of the Shag Point Settlers.
>
> L CAMERON

And so the situation remained for more than 25 years, until the cost of bridge ownership became painfully apparent. Another deputation, again led by Lewis Cameron, waited on the Alexandra Borough Council[7] to point out that the bridge was in urgent need of repair. The council seemed sympathetic but when a committee inspected the bridge and found that extensive repair work was needed, Council became much less enthusiastic.[8] Inevitably it was pointed out that the bridge, after all, belonged to the settlers living on the other side of the river and was not really the Borough Council's problem. Possibly a street light, placed to illuminate the bridge, might be arranged but even this, it was pointed out, would mean depriving ratepayers of a light. "Perhaps they should get a torch — it would be cheaper" was the bright suggestion of one councilor. In the end Council agreed to provide longitudinal planks along the decking as a temporary expedient.

Without proper maintenance 'Cameron's bridge,' as it was called, slowly deteriorated. It was during this period of its life that it became known as the 'Shaky bridge,' not only because of its dilapidated condition but also because of the ease with which resonance motion could be set up in the structure by people crossing on foot, much to the delight of children and alarm of adults. By the 1940s there were gaping holes in the decking and the whole thing was dangerous. As there was by now little foot traffic, it caused no great inconvenience when the bridge was closed entirely and the ends barricaded off. Again there was talk of demolition.

Luckily there were still those who took an interest in relics of the past. A campaign was started in the early 1950s to restore the bridge. Foremost amongst the contributors were Mrs Jean Bringans and Mrs Kate Scott, sisters of Lewis Cameron — the man who had bought the bridge nearly 50 years before for a sovereign. The complete superstructure was rebuilt and the bridge reopened on 7 June 1952 as a metre-wide footbridge. It was named 'Pioneer Bridge' and dedicated to the memory of the pioneers. But no matter what it may be called officially, to the people of Alexandra this 130 year old structure will continue to be known as the 'Shaky Bridge.'

Figure 4.4. The Manuherikia bridge restored as a footbridge.

CLUTHA RIVER BRIDGES

Perhaps it was the decision to make a major realignment of the recently completed Teviot to Alexandra road as it approached the Alexandra ferry, which encouraged a call for a bridge across the Clutha River. The suggestion was made by the Provincial Secretary, George Turnbull, and the Secretary for Goldfields and Works, Horace Bastings, and they further suggested that the residents of Conroys and Butchers Gullies and of Bald Hill Flat could be invited to subscribe to the cost.[10] In February 1874 the Provincial Government called for 'conditional' tenders for a bridge[11] to be built 'contiguous to the present punt,' but it seems that either no tenders were received or those that were, were unacceptable; or perhaps the appeal for subscriptions fell on deaf ears. Not surprisingly, nothing further was heard of this scheme.

Alexandra Bridge

As early as July 1878, the Vincent County Council asked engineers Hay and Macgeorge to report on a proposed bridge across the Clutha River at Alexandra. It decided that the report, when it eventuated, would be sent to the Government with a request for a subsidy.

The need for a bridge was emphasised two months later when the disastrous 'old man' flood damaged the cables which operated the vital punt, and nearly destroyed the punt itself. It was then that the council realised just how vulnerable the district was to floods, and consequent breakdown in communications. But it was the loss, in the same flood, of the Clyde bridge, completed only two years previously, that really tipped the balance. Was Clyde really the place for the replacement bridge? asked those members of the council who represented wards far away from Clyde. Even the *Dunstan Times* suggested that the new bridge should be built 'near Alexandra.'

A strong protagonist for a bridge at Alexandra was Michael Joseph McGinnis, a County councillor who represented Earnscleugh Riding from 1878 until 1885. Only two months after the great flood, McGinnis, supported by Vincent Pyke, the Chairman, successfully moved 'that a bridge be built at Alexandra.' Among the objections made was one that the bridge was not worth building, as it would be redundant when the railway arrived — an event that was not to take place for nearly 30 years. Another councillor was certain that wagons would continue to use the Shag Valley route and so by-pass the bridge.

Figure 4.5. The men responsible for the Clutha River bridge at Alexandra.
Left: M. J. McGinnis — Chairman of Vincent County Council.
Centre: Wm Beresford, J. Drummey, J. Simmonds — contractors.
Right: L. D. Macgeorge — designer and engineer.

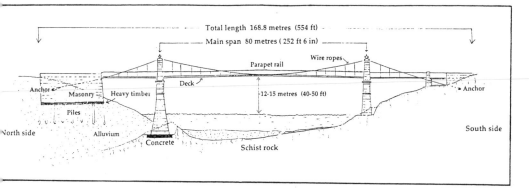

Figure 4.6. Elevation of Alexandra bridge with main features and dimensions.

McGinnis's efforts to have the bridge built at Alexandra did not go unnoticed and he was presented with an illuminated address by the citizens of Alexandra in July 1880. James Simmonds, one of the partners who would build the bridge, went further and suggested

> . . . that upon the Earnscleugh side of the bridge a monument, suitably inscribed, should be erected in recognition of his services, for to him is due all the credit of the project.[12]

Tenders were called in March 1879 for a very elegant suspension bridge designed by the County engineer, L. D. Macgeorge. His plan was for a bridge 552 feet (170 m) long with two stone piers, one near each bank, founded on solid rock and rising 80 feet (25 m) above the river level. The deck would be 40 feet (12 m) above normal water level.

The first tenders received were for over £20,000 and were considered to be too high. Macgeorge was instructed to modify his plans, and by simplifying some of the stonework, he was able to attract a tender price of £16,111 from Jeremiah Drummey, the well-known Alexandra contractor. This was a huge sum for a county that had a population of only about 3,000,[13] but the council was not too worried as its financial position was sound. Revenue from rates was subsidised by £2 for £1 by the Government, and twenty percent of the Land Fund, amounting to £10,000, came to the county. With revenue from mining licences, gold duty and various other fees, the total income was about £25,000; there would be no problem financing the project over a three-year period of construction.

Construction

Work started on 27 June 1879 on the most difficult part of the job, the pier on the Alexandra side. According to drilling carried out by the engineer, solid rock, suitable for the pier foundation, would be reached 6 metres below river level. So while Drummey was away in Dunedin buying a steam engine and pumps, his partners James Simmonds and William Beresford supervised the building of a road down the river bank, and the erection of a sandbag coffer dam around the site of the proposed pier. Once the water was pumped out and the gravel bed of the river exposed, excavation began by 'paddocking,' a method familiar to miners. Work went on night and day in three shifts employing 18 men. For men who were mostly miners, it must have been frustrating to see bucket after bucket of sand and gravel, almost certainly containing gold, being dug out and dumped into the river. But Drummey didn't have time for gold mining, even though he admitted that probably about 20 ounces of gold had been thrown away.

In spite of difficulties such as vital pumps breaking down, bedrock was reached on 1 August. There was concern when it was discovered that the rock was not level, as was expected, but was sloping sharply towards the riverbank. Then it was found that the bedrock was not tough schist rock, as it was first thought to be, but a thin layer of brown conglomerate overlying soft clay and decomposed rock. It was not suitable as a foundation for a pier, so it had to be excavated until firm solid rock was reached. Then a metre thickness of concrete was poured into the hole, and on this the first layers of stonework were laid on 15 August. Using concrete was innovative for the times, but the engineer assured the newspaper reporter that he had closely supervised the operation, and that the foundation would be more secure than the original design.

Figure 4.7. A quarry (centre) in Taylor Place is believed to have been the source of rock for building the northern bridge pier. This 1960 view is now obscured by houses.

Stonework

As well as the men working on the pier foundations, there was a gang on each side of the river preparing stone in readiness for building the piers. Two quarries were established, one on the southern side, which was later opened out to become a rock cutting on the approach road to the bridge, and another in the rocky hill east of the main street of the town.[14]

Different types of stone were required for different parts of the piers. For the unseen 5 metres of the northern pier below water level, the call was for

Figure 4.8. The southern pier today. The lower arch is partly submerged by the waters of Lake Roxburgh. The road deck rested on the floor of the upper archway. The suspension cables passed through the holes level with the top of the upper archway.

large blocks of stone only roughly shaped. Some of these were up to five tons in weight. They were laid in mortar as 'coursed rubble' — meaning undressed rock laid in layers or courses, much like a stone wall, around the outer perimeter of the pier. Within this outer wall the bulk of the pier was filled with stone rubble set in mortar.

From about a metre below the water level up to the road deck, it was specified that the pier would be faced with 'ashlar,' that is, blocks dressed with straight sides and right-angled corners. Although layers were of different thickness, all blocks in the same layer were of equal thickness. For the columns on either side of the road deck, the stonework was of higher quality. Not only were all the blocks cut to equal thickness with carefully dressed sides and corners, but each was given a 'chisel draught'[15] round the outside of the edge of the face. Stone dressers shaped and cut each block of stone according to a numbered plan.

Most blocks were large: many were over a metre long, 35-50 cm thick and weighed over half a ton. When the stone dressers finished the blocks, they were carted down to the construction site on specially built, two-wheeled jiggers with a low tray between the wheels. Here the blocks were handed over to Peter Campbell, the stone setter in charge of the work on the piers.

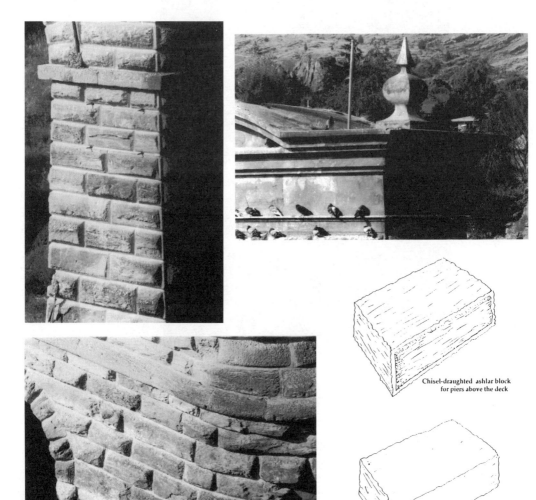

Chisel-draughted ashlar block
for piers above the deck

Ashlar block for piers below the deck

Figure 4.9. Construction details.
    Lower: Ashlar masonry on lower part of pier.
    Centre: Above the deck there is ashlar masonry with each block 'chisel draughted.'
    Upper: Plastered cornice with urns (and pigeons).

Building the Piers

Peter Campbell had learned his trade in Scotland, serving his entire apprenticeship building the stone walls of a basement that was being excavated under a four-storey building. Now he was in charge of setting the stones in the piers, according to the plan supplied by the engineer in which each numbered block was shown.

Progress was good and by early September, eight tiers of rock had been laid and the northern pier was just up to normal river level. Then everything went wrong.

A flood swept down the Manuherikia River and the backed-up Clutha River rose nearly two metres, threatening to overwhelm the excavations. Frantic addition of sandbags to heighten the coffer dam, already 6 metres high, saved the day. Then Drummey fell off the scaffolding and was badly bruised. To cap it all, the partners were threatened with a strike.

On the Saturday pay day, Drummey had dismissed four or five Europeans but had retained a Chinese. The remaining European work force was angry, and regarded it as an insult that Europeans should be dismissed while a Chinese was retained. Then the Chinese made a couple of mistakes that were gleefully pointed out to the boss. The workman had nearly caused a serious accident, they complained, by letting the handle of the crane go, so the load crashed down. Furthermore he had fired explosives without any warning. He had to go, said the workmen, or they would down-tools. Right, said Drummey, anyone who is not satisfied can collect their pay and leave. Fifteen out of the 30 or more workmen went, and that was the end of the matter.

That same week a start was made on the southern pier. Fortunately this pier could be founded on solid rock at just about water level, so there was no need for excavation within coffer dams, or for a substantial foundation of coursed rubble. Ashlar was used to face the whole of this pier and the two piers grew quite quickly at about the same rate. Soon the northern pier was 2 metres above water level, but needed to rise another 2 metres to be safely above all except the worst floods. By early November, the stone setters were beginning to form the first of two archways placed one above the other. This did much to lighten the appearance of the piers, and contributed to the elegance of the whole structure. They also saved masonry. At the end of the month, the northern pier was up 12 metres above its foundation and the southern pier was making good progress.

During the early part of 1880, a start was made on the abutment on which the end of the bridge would rest on the southern bank. But now a serious situation arose which threw the whole project into jeopardy.

Financial and other Crises

In early 1880, the Government became alarmed at the increasing depression of the economy, and decided on a policy of retrenchment. To the consternation of the counties, the mid-1880 budget stopped all subsidies to local bodies and slashed land-fund payments. With the loss of £10,000 in subsidies and grants, Vincent County faced bankruptcy.

Extreme cost cutting was introduced, including dispensing with many staff, abolishing all payments to councillors and even reducing the Chairman's salary from £400 to £250. Payments on contracts had to be suspended lest the bank dishonour Council cheques. Contractors, in turn, could not pay wages. Little wonder it took a long time to finally complete the bridge. But shortage of money was not the only problem plaguing the Vincent County Council.

Since the County system of local government had been established in 1876, Vincent County had been firmly led by its chairman, the legendary Vincent Pyke, after whom the county was named. His had not been an easy task as there was a strong parochial division within the Council, in which councillors from the northern region of the county were matched by equal numbers of those from the south. Nevertheless the business of administering the county was conducted in an orderly fashion until late 1881, when Pyke decided to resign to live in Dunedin.

This gave rise to a desperate struggle to elect a new chairman, and set the scene for what has been described as 'Pickwickian drama which ranged from pure farce to slapstick burlesque.'[16] Among the many unbelievable acts which followed Pyke's resignation was the election of two chairmen. McGinnis was elected chairman to replace Pyke by the southern faction. They promptly locked the door of the chamber against their northern colleagues, who just as promptly broke it down with a battering ram. The northerners then elected one of their number, Colclough, as chairman.

At the next meeting, both chairmen arrived but McGinnis threw his rival bodily out of the chair, whereupon Colclough took up his position at the foot of the table. Both chairmen proceeded to read out the order paper and to chair parallel but separate meetings. As might be expected, the matter ended up in Court where McGinnis's chairmanship was declared illegal. When it was discovered during the long-continuing ruckus that the County accounts had fallen into disarray, councillors pulled themselves together long enough to accept McGinnis as temporary chairman until the election in a few month's time.

To their credit the councillors, in the midst of this internal wrangle, managed to unite in the face of a common enemy, and petition Government for financial relief. They pointed out that, had they known that the subsidies were going to end, they would never have agreed to begin building the Alexandra bridge. Under pressure from almost all counties, Government passed an Act that allowed it to make special grants for specific local works. For the bridge, Vincent County got £3,000 which immediately disappeared into the bank as part of overdraft repayment. It wasn't enough, however, to cover the £8,000 needed to pay for the bridge. In July 1881 the County made a special appeal to Government, admitting that the job was too big for it under the prevailing financial conditions. There was great relief when a further £5,000 for the bridge was placed on the Government's estimates for 1882.

Finishing the Stonework

By July 1880 both piers were up to the roadway level and the southern abutment was finished. While the stone setters turned their attention to the building of the columns on either side of the road deck, other workers turned to the abutment on the Alexandra side. Because the riverbank on this side was a terrace comprised of gravel, preparations were made to drive piles to provide a foundation for the abutment. A steam engine was used to lift a one-ton weight (a 'monkey') which was then allowed to drop freely for four metres down a guide on to the top of the pile. But things did not go well. The ground was so hard that many piles, even though they were of hard totara timber with a steel-shod point, simply shattered.[17] Sometimes it took all day to drive a 5-metre pile successfully. The pile driving, begun in August 1880, and described as 'a heartbreaking job,' was not completed until the end of January 1881. The piles were decked over with heavy hardwood timber planks and the abutment, with its stone facing walls and rubble-filled interior, was built on top of this foundation. Internal cavities were left to accommodate the anchors for the heavy wire ropes which would support the bridge.

The year 1880 ended sadly when the contractors lost a horse and dray which fell into the deep swift water of the river as it was backing to tip its load over a bank.

Perhaps owing to the delays over payment, it seemed to take a long time to finish the seven-metre-high archways over the road, and it wasn't until mid-1881 that the saddles near the top of the piers for the cables to rest on, were installed. These consisted of a heavy iron bed-plate carrying rollers, which in turn supported a metal saddle grooved to accommodate the cables which would hold up the roadway. The devices allowed the cables to move slightly under the influence of loads on the bridge without damaging the piers. A plastered lintel surmounted with two decorative urns, capped each pier.

The Cables

Heavy steel cables supported the bridge decking and the load that it carried. They were anchored securely in the abutments at each end of the bridge, and passed over the rollers in the piers. Vertical steel rods fastened to the cables at short intervals were attached to the deck supports. It was calculated that the maximum load the bridge could be subject to was 200 tons and the safety factor was 4.5. This meant that it would take a load four and a half times greater than any that could possibly come on to the bridge, before it would collapse.

There is now no record of how these 75 mm diameter cables were transported to Alexandra. There were eight of them — four on either side, so presumably they came on eight large drums. They would have been of considerable weight,[18] and each drum of cable must have been a separate load for a bullock wagon on the long journey from the railhead at Lawrence. Nor is there any description of how these heavy, stiff cables were threaded through the rollers on top of the piers. When the contractor, Jeremiah Drummey, was asked about this in his old age he could not remember the details.[19]

The Deck

Once the cables were in place, work went ahead on the wooden roadway which was supported on heavy wooden crossbeams hung from iron rods fastened to the cables. Longitudinal bearers laid on these beams carried the decking planks. The sides of the bridge consisted of upper and lower horizontal beams connected by double vertical posts with diagonal steel bracing. This made up a 'Pratt' truss that stiffened the roadway and prevented oscillation under load or through the effect of wind.

Figure 4.10. A section of the 75 mm diameter wire cable used to support the bridge. There were four such cables clamped together on each side of the bridge. $NZ 2 coin for scale.

While the deck was being finished, a man who was working on the top of a pier thought he would save effort by sliding down a chain hanging from one of the cranes. He leaned out and grabbed the chain, but he did not realise it was not attached to the winding drum of the crane. Fortunately the chain jammed in the pulley at the top of the crane and he was saved from a 24 metre fall into the river.

The Opening

The opening of the bridge[20] on I June 1882 was really quite an occasion, not only for the town but also for the whole of Central Otago. People came from Roxburgh, Ophir and Cromwell, distances that were long in the days of horse transport. The crowd which gathered was estimated at 700. A procession led by the brass band and followed by dignitaries of the district and the public, headed for the bridge. It was appropriate that Mick McGinnis, who had pushed so hard for the bridge and who was, at that moment, the interim and probably illegal, Chairman of Vincent County,

Figure 4.11. The complex system of diagonal braces between the deck and the parapet rail stabilised the deck against swaying caused by traffic and wind.

declared the bridge open. Then everyone moved on to the centre of the bridge where Mrs James Simmonds, wife of one of the contractors, broke a bottle of champagne against the handrail. After crossing the bridge the crowd retreated to the Alexandra end where obligatory speeches were cut short by rain. Everyone moved to the Town Hall for the remainder of the programme.

The bridge, in spite of difficulties, had been completed within three years and had cost £18,360[21] — £2,200 above the tendered price. Drummey and his partners not only had to deal with the physical difficulties of the project, but with a County Council that was in disarray through parochial infighting. As if this were not bad enough, the County Clerk had not only given up any pretence of account keeping, but also had his fingers in the till. It must have been the final straw for Drummey when he had to report to the council in July 1883 that its cheque for £600 as the final payment on the bridge had been dishonoured.

The largest and most elegant of the Macgeorge suspension bridges became famous throughout the land and synonymous with Alexandra. But it was not designed for motor traffic, and after seventy years of faithful service was dismantled and replaced by a modern structure in 1958. Only the piers, somewhat truncated in appearance because the waters of Lake Roxburgh have submerged the lower of the two archways, remain as an inadequate reminder of the abilities of the pioneer engineers and contractors.

Figure 4.12. The opening of the bridge 2 June 1882.

Figure 4.13. The piers stand as forlorn monuments to the skill of the early bridge builders. The steel-arch replacement bridge casts the shadows of its beams on to the piers.

NOTES

1. A clause in the Ferry Act of 1856 made it unlawful to cross the river within 3 miles of the ferry without paying the ferry charge. It was rescinded in November 1864.
2. A letter appeared in the *Otago Daily Times* 30 March 1865 asking for a bridge.
3. *Otago Daily Times* 15 November 1865.
4. Wife of James C. Thomson JP, Goldfields Registrar and Gold Receiver at Alexandra.
5. Reported *Alexandra Herald* 10 October 1906.
6. *Dunstan Times* 8 October 1906,
7. *Alexandra Herald* 1 April 1931.
8. *Alexandra Herald* 8 July 1931.
9. *Central Otago News* 10 June 1952.
10. *Tuapeka Times* 20 December 1873.
11. *Otago Provincial Gazette* 14 January 1874 p. 14.
12. Article by "Uncle Jim" [James Simmonds] *Alexandra Herald* 27 November 1912.
13. Based on the equivalent price of gold this is about $NZ2,500,000 in present-day currency. This seems cheap but was equivalent to about $850 for every man, woman and child in the county.
14. The rock face alongside Taylor Place, now partly hidden by recent building, is believed to mark the town-side quarry.
15. A smoothed area about 50 mm wide cut in from the outside edge of the face of the rock.
16. Angus J. H. 1977 pp. 39-41.
17. Much the same thing happened when contractors were driving piles for the new bridge in 1956. This time the piles were of steel, but as they were driven they bent through 180 degrees underground and their points reappeared on the surface.
18. Each cable, if it were about 180 metres long , would weigh over 4,100 kg.
19. Peter Campbell Jnr taped by Les Thomson, Alexandra 1963.
20. *Dunstan Times* 2 June 1882.
21. Equivalent to about NZ$ 2.8 million.

5.
MAN OF MANY TALENTS

—**James Simmonds**

Perhaps the goldfields attracted men with a wide variety of skills and talents. Or perhaps the environment in which they found themselves encouraged or even forced men to become versatile in order to survive, let alone prosper. Every so often a man turned up who had outstanding versatility — a man who had ability in a wide range of practical skills but was also good at business. If, as so often happened, he also showed a degree of public spiritedness, he quickly became a leader in the community. Fortunately such men were by no means rare. In Alexandra, Louis Gards, James Kelman, Billy Fraser, William Theyers and James Simmonds come to mind. But of these, only Simmonds thought it worth while to leave us some details of his life and some impressions of the conditions in which he lived.[1] These, along with the snippets of information from the local newspapers, can 'flesh out' the dry bones of Simmonds' activities provided by musty records of the Warden's Court. Some life can be brought to the stern face peering at us from old photographs.

Simmonds was born in Hobart, Tasmania in 1841[2] and served his time as a cabinet-maker. Early on he showed an interest in gold mining and spent three years on the Australian goldfields. Then the news of gold discoveries in Otago attracted him and, with a companion, he arrived in Dunedin in late 1861.

Invercargill
A six day tramp took the two mates to Wetherstones, near Gabriels Gully, where they spent five months prospecting without much success, so they returned to Dunedin and Simmonds took a steamer to Invercargill. This town had not yet experienced the short-term boom it was to enjoy after the discovery of gold at Wakatipu. In fact Simmonds counted only 50 dwellings in the whole town. The streets were lines cut through the bush with stumps and fallen logs as hazards to the traveller, and the worst of the bogs made barely passable by bundles of manuka stems laid in the mud. In spite of the town's dismal appearance there was apparently a demand for builders, so he settled down and worked for a year or two putting up

Figure 5.1. James Simmonds 1841-1923.

houses. Although Simmonds' skills as a cabinetmaker would not be called upon very often, he at least knew how to use carpenter's tools and had little trouble handling the simple buildings required.

When the excitement of the gold rushes did engulf Invercargill during 1863, the struggling town hoped it might become the main point of departure for the Wakatipu goldfields. These hopes were dashed when Otago quickly pushed a road through from the Dunstan and diverted the traffic to Dunedin. Nevertheless, prospectors travelling from Southland to the Dunstan had found gold on the way. The first discoveries were in the Nokomai Valley, a tributary of the Mataura River. It was not long before the tales of wealth affected young Simmonds and off he went. He quickly decided, however, that it was easier to collect gold from customers across a bar than it was to dig it from the ground. When in 1865 the West Coast gold rushes drained away most of his customers, his days as an hotel proprietor came to an end.

Nevis

Not far away, and still on the route to the Dunstan, was the Nevis Valley where another gold diggings had opened up. Here Simmonds gained a contract to build an hotel and he recalls the opening day when men, including John Butler, later to become a prominent farmer of Bald Hill Flat, ordered cases of brandy and whisky to celebrate the occasion. Liquor played a big part in the life of the gold diggings, and Simmonds regularly saw trains of 50 or 60 pack horses leaving for Clyde to return with 200 cases of liquor, plus a few other essentials. He did very well at Nevis, demonstrating his versatility by turning his hand at various times to watch repair, boot repair, tin smithing, hair cutting, carpentry and pump and water wheel construction.

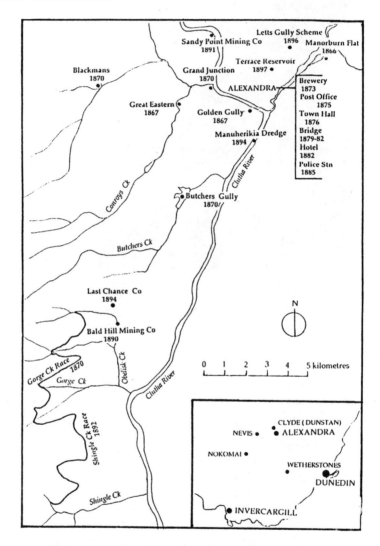

Figure 5.2. Localities connected with Simmonds.

Nevertheless, in the restless way of young people on the goldfields, Simmonds soon sold up and moved on to the Dunstan. Clyde, as the centre of the Dunstan Goldfield, was the largest settlement in Central Otago, its long main street filled with innumerable hotels, stores, and shanties. Business was brisk and money was plentiful, but in 1866 Simmonds moved down to Alexandra — a settlement smaller than Clyde, but in his judgement, with a better future. Several large water races had just been completed and prosperous gold diggings surrounded the town. Like the fabulous Frenchmans Point claims, they were at the peak of their productivity.

Simmonds decided to set up in business as a barber, as this required little equipment apart from a barber's pole — something he thought he could rustle up himself. He arranged to rent a suitable building, and then left for Invercargill to bring back his wife whom he had married several years before. His absence turned out to be a mistake, for when he returned to Alexandra he found that someone else had taken over his shop and was already in business as a barber. Not to be outdone, he set up a bootmaker and leather goods business at the Manor Burn, a few kilometres up the Manuherikia River from Alexandra. He did well but the life was not exciting enough for young Simmonds, so he began the involvement in gold mines that continued for much of his life.

Mining

Simmonds' first mining venture,[3] buying a share in the Golden Gully claim on Bridge Hill, was a failure, owing, as he put it, 'either to bad management or lack of gold.' But this did not put him off. He bought a third share in the notorious Great Eastern mine at the mouth of Conroys Creek gorge. A tunnel had been driven right through the hill and Conroys Creek was channelled through it to act as a sluice. The mine prospered, but when the number of partners was increased to six, the returns could not support them. Simmonds sold out about six months before the remaining partners staged a mock tragedy, during which they led the district to believe that they had been trapped in the mine by a tunnel collapsing. While miners worked frantically to free them, they were well on their way to the North Island, leaving a number of unpaid storekeepers to rue the perfidy of humans.

Book-Keeper

William Theyers was one of the best-known storekeepers in Central Otago. He was a particularly hard-working man who expected everyone else to be the same. So when Simmonds became bookkeeper to Theyers, he found himself working 16 hours a day and 20 hours on Sunday when the ledger was made up. Those were the days when storekeepers delivered their goods, and Simmonds tells of efforts to deliver a large stove to a miner at the Caledonian claim, a kilometre or so down the Clutha River gorge from Alexandra. The stove was tied on to the side of a large horse and, to balance the weight, a sack of potatoes and a bag of sugar were tied on the other side, making a total load of about 350 kilograms. Little wonder the horse sat down, then lay down. In spite of these antics, with Theyers pulling and Simmonds pushing and various others helping, they finally delivered the stove after a long and exhausting day. Billy Theyers was heard to remark in his inimitable way, "If somebody will tie the stove on properly I'll carry the damn thing myself." Having learnt his lesson, Theyers successfully delivered the next stove by carrying it on top of a straw mattress lying across the backs of *two* horses lashed together at heads and tails.

Figure 5.3. Simmonds worked as bookkeeper for storekeeper William Theyers, one of the best known personalities of early Alexandra.

Serious Mining

While working for Theyers, Simmonds still found energy to invest in gold mines. With Joe Knowles, and a group who had just worked out their claim at Frenchmans Point, he opened up a mine in 1870 on the west bank of the Clutha River just above the mouth of the Fraser River. Using horse-drawn trucks running on rails, and employing eleven men, the combined group, calling themselves the Earnscleugh Grand Junction claim, soon had an excavation to a depth of 4 metres over an area of 30 metres square. Then with the help of a large Californian pump turned by two men working in half hour shifts (later replaced by a waterwheel), they made a desperate attempt to reach the bottom on which they hoped the gold lay. Concentrating their efforts on a small area, they went down 6 metres below the level of the Clutha River, and came within less than a metre of the solid bottom before they had to give up owing to the influx of water. Later, others would prove that there was abundant gold in the claim.

Simmonds's luck changed the next year when he bought a claim at Butchers Gully for £350 and, in partnership with James Hesson, developed a very successful gold mine.

During early 1871, Simmonds joined John Mackersey, Henry Young and William Forrest, all well-known mining entrepreneurs, in what they called the Gorge Creek Company. Its purpose was to construct a water race from Gorge Creek to carry 16 heads of water to Bald Hill Flat (the modern Fruitlands). By the end of the year, when construction began, the *Otago Daily Times* was describing the project as the largest work in this district.

It was intended to mine a block in the middle of Bald Hill Flat, and it was Simmonds who came up with the idea of making the mile-long tail race which would be required, a public sludge channel. This would mean that it would be financed by shareholders and Government subsidy. However, this proposal greatly alarmed the farmers who saw it as the thin end of a wedge that would eventually enable the miners to mine most of Bald Hill Flat. There was so much opposition that Simmonds dropped the idea. Later an inquiry was held which resulted in most of the auriferous land being set aside as a Mining Reserve.

Figure 5.4. The Post Office built by Simmonds in 1875 served until 1921 and was then used as a shop. It was demolished only in the mid-1950s.

Contracting

Between mining ventures, Simmonds engaged in various building contracts. One of these nearly cost him his life. With James Hesson and Edward Thomson, he was excavating near the foundation of the Manuherikia Brewery in September 1873 when the whole gable end of the stone building collapsed. Thomson was killed, Simmonds had his hip broken and the other man was also injured.[4]

James Simmonds and George Ratcliffe (a local carpenter) won the contract for a new Post Office for Alexandra with a tender of £568. This wooden building, of a rather imposing design for the size of the town, was erected in May 1875 on the western side of Tarbert Street. It continued to serve until 1921 when a new Post Office was completed, but the old building's life was by no means over. For some years it was occupied by a grocer's shop, and then in 1928 it was moved bodily backwards for about 25 metres to allow a large store to be built for the Co-operative Society. From then on it served as a storeroom for the Society and successive owners of the building, until it was finally demolished in the late 1950s.

A bonus of £5 was offered by the Borough Council in October 1875 for the most acceptable plan for a Town Hall. Of the four plans submitted, Simmonds' was accepted, but by the time the council overcame objections to the building by those who thought a water supply should have priority, Simmonds had been elected to the Borough Council. He was then ineligible to undertake the building contract, but he continued to press for the hall to be built. He finally achieved success when a contract was let at the end of 1876. Although he could not be involved in the construction, Simmonds acted as an unofficial inspector, regularly reporting to Council, not only on omissions by the contractors but on neglect of duty by the official Inspector employed by the council.

Figure 5.5. Simmonds designed Alexandra's Town hall but was prevented from building it himself because he was a member of the Borough Council.

Community Affairs
It was shortly after this that Simmonds' name first appears in reports[5] of community affairs. At a public meeting he supported the mayor against

John Chapple (an ex-mayor), who was in trouble for digging up the road to tap a water race to irrigate his garden. Simmonds told the meeting in no uncertain terms that Chapple was breaking the law.

It is not surprising that such an able and energetic man should be persuaded to stand for the mayoralty, and Simmonds was elected to the office in 1877. During his term, apart from continuing problems with the town water supply, he had to deal with confusion over the building of the Light Traffic Bridge (Shaky Bridge) across the Manuherikia River, and with the effects of the devastating flood of 1878.

It is interesting to note that the man who won the next election (by one vote) was William Hastedt. He had been the Inspector employed by the Borough Council to supervise the building of the Town Hall, and the man whom Simmonds criticised for neglect of duty. But Hastedt never took office, because the election was declared invalid and James Rivers was declared to be Mayor. Simmonds was re-elected as Mayor in mid-1879 and this time held office until 1882.

While he was mayor he entered a partnership with Jeremiah Drummey and William Beresford to build the bridge across the Clutha River at Alexandra (see Chapter 4). It was a big job, and three years were to pass before it was opened on 1 June 1882 and Mrs Simmonds was able to break a bottle of champagne on the bridge rail.

Temperance Hotel
Even before the bridge contract was finished, Simmonds had already entered upon another enterprise which would keep him occupied for the next 10 or 12 years. He had purchased a large section on the corner of Limerick and Ennis Streets, together with the adjoining section in Limerick Street. In April 1882, he began to erect on the corner section, a commodious and substantial two-storeyed stone building, using dressed stone left over from the bridge contract. It was described by the local newspaper as an hotel which would have 40 rooms. As it eventuated, this was a slight exaggeration but the building did have 12 bedrooms as well as dining room, billiard room, bar and so on.[6]

It is likely that the building was erected as a speculation, as it was offered for sale immediately it was completed. But it was a bad time for selling property in Alexandra and this attracted no buyers. So Simmonds decided he would make use of it himself. In December he announced the opening of the "Vincent County Club." The Club would not only provide accommodation, but also cater for weddings and parties and could offer dancing and quoits. It would also provide tea, coffee and stabling. But it seems that the economic depression which was taking a firmer grip on the town, put paid to this enterprise too. Simmonds tried another scheme. He opened a general store in the stone building that was now being described as a Temperance Hotel. But he nearly lost it when a cottage on his adjacent Limerick Street section caught alight and was destroyed in one of the most spectacular fires that Alexandra had witnessed up to that time. On this now empty section and on another to the rear, Simmonds set up a sawmill and timber yard using the whole property as the base for his carpentry and contracting business.

Figure 5.6. Simmonds' building on the corner of Ennis and Limerick Streets.

Figure 5.7. Simmonds erected the policeman's house and adjoining police office and gaol in 1885.

Perhaps the first contract Simmonds undertook from his new premises was the construction, in May 1885, of the new gaol and policeman's residence. These stone buildings, which replaced the original 'Police Camp' burnt down in mid-1884, lasted until they were demolished in the late 1950s.

Bald Hill Flat Mine

Simmonds still had an interest in the Gorge Creek Company which not only owned the large race from Gorge Creek, but also mined a claim at Obelisk Creek at Bald Hill Flat. But now the partners, who had changed a number of times since the enterprise was set up, had a disagreement. It was usual in such circumstances for the assets to be sold by auction, and for the partners to divide up the proceeds. In March 1890 this was done and two of the partners, Carrol and Lynch, paid £1,151 to buy the claim and water race from the others.

The year 1890 was a busy one for Simmonds. With James Hesson, Samuel Simmonds and Peter Jacobs he set up the Bald Hill Flat Hydraulic Mining Company and obtained an 11-hectare claim in Obelisk Creek. Next year the name of the group was changed to the 'Last Chance Elevating Company,' presumably because the previous name was too easily confused with another concern, the Bald Hill Flat Sluicing Company. While all this activity on Bald Hill Flat was going on, Simmonds, with Thos W. Hawley, took time to set up the Sandy Point Mining Company to work an 8.5 hectare claim on the west bank of the Clutha River, about 2 kilometres above the mouth of the Fraser River.

By the end of 1891, in spite of many difficulties, the claim at Bald Hill Flat was ready for operation. A race had been cut from Gorge Creek to a dam, and a line of pipes led to a new innovation — an hydraulic elevator. This was the first to be set up in this district, and its efficiency in recovering gold was amply demonstrated when 60 oz were recovered from the opening 'paddock.'

To help finance the extension of their race to Shingle Creek, some six or seven kilometres beyond Gorge Creek, and to purchase a water right, Stephen Foxwell, a well-known miner from Conroys Gully, was brought into the partnership.

For several months the construction of the extended race went on, with 40 men employed on the project. By the end of February 1893, it was finished and the water was used to work a second elevator. From now on the Last Chance claim regularly returned large quantities of gold and made a fortune for its owners.

Just before Christmas 1892, Simmonds informed the public that he had sold his Vincent County Timber and Iron Yard to J. D. Thomson, who described himself as 'painter, paperhanger and undertaker.' Simmonds was apparently giving up his contracting business, although retaining his hotel and store. His interests were turning more and more to mining, and at the same time, the returns from his investments were allowing him time to spend on public affairs.

Already Simmonds was off on another project. A group of local men,

Charles Leijon, John Mackersey, Thomas Steel, Olaf Magnus and James Simmonds decided to build a gold dredge from various bits and pieces that were available.

The *Manuherikia* Dredge

Using pontoons from an unsuccessful 'pneumatic' dredge, and a bucket ladder discarded from the first steam dredge, *Dunedin*, Simmonds supervised the construction of a vessel which was to be driven by current wheels. The dredge, named *Manuherikia*, was finished in March 1894 but while being manoeuvred into position for dredging, it swung broadside on to the current and sank. It appeared that all their work had gone for nothing. Simmonds set to work, laying pipelines to bring water to sluice the sand out of the hull, removing machinery and finally hoisting the pontoons out of the river.

Figure 5.8. Simmonds' principal mining interest was the Last Chance claim at Bald Hill Flat.

Just before *Manuherikia* was relaunched, James Simmonds made perhaps the costliest mistake of his life. He sold his sixth share in the dredge to Alex McGeorge for £350. The *Manuherikia* went on to become the most successful dredge in the district. McGeorge was doubly fortunate. He used the money he made from the *Manuherikia* to set up the fabulously successful Electric Gold Dredging Company on the Kawarau River, which brought him even greater wealth.[7]

Borough Water Supply

James Simmonds had been elected mayor again in 1892. His wife had died in 1891 and, shortly afterwards, he had moved out to a house at Bald Hill Flat where he could take a closer interest in the Last Chance gold mine. This move annoyed many of the town's people, who did not like their mayor

Figure 5.9 Simmonds and partners built the *Manuherikia* dredge from bits and pieces.

living out of the town, and they complained he was never around when he was wanted. He sold his Temperance Hotel and store to his old mate and brother-in-law, James Hesson, who had retired from mining and had moved into town.

An adequate water supply for the borough was the big problem facing the mayor and council. By this time the water race, which was owned by the Borough and supplied the town, had been leased to the newly formed Molyneux Hydraulic Elevating Company for a peppercorn rental. A condition was that one head of water was to be continuously supplied to the borough. Simmonds had the difficult job of making sure that this happened, even though a number of his councillors had interests in the company.

Finally Simmonds produced[8] his own scheme for supplying adequate water to the town. It involved building a hydroelectric station in Letts Gully, served by a dam filled by the water race already owned by the Borough. The power would be used to pump water from the river. After passing through the power station, the water would continue into Alexandra to be used by those not on the reticulated supply. James Kelman, the owner of the local engineering works, criticised Simmonds' scheme, mainly on the grounds of unreliability of the Borough race's water supply, and for several weeks the pair slogged it out in the correspondence columns of the *Dunstan Times*. [9]

Then Simmonds decided that the Borough should have a piped water supply. The water to be supplied by the Molyneux Hydraulic Company would be fed into street pipes from the company's main pipeline. In preparation for this, Simmonds and a councillor bought secondhand mining pipes from Bannockburn. Unfortunately, when laid and connected to the Molyneux Hydraulic pipeline, they blew apart, in spite of Simmonds' personal efforts to encase the joints in concrete. To his embarrassment, the pipes had to be lifted and sold.

The people who had been waiting eagerly for a piped water supply showed their frustration by electing James Rivers as the next mayor. Rivers was full of ideas about how to supply the town with river water lifted by pumps installed on floating pontoons and driven by current wheels. At public meetings and through the newspapers, Simmonds criticised these schemes, mainly on the grounds that the cost of maintenance had been greatly underestimated.

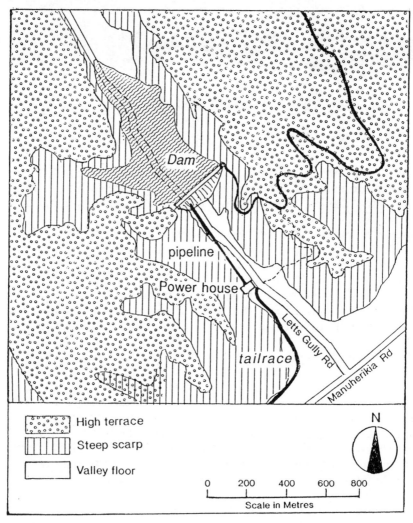

Figure 5.10. Simmond' proposed hydro-electric station in Letts Gully.

Simmonds was elected mayor again in 1896 for the last time. It had almost become mandatory that each incoming mayor produced a proposal for a water supply. This was no problem for Simmonds, the practical contractor. He produced various optional schemes which all made use of the Molyneux Hydraulic Company's pipeline, but when that pipeline was lifted and sold after a bitter row between the council and Company, Simmonds' schemes went with it.

James Kelman replaced Simmonds as mayor in mid-1897 but he remained as a councillor, and was asked by Kelman to produce yet another scheme. Once more Simmonds produced a scheme that used the Borough water race, but this one led the polluted water through filter beds and into a reservoir situated high on the terrace north of the town. With detail designing done by Reynolds, a well-known civil engineer, the council went ahead with the familiar procedures for raising a loan. But the race was giving trouble with washouts and slips, and as the repairs drained the energy and resources of the council, the idea of using it for an upgraded town supply seemed less attractive. James Simmonds did not stand at the next election in 1900 when a new mayor, Henry Symes, took over. Simmonds' latest water scheme faded away when he left the council.

Not long afterwards, Simmonds moved away from Alexandra and took up a farm at Pukerau near Gore. In retirement, he lived out his last years with his son on the latter's farm at Pine Bush, Southland. At Simmonds' death in June 1923, he was the oldest ex-Borough Councillor, and the one with the greatest total length of service.

As a man trained as a cabinetmaker, and with skills in shoe repairing and leatherwork, watch repairing, tinsmithing, hairdressing, pump construction and repair, gold mining, mining investment, dredge construction, carpentry, contracting, store keeping and hotel keeping, he was truly a man of many talents. Coupled with this was a record of community service which covered such diverse fields as Justice of the Peace, Chairman of the Licensing Commission, member of the Library Committee, Dunstan Hospital Board and Central Otago Hospital Board, Secretary of the School Committee and of the Mining Association. Finally he was a councillor of Alexandra Borough for a total of 23 years, including mayor for a total of seven years.

Truly, James Simmonds had served his community well.

NOTES

1. Much of the detail in this chapter is taken from an article written by James Simmonds in the *Alexandra Herald* 27 November 1912.
2. *Cyclopedia* p. 712.
3. It is not clear just how much physical mining Simmonds did. He was a very practical man and it is likely that in many cases he would keep in close touch with those claims in which he had invested. But phrases such as "he opened up a mine" or "he bought a share in a claim" may only mean that he provided all or part of the necessary money.
4. *Dunstan Times* 12 September 1873.
5. *Dunstan Times* 7 November 1873.
6. This building is still one of the landmarks of Alexandra. For nearly a century it

had served as a private boarding house, first as Simmonds' 'Temperance Hotel,' then as 'Hesson's Boarding House,' then as 'The Lodge.' It is now used as solicitors' offices.

7. Sinclair 1962 p. 36.

8. *Dunstan Times* 22 May 1896.

9. In one letter Simmonds made reference to the "Molyneux-Borough-Hydraulic Council." At least half of the Councillors were directors or shareholders in the Molyneux Hydraulic Elevating Company.

6.

WATER AND FIRE

—The First Fire Engine.

November 13, 1903 was a public holiday in Alexandra. For the first time since the township had been established forty years before, residents no longer had to dip into a polluted water race for their water, or pay extravagant prices for river water brought to their doors in barrels. At last they had water piped to taps in their houses, and they made the most of the occasion. It was just as well they did not know that the scheme would fail within a few weeks, and would eventually leave the town practically bankrupt.

One immediate consequence of the arrival of high pressure water mains was the formation of a properly constituted volunteer fire brigade. Just a month after the opening of the water supply scheme, Mayor Kelman called a public meeting on 12 December 1903. Some twenty of those present offered their services, and what was to be the first of regular meetings of the Alexandra Volunteer Fire Brigade was held just four days later.

Equipped with manual hose reels, on which were mounted brass standpipes and branches, the brigade formed an effective fire fighting unit, providing protection that was judged adequate for the time. The pressure in the mains, provided by the fall from the new reservoir situated 110 metres above the town, was often more than the fire hoses of the time could stand. Nor could the firemen always control the hoses charged with such pressure. It is said that at a fire in a shop in the main street, the fire hoses blasted the sheets of corrugated iron from the walls and caused as much damage as the fire. From that day in December 1903 when the first meeting was held, Alexandra has never been without an efficient fire brigade. But it had not always been so.

Over the years a number of fire brigades had been formed, but the initial enthusiasm with which each group was set up, faded after a short time, and the town was left for long periods without any organised fire protection.

Early Fire Protection

In the early days of the township, when most of the buildings on the main street were described as constructed of 'wood and canvas,' fire was always of concern. There was, however, little that could be done towards controlling a fire in the absence of an adequate supply of water, and most burnt themselves out. By the time water was carried from the river, the flimsy building had disappeared.

Nevertheless, as early as December 1863 an attempt was made to make some provision for fire fighting. It was reported[1] that every person in the town, with the exception of two, had subscribed towards setting up a fire brigade. The proposal was to provide buckets and casks full of water at stated places. Early in the new year the brigade held its first meeting in the Caledonian Hotel when a Captain, Lieutenant, Inspector, Secretary and Treasurer were appointed, and it was reported that:

> Buckets, casks, ropes, ladders and all necessary materials have been purchased and everything is in perfect order and ready prepared for use, should that dire calamity for which all this paraphernalia is provided to mitigate the evils if ever it shows its head amongst the buildings of the townspeople.[2]

Unfortunately nothing more is heard of this intrepid group.

Alexandra's Folly

The newly constituted Borough Council soon concerned itself with fire protection for the town, and early in 1870 decided to buy seven 400 gallon malting tanks from William Theyers, who used part of his store in Tarbert Street as a brewery. Now that he was setting up a separate brewery in partnership with C. P. Beck on the outskirts of the town, the tanks were surplus.

Seven large, expensive brass taps of 2 inch (50 mm) bore were ordered from Dunedin, but in the end only four tanks were actually bought for a figure said to be in excess of £100. Two were placed in each ward with four buckets apiece. Each tank was mounted on a stand 45 cm high made of stone and mortar, and each was emblazoned with the painted notice TO BE USED IN CASE OF FIRE ONLY. It was fortunate that they were never called upon for this purpose, as the taps were so stiff they could not be turned and there was seldom any water in the tanks. We are not told how it was intended to keep them full of water, nor is there any reference to a fire brigade. Apparently it was up to the citizens to organise a bucket brigade from the tanks when required. The correspondent of the *Cromwell Argus* who implied that the council had paid far too much for them,[3] referred to the tanks as 'Alexandra's Folly.'

When the Borough Council bought the Ovens Water race early in 1873, it was expected that this would provide water for fire fighting, so three of the tanks, together with the spare brass taps, were sold at public auction. According to a correspondent, they 'did not realise a tithe of the first cost.' The fourth tank was retained for borough use.

The First Fire Engine

Alexandra got its first fire engine in 1881. Its only similarity to the red monsters that wail their way along the town's streets nowadays was the fact that it had four wheels. It was a manual pump activated by men at each end of a long handle which they worked up and down like a seesaw. A primitive contrivance, it was effective and served the needs of the time quite well.

Although no known photograph exists, it is still possible to identify and describe the machine with a fair degree of accuracy. Apparently Messrs A. & T. Burt of Dunedin were the agents, and it is unfortunate that their letter setting out the specifications and description of the machine they were offering has not yet been located. But the Borough Council's order placed with the firm in November 1880 was for:

> . . . a force pump mounted on a 4-wheeled carriage as specified in your letter of the 6th. Include also 12 ft TR suction hose and 50 ft TR delivery hose and one nozzle and hosepipe and brackets. If you have not got these in stock please say when you have same ready for delivery.[4]

The quoted price was £38. We may assume that Merryweather of England made the pump, as the council minutes of June 1885 refer to correspondence with that firm about Alexandra's pump. Further information comes from Tauranga where a fire brigade was being formed, and two Merryweather manual fire engines were ordered late in 1881[5]. The quoted price was £37 each, so it is probable that they were machines similar to that bought by Alexandra. Their order to the Auckland agents, E. Porter & Co, mentions that the machines are on 12 inch (30 cm) diameter wheels. Later, tests showed that each machine could be satisfactorily worked by two men.

Some remnants of the first Alexandra fire engine were still lying in a yard in Deel Street as late as 1950. Mr E. V. King of Alexandra remembers a copper air chamber with a domed top and a pulling handle with a rounded Y-shape at one end.

The only two- or four-man manual fire engine listed in the Merryweather catalogue[6] of the time which fits the specifications of 12 inch diameter wheels, pulling handle with a large Y-shaped yoke for attaching to the front axle, a domed-top air chamber and with a price (including the delivery hose) of less than £40 is the so-called 'Railway' fire engine.[7]

The catalogue gives an illustration (Figure 6.1) and provides specifications of construction material and performance. The engine was a little over a metre long, half a metre wide and about the same in height. It consisted of a sheet-metal, open tank mounted on a cast metal base that had four iron wheels. The two rear wheels were about 30 cm in diameter, but the two front ones were smaller and attached to an axle which, for steering, swivelled like that of a child's trolley.

Inside the tank was a vertical, cylindrical, copper air chamber about 50 cm high and 25 cm in diameter, with a domed top. It was flanked on either side by a vertical pump barrel made of gunmetal. A wrought iron handle, perhaps two metres in length with rounded, wooden cross pieces at the ends, was pivoted at the centre on an axle which was attached to two supports fastened to the base plate. The pump shafts were attached to the long handle, so when it was worked up and down the pumps were activated.

The machine was pulled along by a handle attached to the front axle, or it could be carried by four men with poles run through brackets attached to

Figure 6.1. A 'Railway Fire Engine.' from Merryweather's catalogue of 1896,

the sides of the tank. Once at the scene of the fire, one end of a length of rubber suction hose was connected into the side of the tank and the other end, covered by a strainer, was thrown into a water race or pond. In the main street, a sack placed in the gutters temporarily dammed the water which was now flowing more or less constantly from the Borough's Chatto Creek race. A few buckets of water thrown into the tank primed the pumps, as volunteers, two at each end, began to work the long handle up and down. Meanwhile the 50 ft (15 m) length of canvas delivery hose was connected to the pumps and run out towards the fire, where eager hands would be grasping the long brass branch or 'nozzle,' as it was referred to in the correspondence.

A surprisingly effective jet of water could be obtained as the pulses of the two pumps were evened out by the air chamber into a constant flow. The pressure obtained depended largely on the enthusiasm of the men working the handles, but we can be sure that there would be a fair supply of willing hands ready to take their place as others tired. According to the catalogue specifications, the pump would throw a jet of 35 gallons a minute to a height of 75 feet (23 m).

This particular model of manual fire pump was popular with country fire brigades of the time, and for many it was their first step up from the ubiquitous bucket brigade. A good example, similar in every respect to Alexandra's pump, is preserved in working order at the museum of the Fire Services Historical Society at Ferrymead, Christchurch.

Figure 6.2. The Merryweather 'Railway' pump in the Fire Services Historical Society Museum at Ferrymead, Christchurch.

Burts' must have had the pump in stock and sent it to Alexandra fairly smartly, because a meeting was called on 10 January 1881 to organise yet another fire brigade.[8] Evidently the previous fire brigade had gone into abeyance.

There was some discussion at various council meetings as to where the fire engine should be housed, and in the end tenders were called to build a small shed, 2 metres by 2.5 metres, with stone sides and wooden gate. James Simmonds erected it in what is now McDonald Street at the back of the old Town Hall (which was opposite Limerick Street), for the surprisingly small sum of £4 17s. 6d.[9] A group of men was appointed to look after the engine and practise with it, and apparently they became quite effective fire fighters.

The Big One

Their finest hour came shortly before midnight on 1 February 1902, when fire broke out in the shop of J. T. Duggan, cycle repairer in Tarbert Street. The shop was situated a couple of doors up from the Limerick Street intersection, and the fire quickly spread to the shop on either side as the partitions were only of scrim and paper. On one side was the bakery and residence of W. Wittich, and on the other side the shop was occupied by Reid, a watchmaker. There was some difficulty in getting Mrs Wittich, who was an invalid, out of the building.

The pump, then more than 20 years old, was dragged to the scene and worked at the fire for several hours.

> The old antiquated fire engine did good work under the direction of Captain Reid,[10] whilst there were many who assisted to man the pump. Luckily there was no wind blowing, or one half of the town would have been destroyed.[11]

The three shops were destroyed, but the efforts of the fire brigade (a new group formed a few months before), and the old pump were greatly praised for the fact that they had saved the business section of the town.

Figure 6.3 Manual pumps in action — an illustration from the Merryweather catalogue. A large pump is drawing water from a well (right background) and sending it on to the two smaller pumps attempting to douse the fire. Reinforcements are arriving from the left.

Last Appearance

When high pressure water became available in the street mains in November 1903, the newly formed Alexandra Volunteer Fire Brigade used standpipes from hydrants in the mains. The old pump was to be used only for fires beyond the water mains reticulation.

As far as is known, the last time the pump was used was at the famous coal mine fire of July 1906.[12] An interesting question arises as to how the pump was transported the 2 kilometres from the fire station in Skird Street to the burning coal mine. This lay a considerable distance beyond the end of the present Eureka Street. Was it pulled all the way with its small trolley-like wheels sinking into the sand of the streets? Was it carried by relays of men, or was it thrown into a cart that had been quickly yoked up by some public-spirited citizen? No doubt the hindrance of the pump and other gear that the brigade had to take with them, accounted for the fact that, according to reports, it took members half an hour to arrive at the scene.

Perhaps the old pump wasn't working very well at the coal mine fire, as there is newspaper comment about the 'thin jet of water'[13] produced. Shortly afterwards the Borough Council asked the Town Clerk to get a report on the old fire engine from the Captain of the Fire Brigade, and what it would cost to put it in repair. The answer was £5, but this must have been considered excessive, as there is no record of any repair work being done. In fact, the last we hear of the old pump is an offer from a dredgemaster of one pound for 'the old pump lying beside the fire station.' For some reason the offer was declined.

Forty years later a few remains of the fire engine were still lying outside the Otago Central Power Board workshops in Deel Street, but the tank and wheels had long gone. In the late 1950s when a suggestion was made that the old machine should be restored for use in the Blossom Festival procession, a search was made but by then no trace of the old engine could be found.

NOTES

1. *Otago Daily Times* 21 December 1863.
2. *Otago Daily Times*, 11 January 1864 .
3. *Cromwell Argus* 7 and 28 October 1873.
4. Minutes of Alexandra Borough Council 26 November 1880.
5. A. C. Bellamy, p. 8.
6. Merryweather catalogue 1896.
7. So called because it was suitable for use at small railway stations.
8. *Dunstan Times* 3 September 1901.
9. The Borough Council's estimate for the work was £24. Council Minutes 26 June 1883.
10. If Mr Reid, the watchmaker whose shop was destroyed, was also Captain Reid of the Fire Brigade it is likely that the newspaper would have mentioned the fact. The Electoral Roll of the time also lists a Henry Alfred Reid who was, perhaps, more likely to have been the Captain of the fire brigade.
11. *Dunstan Times* 4 February 1902.
12. For a description of this dramatic event, see *Mine Fire* by John McCraw. 1992.
13. *Otago Witness* 23 July 1906.

7.

'LORD LOCK'

— A Mystery of the Goldfields

In Conroys Gully, at the junction of Chapman Road with Conroy Road, stands a rather picturesque stone cottage in reasonable order and still occupied. A notice at the gate proclaims that this is 'Lord Lockie's cottage.' Who was this Lord Lockie[1]? The present occupier of the small house will tell you that he was a British aristocrat who, after living in the house for some time, went 'home' to inherit a title.

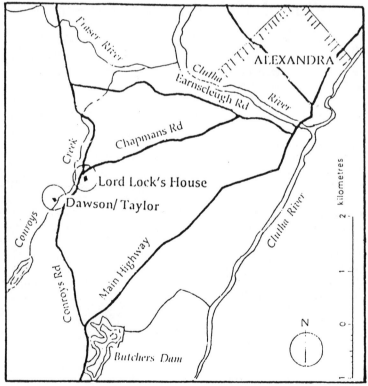

Figure 7.1. Location of 'Lord' Lock's house in relation to Alexandra and Dawson's (later Taylor's) property.

Figure 7.2. The house in Conroys Road built by Stephen Foxwell and rented to 'Lord' Lock.

It seems that this story originated with the Taylor family of Conroys Gully. Although the late June Wood[2] was the first to mention the story in print, it is probable that her source was the late Mrs Gladys McArthur (*nee* Taylor).

The Story
The following version of the story was related by the late Geoff Taylor, who heard it from his grandparents, Richard and Mrs Dawson, pioneer settlers in Conroys Gully:

> The Dawsons were neighbours and friends of Lock and his wife. Lock was an aristocrat who returned to Britain to inherit a title and became 'Lord Lock.'
>
> It was obvious to everyone that Lock had rather more funds than the average miner. He did little work and was believed to be a remittance man.[3] Shortly after their arrival, the couple commissioned Stephen Foxwell, a well-known local resident and miner, to build the stone house at the road junction. Lock and his lady left New Zealand after a few years and, before departing, presented the house to its builder, Stephen Foxwell, who lived in it until he died in 1913.[4]

Mr Taylor commented that because Mrs Dawson, an Irish Roman Catholic, quickly became very friendly with her, Mrs Lock may have been of the same faith and perhaps also Irish. Furthermore, the fact that the wife was not referred to as 'Lady Lock' — she was always 'Mrs Lock' — tends to support the view that Lock did not have a title while in New Zealand.

The Locket

An odd twist to the story is the gift Lock made to Agnes, the young daughter of Sarah Cameron, proprietor of the Caledonian Hotel. Lock was a regular and good patron of the hotel, and was in the habit of staying at the establishment for periods when he came to town and so became friendly with the girl. On her sixteenth birthday, which was on 19 February, 1880, he presented her with a small gold locket. The locket, which is about 25 mm long, is fronted by a carved agate stone and the back has decorative engraving. It is hinged, and when opened reveals a tiny photo or painting of a figure reputed to be Lock, but it is so badly deteriorated that it is only recognisable as a male figure. The present owner, Mrs Noel Watts of Cambridge, remembers a similar photo of a woman in the other half of the locket.

On the back of the mounting paper of the photo is written:

> Hart Campbell & Co
> Photos
> Arrowtown
> Feb 6th 1880

Hart, Campbell & Co was a well known Invercargill photographic firm which apparently had a branch in Arrowtown. Presumably there was no photographer in Alexandra at this time, so Lock had the Arrowtown firm either take the photos or reduce existing photos to fit the locket. This locket was passed down to Agnes's granddaughter, Mrs Watts, who has presented it to the William Bodkin Museum at Alexandra.

Search for a Peer

In spite of an extensive search through such standard works as *Debretts Peerage* and *Who was Who*, no reference to a 'Lord Lock' or 'Lord Locke' can be found. There is a 'Lord Loch' — however, this peerage was not created until 1895, and the man who was to become the first Baron was far away from Central Otago during the relevant period. He was Governor of the Isle of Man from 1862 to 1882, Commissioner of H. M. Woods and Forests from 1882 to 1884, and then Governor of Victoria for the next five years.

The Baron had a son but, as he was born in April 1873, he was only six years old at the time of the presentation of the locket in February 1880.

A search of the passenger lists of assisted immigrants disclosed a number with the name 'Lock' or 'Locke.' Some had landed at Port Chalmers during the 1870s, but all were married couples with children. It is unlikely that an aristocrat would be an assisted immigrant, but a search of the lists of passengers held by the Otago Settlers Association did not produce any further information.

The Electoral Rolls of the time do not list anyone with a name resembling 'Lock.'

The House

On 18 April 1870, Stephen Foxwell, who was mining in the upper part of Chapmans Gully, applied to the Alexandra Warden's Court[5] for a

Figure 7.3 The gold locket presented to Agnes Cameron by 'Lord' Lock on her sixteenth birthday.
Upper left: The front has an agate stone. Upper right: The reverse is engraved.
Lower left: Inside is a small indistinct photograph. Lower Right: The photographer's name and the date are on the back of the photograph.

'Residence Area' of one acre and it was granted shortly afterwards. Foxwell had taken advantage of a clause in the Mining Act that allowed the warden to grant a genuine miner a small area on which he could build a hut or house. This Residence Area, for which the miner paid £1 a year, was protected against mining, unless compensation was paid. Foxwell would have been required to erect some sort of dwelling on the site within three months of the licence being granted, but this may not necessarily have been the two-roomed stone house that stands today. In fact it would have been more usual for a bachelor, such as Foxwell, to erect a single-roomed hut rather than a more elaborate house. So the story that Foxwell was asked by the Locks to build the house for them may well be true. But why a couple, without apparent interest in either mining or farming, should choose to live in an isolated place at least 5 kilometres from the nearest settlement, Alexandra, is a matter of speculation.

According to Glad McArthur,[6] her mother Evelina Dawson, who was born in 1869, was only a 'small girl' (presumably in her pre-teens) when the 'Loches' lived at Conroys. This perhaps confirms they were there during the 1870s.

As there is no record of the Residence Area having been transferred to Lock, Foxwell would have continued to pay the ground rent, and it is possible that he himself may have occupied a hut on the same Residence Area. When another Conroy miner, John Bennett, applied for a Residence Area in 1883, the Application gave the location as 'adjoining Foxwell's residence (south side).' The use of 'residence' rather than 'hut' may indicate that by this time the Locks had left and Foxwell was living in the house. After Foxwell died on New Years Day, 1913, the cottage was sold and the Residence Area included in a block of 3 acres 2 roods 6 poles surveyed off as Section 79, and purchased by Alexander Taylor of Conroys Gully.

Who Was Lord Lock?

So it seems that our man of Conroys Gully could not have inherited the title of 'Lord Lock' or' Lord Locke' as no such peerage has been created. Nor could he be 'Lord Loch,' as Henry Brougham Loch was not created a peer until 1895, and until that time had been engaged far away from New Zealand. There are, however, still a number of possibilities.

Mr Lock may have invented the story of his expectations for his own reasons. Although miners were tolerant of 'characters,' and generally followed a strict code of minding their own business, they disliked being misled or lied to. They were quick to recognise a deception of this sort and the perpetrator would have been given a hard time.

It could be that Lock spoke with an educated, English accent and had the manner of a gentleman. Miners may have assumed that he was someone from well up the social scale and enlarged the story by speculation and rumour.

It is also quite possible that the original story is partly correct. The man may well have been the son of a landed family (such as, for example, Loch of Tittensor, who had an estate near Stone in Staffordshire[8]) who finally went back to Britain to inherit, not a title, but the family estate.

NOTES

1. No one seems to know how the name was spelt. The sign on the cottage says 'Lockie.' Wood[2] uses 'Locke' and Mrs McArthur both 'Loche'[6] and 'Locke.' The simplest version, 'Lock.' is adopted here.
2. Wood, J. A. 1970 p. 27
3. A man who had been 'sent out to the Colonies' and supported with regular funds (the 'remittance') to stay there. He was often well educated and from a 'good family' but presumably had transgressed in some way.
4. Late G. D. Taylor. Oral Communication to author 1995.
5. Records of the Warden's Court Alexandra held by National Archives, Dunedin Regional Office.
6. McArthur, Glad. 5 May 1977 Stone Cottages. Letter to Editor Otago Daily Times.

7. McArthur, Glad. 1992

8. Burke, B. *A. Genealogical and Heraldic Dictionary of the Landed Gentry of Great Britain and Ireland.* Edition 4. 1868

8.

BEER AND BUNNIES

It must have been a good brew. So good, in fact, that the *Otago Daily Times* was worried about the effect on Dunedin breweries:

> Theyers and Beck have succeeded in producing a malt beverage of superior quality such as is calculated to drive competitors out of the Dunstan market. The industry will boost local agriculture as the climate is adapted to grow excellent barley and in one case 80 bushels to the acre has been grown.[1]

'Theyers' was the inimitable William Theyers, a Gloucestershire man who had arrived at the Dunstan in 1862, by way of the Victorian goldfields and Gabriels Gully. Now, in 1870, he was well established in Alexandra as the proprietor of a flourishing general store. He had 'a finger in many pies' and all through his life he continued to invest in gold mines and dredges and in a host of other enterprises. He apparently also had a liking for 'home brew.'

Figure 8.1. Men of the Manuherikia Brewery.
Left: C. P. Beck, partner.
Centre: Wm Theyers (in centre), partner
Right: F. J. Kuhtze, brewer.

Canute Petersen Beck, a Dane, came to New Zealand from Australia. He had worked for a number of years as an assistant to a storekeeper and butcher before setting up his own business. While in Australia he met Vincent Pyke and began what was to become a life-long friendship. No doubt it was Pyke who told him about the gold discoveries in Otago.

The thirty year old Beck arrived at Port Chalmers in January 1862, and later in the year joined the rush to Arrowtown. He was not one of the lucky ones and soon returned to Manuherikia (Alexandra) where, on the river bank opposite the town, he set up a butchery business. But the gold fever had not abated, and soon he was off with the rush to the Hogburn (Naseby) in mid-1863. Because Beck was one of the few with a horse, he was able to cross the flooded Manuherikia River ahead of the hundreds camped on its banks waiting for the river to fall. But to no avail: the gold still eluded him, and he fell back to what he knew best — butchering.

Nevertheless, Beck continued to follow the various gold rushes to Mt Buster, Hyde, Macraes, etc. but without much success. Finally he entered into a partnership with two Americans, Peter Hopper and Ben Delany, who were making ginger-beer and cordials in Naseby. They sold this business and bought J. D. Feraud's extensive cordial business at Clyde. Hopper and Beck ran this until 1867, and then Beck took over the business himself and kept it going for another 11 years.[2]

Manuherikia Brewery

William Theyers had set up a brewing plant in early 1869[3] at the rear of his shop which at that time was in Tarbert Street, below the Bendigo Hotel. Within a few months he had entered into partnership with Beck to brew commercially, and plans were made for establishing a brewery on the outskirts of Alexandra. Theyers had already successfully applied for a 2.5 hectare block on the river side of the Manuherikia road overlooking the Manuherikia Ground Sluicing Co's claim. A 24 by 7.5 metre building was pushed ahead, and the first brew, started in March 1870, was described as 'light, clear and sparkling — as good as any in Dunedin.' The brewer was Frederick Kuhtze. He had learnt the trade in his native Germany, and had arrived in New Zealand unexpectedly when the ship, *Ida Ziegler*, in which he was a crew member, was wrecked at Napier in early 1869.

Unfortunately, the early promise was not fulfilled and the enterprise was soon struggling. It was offered for sale but did not find a purchaser. Accordingly, Beck moved down from Clyde to Alexandra, merged his cordial business with the brewery, and gave the management of the whole concern his personal attention.

Under Beck's management, the product was soon in great demand over a wide district, and a number of additions and alterations had to be made to the brewery. It was during these alterations that James Hesson and James Simmonds were injured, and Edward Thomson killed, by a falling wall.

The brewery reached its peak production around 1880, when output was 90 hogsheads (about 20,000 litres) a month. The stone-walled buildings were quite extensive, and were built on several levels on a slope leading down from the road towards the Manuherikia River. This assisted

Figure 8.2. The brewery about 1900. C. P. Beck is on the left.

the movement of the barley, which was unloaded into the brewery on the upper level, down through the various stages of the process. The power for crushing the malted barley came from a large water wheel.[4] Water for the wheel, and for making the beer, made a long journey from the headwaters of Chatto Creek by way of the Golden Gate race that ran along the foot of the Dunstan Mountains. Beck's quota of water was discharged into the head of Tumatakuru Gully and, after flowing for several kilometres down this gully, was picked up by a second race[5] which conveyed it across to the head of Letts Gully. The water followed this gully until it entered the old race of the Manuherikia Ground Sluicing Co (Drummey's race), which led it to the water wheel.

Beck bought Theyers out in 1890, and from then on the brewing side of the business was gradually phased out and replaced by cordial manufacture. This continued until the time of Beck's death in November 1906 when the factory closed.

Empty soft drink bottles, with 'Theyers & Beck' cast into the glass, still turn up occasionally in excavations around Alexandra. Some have a small, round glass ball[6] trapped in the neck to act as a seal. Others have an elongated rounded base so the bottle had to be stored on its side to ensure the liquid always covered the cork, which was thus prevented from drying out and leaking.[7]

In October 1907 the factory, together with its land, was sold. The new owners made an unsuccessful attempt to start production again, but within less than a month the factory had passed into the hands of Lanes &

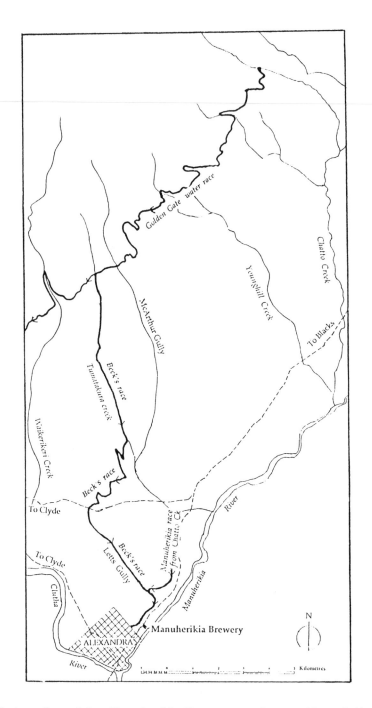

Figure 8.3. Location of the Manuherikia Brewery on the outskirts of Alexandra. Water races brought water more than 30 kilometres from Chatto Creek to drive the water wheel.

Figure 8.4. A 'Theyers and Beck' cordial bottle. The shape was designed to ensure that the bottle was stored on its side so the liquid covered the cork and prevented it drying out and leaking.

Co. of Dunedin, the cordial manufacturers. They used the buildings as a distribution centre for their own products.

The Cordial Factory

Two Dunedin men, Thomas Grant and Walter Maynard, bought the factory and its plant in June 1909.[8] They set about overhauling the equipment, which had been lying idle since Beck's death. Their intention was to manufacture fermented beverages as well as cordials. First a concrete floor was laid throughout the premises. This was seen by the inspecting reporter as a 'vast improvement on that which Nature provided in the way of earth.'

Next they turned their attention to the equipment, and the two bottling machines were cleaned and overhauled. The 2 h.p. oil engine, which did not perform very well, was overhauled and new parts fitted where necessary, so that it worked 'sweetly and satisfactorily.'

The partners began by selling their products in gallon earthenware jars with screw tops. This was in itself an innovation. The jars were made in New Zealand, and they acquired 2,000 of them. Filled with cordial they were retailed to private customers at 1s. 6d. each, and were returnable when empty.

Grant had had 14 years brewing experience with Speight & Co of Dunedin, another four years with Hill's cordial factory in Christchurch and yet another four years on his own, so he was experienced in the manufacture of a wide variety of products. Special features of the output of the Alexandra factory were fermented beverages such as cider, ginger beer and hop beer, but it also turned out soda water, lemonade, ginger ale, raspberry and ginger wine and other cordials. Although the old brewery was still intact, Grant and Maynard did not start it up, but preferred to stay with the manufacture of high-class cordials.

Grant was particularly impressed with the quality of the water from a spring on the property, which replaced the long-abandoned water race. He attributed the high quality of his beverages to this water. Within a short time of beginning, orders were coming in from all over Central Otago, and the partners purchased a specially built wagon for delivery of their cordial jars.

Figure 8.5. The storeroom, across Manuherikia Road from the brewery, is the only surviving brewery building.

In spite of the owner's enthusiasm and experience, the cordial factory closed down just before World War I. The building was sold in 1915 to S. T. Spain for his canning factory.

PRESERVING THE RABBIT
Stephen T. Spain had been a butcher in Alexandra. He had taken over Earnscleugh Station from his father, which also meant taking over the continuing, and losing, battle against rabbits. Although the station

employed dozens of rabbiters, and hundreds of thousands of skins were sold each year, it seemed to make little difference to the number of rabbits which swarmed over the sunny slopes of the station's low country.

Although the skin trade was lucrative, and was the means by which many young men accumulated sufficient money to begin farming on their own account, nothing was done with the carcasses of the rabbits. They were simply left to rot. Steve Spain, as a butcher, was concerned about this waste of meat, and made a number of attempts to interest local investors in some sort of meat preserving process, but without success.

Figure 8.6. Stephen Spain of Earnscleugh Station was the instigator and principal shareholder of Central Otago Preserves Ltd.

It was Britain's demand for food, following the outbreak of the Great War in 1914, that decided Spain to set up a factory for preserving rabbit meat himself. By the time he made his first public announcement[9] on 10 May 1915, he had obviously done much negotiating behind the scenes. The buildings of the old Manuherikia Brewery on the outskirts of Alexandra had been purchased, and already modifications were under way. The necessary machinery had been bought from the freezing works at Woodlands in Southland, and it was intended to start preserving rabbit carcasses at the rate of 2,000 to 3,000 a day, with a possibility of raising the daily output to 15,000.

Spain revealed that the British War Office had offered to pay 14 shillings a dozen for two-pound (about 900 grams) cans of rabbit meat, and though he had hoped for a higher price, the factory would still make a profit at this figure.

98

By the following month the machinery was on its way, and it was announced that Mr Dan Hannon, late manager of the Woodlands plant, had been appointed manager at Alexandra.[10] August 4, 1915 was the date set for the factory to commence operations.

Figure 8.7. An Argyll truck collected rabbits for the factory. Resurrected but unrestored, it takes part in a Blossom Festival procession in the late 1950s.

It was planned that rabbits trapped within a 60 kilometre radius of the factory would be collected and brought in by motor lorry. But already there were difficulties. Because of the war, rabbit trappers were becoming scarce, and to prevent rabbits getting out of hand, property owners were resorting to poisoning as a method of rabbit control. Poisoned rabbits were, of course, not acceptable in the preserving plant.

Nevertheless by March 1916, the plant was fully occupied processing 3,000 rabbit carcasses a day, and Spain had demonstrated that the process could be carried out successfully and profitably. With a view to expansion and development, he now decided to set up a public company with a capital of £7,200. It was incorporated on 18 March, 1916 with a Directorate of prominent runholders comprising S. T. Spain of Earnscleugh, John Wilson of Lauder, William Laidlaw of Matakanui, Robert Jopp of Moutere and James Ritchie of Bannockburn, with Charles Richards of Alexandra as Secretary. By June, shares had been allotted to 86 shareholders, all of whom were Central Otago people, and most took up five to fifty shares. The Directors, and a few senior employees, took up allocations of 100 shares each. S. T. Spain initially took up 1,800 shares but later increased his holding to 2,500.

Figure 8.8. The old brewery buildings after conversion to the canning factory. A 'retort room,' (on the right with the tall chimney) has been added to the original buildings.

Canning rabbit meat was not a very complicated process. A newspaper reporter shown through the factory was much impressed by the cleanliness of the place, which was ensured by the copious amount of water used in the constant hosing down of floors and work benches. Rabbits were being skinned at the rate of about 15 per minute by a team of local men who had rapidly become experts in the procedure. The desirable cuts of flesh were stripped off, washed in a large tub of water, then transferred for a few seconds to a cauldron of boiling water before being placed into the cans. The cans were made in the tinsmith's shop on the premises. After closing, the cans were heated in the 'retort room' so that their contents were cooked for four hours. Then the cans were dipped into lacquer, and with the application of a colourful label they were ready to be placed in boxes for export to the markets of the world.[11]

It was found impractical to operate the factory during January and February — the hottest months of the year — because, in the days before refrigerated trucks, it was not possible to keep carcasses sufficiently fresh before they could be processed. So Spain suggested that during this period other produce could be canned, and put his proposal to a public meeting. He proposed that a new co-operative company be formed with a capital of £10,000, and with the suppliers of both meat and fruit as shareholders.

Figure 8.9. The can-making room in the factory.

The Fruitgrowers' Association was interested but, inevitably, had to set up a committee to look into the proposals. While this 'looking into' was going on, the Directors of the Company ordered £2,500 worth of extra machinery so that they could begin canning beef and mutton during the following summer. During the summer recess of 1916-17, the company erected a large concrete building[12] to replace the old stone-walled brewery building which was being used as the main processing room.

This was the time of peak production for the Central Otago Preserving Company, known locally as 'the Canning factory' or 'the Rabbit factory.' It, along with the newly established freezing works near the Railway Station, provided much needed work to replace the loss of jobs that accompanied the demise of the gold dredges. Business had been at a standstill, and there were many empty houses. Now the town had an air of prosperity and the future looked bright. Both new industries were particularly suitable for those who needed temporary or part-time work while their orchards were coming into bearing. But the frenetic activity didn't last long.

Owing to a wartime shortage of shipping, cases of cans began to pile up on the wharf at Dunedin. Although all had been ordered by agents in Britain, and could be regarded as sold, no money had so far appeared. The cannery began to suffer what is nowadays called a 'cash-flow problem.' In September 1917, the factory came to a standstill simply because of shortage of storage space. The chance was taken to carry out much needed alterations and extensions. We are not told how the shipping problem was resolved — presumably the backlog was finally cleared.

Figure 8.10. The 'tinning room' where tins were packed with rabbit meat.

There was jubilation, not only in the cannery, but also throughout the town when it was announced in December 1917 that the British Government had ordered 8,000 cases of canned food. This was followed in March 1918 with another order for 20,000 cases from the British Admiralty, which completely absorbed the year's output. The factory was flat out and it began to give out nasty odours that drifted over the town, but the town couldn't afford to complain. As the newspaper put it, any move on the part of the town to close the factory down would be to destroy the golden egg. But it did suggest that the offending gas should be bottled and sent to the Western Front where it would without doubt prostrate the German army.[13]

With the end of the War, orders fell away, and once more cases of cans began to pile up. In a short time there were again 20,000 cases of canned goods and 22 bales of rabbit skins in store. At the end of 1919 the factory closed as usual before the hot weather set in, but an emergency meeting in March 1920 declared that it remain closed. The outlook was bleak. There was a glut on the British market, and prices realised for the product came nowhere near covering the cost of production, transport and other charges. Before the stocks lying in Britain were written off at a cost of £2,100, Archie Ashworth, a Director, suggested that a subscription fund should be raised to pay the standing charges levied in Britain, and then the cans should be given to the starving people of Russia.

When a shareholders' meeting was called in February 1923, the factory had not opened but at least all the stocks of canned meat had been disposed of and the rabbit skins had been sold. A shipment of cans sent to Europe was returned to Britain with the possibility of having to sell at 8s or 9s a case — far below cost. The United States market was being explored without any real hope of success. Consideration was given to a motion to wind up the company. W. A. Bodkin opposed this course of action until he had held another meeting with fruitgrowers, to see if they had changed their minds about preserving fruit. But they had not, and on 8 October 1924 the Central Otago Preserving Company Ltd went into voluntary liquidation.

Figure 8.11. The 2 lb (900 gm) can of cooked rabbit meat produced by the Central Otago Preserves Co Ltd. Directions on the label: IF DESIRED HOT BOIL FOR TWENTY MINUTES BEFORE SERVING

The buildings lay empty for most of the next 16 years under the charge of a caretaker, but during the drive to develop an apple export industry in the 1920s, the large hall was used for several seasons as a packing house for the fruit.

The finale was an auction sale held on 1 April 1939 when the land, buildings and the machinery were offered for sale. It was a 'satisfactory' sale according to the auctioneer, with all of the gear being sold. Some people had travelled from Dunedin and Invercargill to the sale. The land comprising more than two hectares, together with the buildings, which included the large hall built for the canning factory as well as the old Brewery buildings, were sold to G. H. Fox for £270.

Figure 8.12. The large building in the centre of the photograph, built in 1917, is the only surviving building of the canning factory. It is used now as the recreation hall for a holiday camp here seen at an early stage of development.

Fox demolished most of the old buildings, as he developed the site into a holiday camp during the early years of World War II. The only remaining brewery building is the bottling store that still stands on the roadside opposite the site of the brewery. The large concrete building, built for the Preserving Company, is still in use as a recreation hall for the flourishing holiday camp.

NOTES

1. *Otago Daily Times* 17 August 1870.
2. Obituary *Otago Daily Times* 28 November 1906.
3. *Dunstan Times* 19 February 1869.
4. *Dunstan Times* 11 December 1885 and Recollections of Olaf Magnus, taped by L Thomson 1988.
5. The geological map of Leaning Rock Survey District included in J. Park, 1905, shows this race clearly.
6. These glass balls were in great demand by children as a cheap source of the marbles known as 'bottlies.' The late Alex. Taylor of Alexandra told (personal communication) how an empty bottle with its ball still in place could, when shaken vigorously, be used to encourage a horse pulling a gig to greater speed.
7. Collectors refer to these bottles as 'torpedoes.'
8. *Alexandra Herald* 8 September 1909.
9. *Dunstan Times* 10 May 1915.
10. *Dunstan Times* 21 June 1915.

11. *Dunstan Times* 20 March 1816.
12. This building still exists as the recreation hall for the holiday camp.
13. *Dunstan Times* 13 May 1918.

9.

SCRAPING THE BOTTOM

—Development of the Gold Dredge

It all started with 'blind stabbing.' A miner, standing as far out in the turbulent river as he dared, jabbed his shovel into the sand of the river bottom, lifted it carefully, and tried to save as much of the contents as possible from the ravages of the strong current as he waded ashore. Whatever was left on the shovel was carefully panned or cradled. It wasn't long before someone made a raft out of barrels or spare timber, and securely moored it out in the river so that the shovelfuls of sand could be thrown on to it, instead of the miner wading ashore with each one. When the raft was fully loaded, it was pulled ashore and the sand washed through a cradle. Working up to his waist in the freezing water of the fast-flowing river, a man could tolerate only about 15 minutes at a time. And no doubt during that time he wondered if there wasn't an easier way to make a living. Why not, for instance, work from the raft?

Hand Dredging
According to W. H. Cutten[1] the engineer, it was a man named Brown, working with his mates near Alexandra, who developed the technique. He made a much larger 'shovel' from a ring of heavy iron, up to 45 cms in diameter, to which was attached a leather bag and a long wooden handle. This was the scoop or 'spoon.' Men on the raft, moored 15 metres or so from the shore, dropped the scoop down into the river bed, and then their mates on the beach pulled it towards them by means of a simple windlass and a rope fastened to the scoop. The raft men steadied the contrivance with another rope fastened to the top of the handle. This was paid out as the scoop was drawn away from them.

This 'hand-dredging,' as it was called, worked best in water less than 8 ft (2.4 m) deep, and became very popular because it required only simple equipment. Often several neighbours joined forces to dredge the under-water parts of their adjoining claims because the procedure required seven men — two on the raft or boat, two on the windlass and three working the cradle, one of whom would lift and empty the bag.

The next step was to carry out the entire operation from the raft or barge. The spoon was pulled along the riverbed for the length of the barge by a windlass mounted at one end of the vessel, and emptied into cradles or sluice boxes on the barge. Then a current-driven wheel was fitted to lift river water for washing the sand through the gold-saving devices. So step by step, with contributions from many innovative but unknown miners, the 'spoon dredge' was adapted to gold mining.

SPOON DREDGES

Spoon dredges were not new. They had been used in China for centuries and are still used for cleaning out irrigation canals. They were also used on the River Thames for recovering ballast tipped overboard from loading ships. In fact it was a group of ex-Thames dredgers who formed a company which built the first large spoon gold dredge in the district.

Ben Knight and his mates formed the Molyneux and Kawarau Gold Dredging Company in mid-1863, and after some experimenting on the Kawarau River with a punt washed down from the lakes, set about building a dredge. The hull, with complete decking, had been built at Queenstown and brought down the river to Clyde. Here it was fitted with a crane which hung over the side amidships, a winch at the bow and an undershot water wheel which delivered water to the sluice boxes on the deck. The finished craft had a displacement of 40 tons and cost £600. *Alabama*, as it was named, was launched in November 1863 amidst festivities that included having a brass band on board, as the vessel was taken down the river to its claim.

Operating these spoon dredges was hard physical work.[2] First the vessel had to be securely moored in the river. A ship's anchor held the stern, and three wooden poles with steel-shod points were driven into the riverbed and clamped to the hull at the bow and amidships. From the windlass on the bow, a substantial chain was led over a roller at the end of the davit or crane and fastened to the spoon. On the *Alabama* the spoon consisted of a circle of 12 mm-thick iron, 60 cms in diameter and 10 cms deep, with a hardened iron lip fastened around the front edge for half the diameter. Fastened to the rear of the iron ring was a bag made from bullock hide which would hold 'about as much as a porter hogshead'[3] (about a quarter of a cubic metre). A wooden handle, about 6 metres long, was securely fastened to the ring so the whole contrivance looked like a giant spoon.

It was the dredgemaster's job to position the spoon on the riverbed. The chain was wound in until the spoon hung midway between the deck and the top of the crane, then with all his strength he pushed the heavy, cumbersome contrivance outwards and at the same time shouted for the chain to be slackened. He was careful to keep clear of the long handle that whipped across the deck as the spoon fell into the water. His experience allowed for the effect of the current on the sinking spoon, so that it hit the bottom just where he wanted it. The weight of the spoon ensured that the handle stuck vertically out of the water. A rope, called a 'stopper,' already tied around the upper end of the handle, was fastened to a rail so that it could slide along as the spoon was pulled by the chain and winch, but at the same time prevent the spoon from rising from the bottom.

As the strain came on from the winch, the spoon's hardened lip bit into

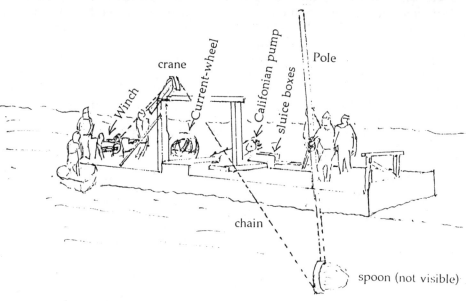

Figure 9.1. A. spoon dredge on the Buller River. On the right the dredgemaster is holding the long pole which is attached to the spoon about two metres under water. A sturdy chain, attached to the spoon, leads through the davit or crane to the winch at the bow. An current-wheel drives the Californian pump which lifts water into the sluice boxes.

the river bed, and by the time the spoon was under the crane and lifted out of the water, the bag was, with luck, full of gold-bearing wash. It was emptied out and washed through the sluice boxes, with the tailings falling over the stern. Three men worked at the sluice boxes, three more on the winch and one operated the spoon. The dredge was effective in water up to 6 metres deep, and an area of river bed about 3 by 2 metres could be worked without moving the dredge.

Alabama did not prosper on the river between Clyde and Alexandra, so it was slowly and laboriously winched up through the fierce currents of the Dunstan Gorge to Hartleys Beach. It was worthwhile, as the dredge soon began to reap a golden harvest. Returns of one ounce of gold to the scoop were reported but it did not last long — the dredge sank in March after only a couple of months' work.

This was a common fate for these dredges. As sweating miners heaved and tugged on the winch to drag the reluctant spoon through boulders and compacted gravel, the flimsy hull was often strained until seams opened up. Some dredges even capsized during efforts to free a jammed spoon.

SPOON GOLD DREDGES
ALEXANDRA — CLYDE DISTRICT.

NAME	OWNER	LIFE	FATE
ALABAMA	Knight & Halliday	1863-	
ALEXANDRA	Alexandra Gold Dredging Co.	1865-1868	Broke away, wrecked.
TWIN	F.D. Siedeberg	1865-1871	Dismantled.
SALAMANDER	F. D. Siedeberg	1865-1871 1872-1874	Converted to steam. Steam spoon dredge.
	McLellan & Party	1876	Converted to current wheeler,
		1879	sank
CLYDE	Hastie & Hawthorne	1868-1874	Sank in flood.
GALATEA	Knight & Halliday	1868-1874	Sank.
GARIBALDI		1869- 1872	Sank.
YORKSHIREMAN	Mackersey	1869	
DREDGE	Beattie & party	1869- 1871	To Upper Clutha.
KEARSAGE	Young & party	1870- 1872	Converted to pneumatic dredge.
HARTLEY	McMarron & Veitch	1870-Jan	Dragged anchor in flood
DREDGE	Eames & party	1882	Manuherikia River.
DREDGE	Quayle & party	1893	Prospecting dredge at Twelve Mile.

Figure 9.2. S Summary of information about spoon dredges known to have operated in the district.

Alabama was raised and fitted with stronger machinery. She was taken back down the river to Prospectors Point at the junction of the Clutha and Manuherikia Rivers. Here, during the big flood in the Manuherikia River in October 1866, she was the saviour of Leslie's punt that was being washed down the river until it became entangled in the dredge's mooring chains. However, it was off Sandy Point above the junction of the Fraser River that *Alabama* struck rich gold, returning as much as £175 per man for a fortnight, and there she spent the remainder of her career.

Alabama set the pattern. Even before she had met with success, other larger dredges were under construction. One, the *Alexandra,* became involved in a boundary dispute with *Alabama.* Apparently the digging of a trench near the boundary of a claim by one dredge's spoon, caused valuable gold-bearing sand from the adjoining claim to fall or wash into the trench. No one had thought of this, and the Warden was asked to make some rules about leaving a strip of neutral territory between claims.

In January 1868 *Alexandra* broke away ('cut away' according to one report) from her moorings and was found bottom-up on rocks at McKenzies Beach, far down the Alexandra gorge. Halliday and Knight rebuilt her as the *Galatea* which, launched in June 1868, was the most successful of all the spoon dredges. Many of its returns of £100 per man per week matched, or were better than those of later steam bucket dredges. In 1871 it dredged a small bar in the river which returned £5,000 worth of gold. With the claim worked out and too much 'drift'[4] (gravel moving along the river bed) to cope with, the dredge was sold in November 1873, and met its end in 1874 when it sank at its moorings.

Siedeberg's Dredges

Although Ben Knight was undoubtedly the first to introduce a large spoon gold dredge to the district, Franz David Siedeberg also deserves a place as a pioneer. It was he who, with Herman Schultz as a partner, built a dredge in February 1865 which shadowed the design of future dredges. It consisted of two pontoons connected at each end (so it was referred to as the 'Twin dredge') but with a space (the 'well') 1.2 metres between them. The spoon was dragged along the riverbed under this well and lifted out by winches. Then the recovered material was run through a specially designed cradle that was mechanically shaken. The power for this and the necessary water were provided by a 1.2 metre diameter undershot wheel mounted at the stern. It was a reasonably successful dredge and it was said that it could lift 80 spoonfuls, each of a quarter ton of gravel, in a 10-hour shift.

Siedeberg built another similar dredge in mid-1865, and the two dredges worked up and down the river for many years. The older dredge was dismantled in 1871 and the materials used to alter and lengthen the newer dredge, now named *Salamander*. He installed two steam engines, one to power the windlass for pulling the spoon, and the other for pumping water.

It was while attempting to board this dredge in March 1871, that Siedeberg's boat fouled a rope and all six men in it were tipped out. Five of them scrambled aboard the dredge, but Siedeberg climbed back into the boat which, without oars, began to drift down the river. He was a mile downstream before a miner rescued him.

Salamander began work in August 1872 and the machinery operated well. However, the drift was so bad that little gold was obtained, in spite of various devices used to keep the drift away from the working area. Finally an accident to the spoon put the dredge out of action. Disappointed and frustrated, Siedeberg decided to give up, and sold the dredge to McKenzie for conversion to a current-wheeler.

Spoon dredges were inexpensive to build but they had disadvantages. They were only suitable for shallow, calm water up to 6 metres deep; they had difficulty breaking through the surface of the riverbed where it was armoured with a pavement of close-set stones interspersed with large boulders, and they were expensive in labour. But in the end, it was the 'drift' that defeated them. This was the mass of moving gravel that began to flow down the bed of the river from sluicing operations along the banks. As it moved down the river it successively affected the spoon dredges. By 1871 it had reached Roxburgh, and by 1874 all the spoon dredges in the district were out of action.

ODDITIES
The lure of untold wealth supposedly lying on the bottom of the river was strong, and many schemes were dreamed up to overcome the problem of the gravel drift so that the gold, reputed to be lying beneath, could be scooped up. These included submarine boats, diving bells, Priestman grabs and so on.

In October 1872, it was reported that the 'Pneumatic Company' had bought the spoon dredge *Kearsage* and intended using it as a basis for a 'pneumatic dredge.' The device started work in the river near Clyde in February 1874.[5] Two men entered a heavy iron tube about 1.5 metres in diameter, which had been lowered to the river bed through a well in the pontoon. Air was pumped into the tube until pressure at 120 lbs per square inch forced the water out so the men could work on the exposed river bed. After an initial 'shock to the system' which apparently caused 'but little inconvenience,' the men were able to work for up to four hours in the tube.

There was difficulty in supplying sufficient power to drive the pumps on *Kearsage*. Current-wheels temporarily replaced the steam engine, but to no avail. When someone forgot to loosen the mooring lines as the river rose, the dredge was pulled over on to its beam-ends. It was totally wrecked, and so was the company.

CURRENT-WHEELERS
With the decline of spoon dredging and the failure of pneumatic dredging, thoughts turned to the dredge which had been working away quietly at Teviot. It had a chain of buckets driven by paddle wheels turned by the current of the river. Perhaps this could handle the gravel drift that had scuppered the spoon dredges.

This 'current-wheeler' had been designed by William Ward of Teviot, built in 1866, and operated for a number of years by the Moa Gold Dredging Company. It was over 16 metres long, with paddle wheels five metres in

CURRENT-WHEEL GOLD DREDGES
ALEXANDRA—CLYDE DISTRICT.

NAME	OWNER	LIFE	FATE
SALAMANDER	McLellan, McKenzie	June 1876-June 1879	Sank 1879.
DUKE OF SUTHERLAND	Fraser, McKenzie	March 1879-Dec 1881	To Teviot.
EUREKA	Scott & party	June 1884-May 1898-	Converted to steam.
PERSEVERANCE	Cards, Finlay Mackersey Spencer	May 1886-Ap 1899	Sank and dismantled.
MANUHERIKIA	O Magnus & Party	Sept 1894- June 1899	Sank.
VICTORIA	Spencer & Party	Dec 1895-July 1897	Converted to steam.
GOLDEN FALLS	Golden Falls Gold Dredging Co	Feb 1901-Mar 1903	Converted: oil engines.

Figure 9.3. Summary of information about current-wheel dredges known to have operated in the district.

diameter. It could dredge to a depth of nearly five metres with a string of 25 buckets. It was certainly a technological advance on the spoon dredges, as it could deliver a continuous supply of gold-bearing material to the dredge deck.

The current-wheeler had one great disadvantage. It only worked effectively in a strong current, and that was usually out in the middle of the river where the water was too deep to allow the buckets to reach the bottom. If it came into shallower water where the current was weaker, the dredge lost power and finally stopped working. Nevertheless, the current-wheelers were cheap to build and to run, and despite their shortcomings, they were the main type of dredges used in Central Otago during the 1870s and 1880s.

The first current-wheeler in the district was based on the *Salamander*. Taken over from Siedeberg by McLellan and McKenzie, and converted from a steam spoon dredge to a current-wheel bucket dredge, the vessel began work at Sandy Point where, in spite of the drift, it managed to pay a small dividend over the three years of its existence. Then at 5 am one morning in June 1879, McLellan and a dredgehand were awakened by water in their bunks. They had to swim ashore as the dredge sank in deep water, caused it was thought, by the bucket chain chafing a hole in its planks The wreck was sold where it lay, and whatever machinery was accessible was removed for use in a later vessel.

William Fraser, John McKenzie and Mcleod used parts of the *Salamander* on the *Duke of Sutherland*, launched by Mrs William Fraser on 27 February 1880.[6] The current wheels drove the bucket chain through reduction gears instead of directly from the main axle, and the motion was transferred to the bucket chain through big square 'tumblers' at each end of the ladder. These features were new but became commonplace on subsequent dredges.

In 1886 a man who could well be regarded as the 'father' of gold dredging in the Alexandra-Clyde district, Louis Gards, placed the *Perseverance* on the river. Gards had wisely abandoned prospecting for gold after nearly losing his life in a storm on the Old Man Range, and turned instead to his trade of wheelwright and blacksmith. But the quest for gold still had its attraction for him, and the *Perseverance* was the first of a fleet of dredges in which Gards was to have an interest. With a length of 25 metres, it was by far the largest dredge built so far. The buckets, of 2-3/4 cubic feet capacity, were made in Gards' blacksmith shop by James Kelman, the recently appointed manager. He was the man who, a few years later, would buy the business and develop it into an engineering workshop, renowned for its ability to repair and manufacture components of dredges. Gards later sold his share of the dredge to his partners, Finlay and George Spencer. 'Finlay's dredge' became well-known because it was working close to the track to Clyde, and luckily attracted the attention of photographers even after it sank and became derelict.

Figure 9.4. *Perseverance No 1* was a large current-wheel dredge built by Louis Gards and party in 1886.

Perhaps the most successful of all the current-wheelers in the district was the *Manuherikia*. Home-built out of bits and pieces of other dredges, it was completed in March 1894, and after an initial set-back when the dredge sank, it began work in the upper part of the fearsome gorge below Alexandra. Its consistently high returns of gold allowed its fortunate owners, within a short time, to build a steam dredge that went on to increase their fortunes.

Not all were successful. A huge current-wheel dredge built in 1900, at a cost of £9,000, to work in the same gorge, was supposed to be the answer to the difficulties of coaling steam dredges in the gorge. In spite of the very large paddle wheels 6 metres in diameter and 3.5 metres in width, the *Golden Falls* was an abject failure. Not one flake of gold did it recover. The claim was just above the rocky obstruction that gave rise to the falls in the gorge. This same obstruction slackened the current for some distance upstream so the paddle wheels, big as they were, could not generate enough power to work the machinery. When the buckets did manage to bring up some gravel, the tailings piled up at the rear of the dredge, further obstructing what current there was.

New owners replaced the paddle wheels with oil engines, and a small amount of gold was recovered, but at great expense. In February 1905, perhaps to many people's relief, the dredge sank at its moorings and the wreck was sold for dismantling.

STEAM DREDGES

It seemed obvious that the bucket chain should be driven by steam, but it seemed to take a long time for this to eventuate. Certainly, as far back as March 1873, a company headed by John Chapple and John Mackersey, and strongly supported by McQueen and Kincaid, the engineering firm, had been formed in Alexandra. It was intended to build a steam powered bucket dredge, but had faced difficulties. Problems in obtaining cheap coal, opposition by the Miners Association over the size of the claim applied for, and lack of local support saw the project abandoned. But the Alexandra correspondent of the *Tuapeka Times*, with heavy irony, suggested that the scheme was 'too simple and commonsensical' to appeal, and blamed the wording of the prospectus:

> Had the prospectus simply stated that the wash-dirt was to be blown in the air by nitro-glycerine, and the gold extracted from the flying debris and deposited in a fire-proof safe by means of a strong current of hydro-sulphate of chinanikan gas, there would have been no difficulty in disposing of the shares and the shareholders in all probability would have been smiling over their dividends, instead of mourning the money sunk in the preliminary expenses of the defunct company.[7]

It was not until 1881 that steam bucket dredges made their appearance. *Eureka,* owned by Scott and party of Dunedin, was at work in July of 1881 but was not a success. Apart from the fact that the second-hand engine and boiler were worn out and far too heavy for the dredge, coal was consumed at the rate of 25 tons per week. The vessel was soon converted into a current wheeler.

Another dredge, *Dunedin,* launched in September and at work a few months later, must be regarded as the first successful steam bucket dredge. Charles McQueen of Kincaid and McQueen designed it but it had a bad flaw. It was provided with two-bucket ladders — one on each side of the dredge. This was intended to allow the vessel to work close up to the banks of the river, but in practice each line of buckets would bite on obstacles at different times. The dredge was tugged to one side and then the other, and ended up rolling alarmingly.

Figure 9.5. In 1881 *Eureka was* the first steam-driven bucket dredge on the Clutha River but was soon converted to a current-wheeler. Later, as shown, it was re-converted to steam with a current-wheel mounted on one side to lift water for washing the gold-saving tables.

It started work at Sandy Point, up-river from Alexandra but did not do particularly well. In 1888, much to the disappointment of the town, it was taken down through the gorge, converted to a single ladder dredge, and began work at Coal Creek. It had recovered 16,000 oz of gold and paid dividends of more than £15,000 by the time it was sold off, hopelessly out of date, in 1901.

A Diversion.

There was excitement over announcement[8] in the newspapers of 1886 that the intention of the New Zealand Gold Dredging Co Ltd, being set up in London, was to dredge the Clutha River with a new type of machine. It turned out to be a suction dredge invented by James Welman of Poole. The news caused a flurry of pegging out of river claims in anticipation of the success of the new dredge.

The dredge was launched at Alexandra in April 1887 for the trials, but it was immediately obvious that the centrifugal pump was neither large enough nor powerful enough to suck up stones, let alone gold. Larger pumps and pipes had to be imported, and while awaiting these, the dredge sank at its moorings. Refloated, it was tried out with the larger equipment, and this time it seemed to work well in that it lifted a stream of gravel and water. It was taken to its claim on the Manuherikia River to be fitted with gold-saving apparatus.

The Welman vessel started dredging in earnest on 7 July 1888, but had only been working for a couple of weeks when stones smashed part of the pump. Before it could be repaired, a flood swamped the dredge and swept away the gold saving boxes. The hull sank into the sand and it was more than 12 months before it could be raised. And that was the end of that particular enterprise.

On the basis of its fortnight's work the Welman dredge was hailed as a success by its promoters, although nowhere is the quantity of gold recovered, if any, reported. But such was the mood of the time that, during 1887, the entire Clutha River from Albert Town to Tuapeka Mouth was taken up in Special Claims, on which it was intended to install Welman dredges. In the end, the Welman-type suction dredges were successful only on sandy beach claims such as at Waipapa in Southland, and at Hokitika on the West Coast.

Steam Dredges Ascendant

The continued success of the *Dunedin* coupled with the excitement of the Welman dredge saga, heightened interest in gold dredging. But it was the news that a small dredge, placed on the Shotover River by a wealthy Chinese merchant of Dunedin, Choie Sew Hoy, was winning large quantities of gold that really excited the investors.

Figure 9.6. *Dunedin* was the first *successful* steam-powered bucket dredge and started work on the river in February 1882.

Within a few months, no fewer than 28 companies had formed, and of these, nine managed to build dredges and place them on the Shotover and Kawarau Rivers. All but two of these companies were liquidated within two years.

Not everyone lost through the disastrous collapse of the first Otago dredging boom. Entrepreneurs of Alexandra took the chance to acquire several of these steam bucket dredges at a fraction of the cost of new ones.

Louis Gards, owner of the successful current-wheeler *Perseverance,* bought the Shotover Dredging Company's vessel, dismantled it and re-erected it at Sandy Hook at the mouth of the Fraser River. It was launched in late August 1892 as *Perseverance No 2*. It was reported that the total cost of the dredge, transport and re-erection was £3,000. Gards' two dredges were said to have recovered 1,250 oz of gold during the following year — more than enough to pay for both dredges. The Alexandra Gold Dredging Company, headed by James Kelman and George Spencer, bought the Kawarau Big Beach Dredging Company's dredge and re-erected it as the *Chicago*. Dr Hyde and his Dunstan Dredging Company bought the Frankton Beach Company dredge, which had cost £3,800, for £400. It was soon working on the Clutha River as the *Clyde*.

A couple of years later, the Horseshoe Bend dredge was brought down by a Dunedin group and set up as the *Enterprise,* a vessel which was distinguished by the presence of a tailings elevator. This device was designed by Cutten, a Dunedin engineer, although J. F. Kitto, a local miner, claimed he had invented it in 1889.[9] A tailings elevator stacked

Figure 9.7. *Enterprise No 1* was an old Wakatipu dredge. It was the first dredge to have a tailings elevator.

tailings well to the rear of the dredge and allowed the vessel to work into the river banks. By 1895, the *Clyde* and *Chicago* had also been fitted with elevators.

In the middle of 1892 there had been only two current-wheel dredges working on the river between Alexandra and Clyde, the *Perseverance* and the *Eureka*. But *Eureka* underwent yet another change when a steam engine, this time of appropriate size and weight, was installed. By mid-1894 there were, in addition to the current-wheeler, five steam bucket dredges at work. With this fleet of small second-hand dredges, the foundation of the gold dredging industry of Central Otago, and of New Zealand, was established.

Although the ex-Wakatipu dredges were successful in winning substantial amounts of gold, it was soon realised that they had serious limitations in power, and particularly in the depth to which they could dredge. They also had weaknesses in their gold-saving equipment, and the early dredges were accused of discharging more gold back into the river with the tailings, than was saved. Dredge designers took these criticisms into account in planning their new vessels which steadily increased in size and power. They could dredge deeper, bring up more material in their larger buckets and stack tailings to greater heights. Attempts were made to improve gold-saving by substituting screens and tables for sluice boxes.

Milne and party's *Ngapara*, which started work in October 1895, was the first new steam dredge to be built at Alexandra since *Dunedin* had been launched 14 years before. The owners of the old Wakatipu dredges also decided it was time they ordered more modern vessels.

The first of these new dredges to begin working, in May 1896, was Leijon's *Eureka No 2*, closely followed by the dredge of the Clyde Gold Dredging Company. This was a public company formed by Dr Hyde to finance the *Moa*, which started at Poverty Beach in August. At about the same time, new companies put the first *Earnscleugh* dredge to work at Sandy Point, and the *Manorburn* on the Manuherikia River.

Manorburn

Dredges such as *Moa* and *Manorburn* were good examples of how the bucket steam dredge had been adapted in New Zealand to gold dredging. Later vessels would be larger, more powerful and able to dredge to greater depths, but their overall layout would be similar. Plans of *Manorburn*, which began work on the Manuherikia River in 1896,[10] illustrate the main features of a gold dredge of the period.

The pontoons were made of three layers of kauri timber laid diagonally. They were 72 ft (22 m) long, 24 ft (7.4 m) wide and had a draught of 3 ft (90 cms) There was a well 4 ft (1.2 m) wide which ran back from the bow for about two thirds the length of the dredge. In this well was the ladder which was 50 ft (15.25 m) long and carried an endless chain of 30 buckets, each one pivoted on heavy steel pins and joined by steel links. The buckets, each of 2-3/4 cubic ft (0.08 m³) capacity, had hardened steel lips. At each end of the ladder the buckets passed round a large square pulley, the tumbler, which transferred the motion of the engine to the bucket

Figure 9.8. *Manorburn,* (1896), a second generation steam dredge, was larger, more powerful, could dredge deeper and bring up more material each hour than the old Wakatipu dredges. A tailings elevator was fitted and the machinery covered in.

chain. The inboard tumbler was supported high above the deck of the dredge on an axle, which was in turn supported by heavy timber posts. A gantry with block and tackle at the bow allowed the ladder to be lowered or raised. It was found that a ladder angle of 45 degrees was the most efficient for dredging.

The bucket chain was driven at such a speed that about 12 buckets a minute came up and deposited their loads into a hopper, which in turn fed the material into a revolving cylindrical sieve or screen 16 ft (4.8 m) long. Stones which could not pass through the screen holes were carried up the tailings elevator and stacked behind the dredge. The finer gold-bearing material, with the help of copious water, was washed through the holes in the screen on to sloping steel tables. These were covered by plush, baize or canvas overlain by coconut matting and expanded metal. Here the gold was trapped, whereas the sand was washed over the tables into the river.

The bucket chain and the pumps were driven by a steam engine which also powered the six winches. Five of these controlled the five rope lines which enabled the dredge to be manoeuvred. Each line was anchored to a large log of wood buried on the bank, so that when a line was tightened by its winch, the dredge was pulled towards the anchor. When the bowline was tightened, the dredge was pulled forward and it was used to keep the buckets hard in against the face in which they were digging. Two lines on either side of the bow, and two on either side of the stern, allowed the

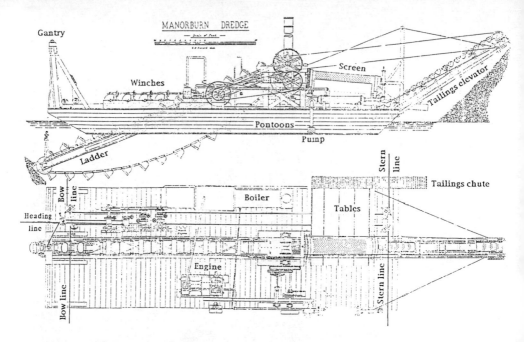

Figure 9.9. By the time *Manorburn* was designed, layout had become standardised and the pattern set for future dredges. They would become larger and more powerful but improvements would be minor.

dredge to be moved sideways. The sixth winch raised and lowered the heavy dredge ladder with its bucket chain.

When a dredge was working, the winchman was the most important man of the crew. He stood at the winches with his hands on the levers, tightening and loosening the various ropes to keep the buckets constantly biting into the gravels far beneath the surface. It was a crime to allow buckets to come to the surface less than full. The winchman had to constantly move the dredge sideways as it worked along the face of the cut. He also had to be ready for problems such as when buckets struck a big boulder, or more seriously, when a fall of gravel buried the lower buckets so that they jammed, and the power of the engine was insufficient to move them.

Weaknesses of the dredges of the mid-1890s were the shortness of the bucket ladders, which meant that often the buckets could not reach the bottom of the Clutha River, and the inefficiency of the gold saving devices which still allowed quantities of gold to be lost. Nevertheless the basic layout had been established, and future dredges would simply be progressively larger and more powerful. Other improvements would be of a minor nature.

Calm before the Storm

The number of dredges increased steadily during the late 1890s, with the appearance of larger and more modern vessels such as *Moa*, *Golden Beach*

120

and *Molyneux Hydraulic* at Alexandra. *Unity* and *Vincent* worked near Clyde, and *Chatto Creek* and *Nil Desperandum* far up the Manuherikia River. No doubt the numbers would have continued to increase steadily, but the rich harvest reaped by *Moa* working off the legendary Frenchmans Point, and the old current-wheeler *Manuherikia* a few hundred metres down the gorge, grabbed the attention of the stock market. But above all, it was the record returns of the *Electric* and the *Hartley and Riley* dredges working near Cromwell that had set the investors alight. This led to the boom in floating dredging companies and in speculating in their shares.

Figure 9.10. *Moa No 1*, (1896), won high returns off Frenchmans Point and made the Clyde Gold Dredging Company the most profitable gold dredging company in the district. *Moa 1* rests in the mud at the mouth of the Manuherikia River under a clump of willow trees.

Climax of the Dredging Era

Many of these newly floated companies actually ordered a dredge from contractors, but it was 1901 before they began work on the rivers. Their numbers increased rapidly until 1903, when there were no fewer than 35 working dredges within a 17-kilometre radius of Alexandra. These dredges were much larger and sturdier than those of the 1890s. Pontoons were up to 130 ft (40 m) long and buckets had much greater capacity. Ladders and elevators were longer, so greater depths could be reached. Tailings could be stacked well behind the dredge, allowing the vessel to work into high river banks without burying itself in tailings. To drive all this machinery, larger boilers and more powerful engines had to be installed.

The open decks and exposed machinery that were a feature of the early dredges, were now completely covered in by corrugated iron, so that working conditions became more comfortable. Electric light was installed, and watertight bulkheads in the hulls. Much more attention was given to safety, with strict rules enforced by inspectors, often under threat of prosecution.

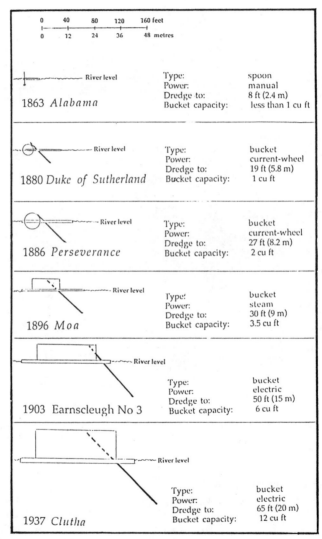

Figure 9.11 The increasing size of vessels and depth of dredging over the years is shown by scale diagrams of representative dredges for each period. Included also is information about the type of dredge, motive power and capacity of buckets.

Because coal for the steam engines was a major expenditure, other ways of powering dredges were investigated and sometimes tried. Supplying coal to the dredges that had begun to work in the depths of the Alexandra gorge, was very difficult.[11] Boating bagged coal down the gorge in small open boats was perhaps the most dangerous operation connected with dredging. The alternative was to cart coal to the brink of the gorge and sledge bags down rough zigzag tracks. This was very difficult and dangerous in the winter with the ground frozen, but it was the same frost that lowered the river level so the dredges could work. Electricity was tried on the *Fourteen-Mile Beach*, but was deemed a failure owing to shortage of water for power generation in the winter. Electricity was, however, successfully used in 1903 to power the large *Earnscleugh No 3* which operated for nearly 25 years on power generated by a station on the Fraser River. Later *Earnscleugh No 5* also worked on power from this source.

Golden Falls, another dredge designed for work in the gorge, tried large current-wheels and when they proved a failure, oil engines were installed. Fuel for these was carted in cans to the top of the gorge where it was fed into a long line of small diameter pipe. This discharged into a holding tank beside the river, where cans were refilled and taken out to the dredge by boat, and the kerosene finally emptied into the fuel tank of the engine. Water-driven Pelton wheels were used on *Golden Beach* and on *Olrig,* and suction gas engines were successfully used on *Lady Annie*.

Figure 9.12. The dredge of the Clutha Dredging Company was the largest built in the district. Launched in 1937, it worked in the Alexandra gorge, then on the terraces adjacent to the town, and finally across the river on Earnscleugh Flat where it was dismantled in 1963.

The Big Ones

Ten years after the last feeble attempt to dredge for gold in the Alexandra Gorge, two huge electric-driven gold dredges were launched in 1937. English companies financed both. The Molyneux Dredging Company's dredge, built at Clyde, was 154 ft (47m) long and could dredge to a depth of 55 ft (17 m). It began work in April 1937 and worked its way rapidly up through the Cromwell Gorge and into the Kawarau River. It passed under the bridge at Bannockburn with difficulty, and came to a standstill in 1943. For ten years it lay moored in the river and was finally dismantled in 1955 without paying a cent in dividends.

The second dredge, built at Alexandra,[12] was even larger. Owned by the Clutha River Dredging Company, it was 164 ft (50 m) long and could dredge to a depth of 65 ft (20 m) with buckets that held 12 cubic ft. The vessel weighed 1,150 tons. It began work in March 1937, dredging down the river for some distance, and then returning to have a long elevator fitted in preparation for dredging the river banks. This it proceeded to do during the 1940s before crossing the river to Earnscleugh Flat, where it finally ceased work in April 1963 and was dismantled. It had recovered gold worth £680,000[13] (about $NZ82 million today) during its 26-year working life.

NOTES

1. Cutten, W. H. 1899.
2. Based on a description in the *Otago Witness* 3 September 1864.
3. A hogshead held 54 gallons, so the bag of gravel which would consist of sand and pebbles made up of schist, quartz and greywacke, would weigh about 700 kilograms.
4. Gravel 'drift' was the bugbear of early dredging and eventually caused the downfall of the spoon and current-wheel dredges. It was described as 'a moving carpet' of gravel and sand, several metres thick, moving down the bed of the river with the current. The drift was derived from material washed into the river by the numerous sluicing claims along the banks.
5. An article in *Otago Daily Times* 17 September 1872 describes the vessel.
6. The vessel was 61 ft (18.5 m.) long and 16 ft (4.8 m.) wide. The current-wheels were 13 ft 6 inches (4 m) in diameter and 4 ft (1.2 m.) wide. With a bucket ladder 36 ft (11 m.) long the 25 buckets could dredge to a depth of 19 ft (5.8 m.). There is a possibility that the 'John McKenzie' listed as an owner of both *Salamander* and *Duke of Sutherland* was actually John Mackersey (often spelt 'McKersie')
7. *Tuapeka Times* 8 July 1874.
8. *Dunstan Times* 23 July and *Tuapeka Times* 7 August 1886.
9. Kitto, J. F. 1900 p.31.
10. *Dunstan Times* 2 August 1896.
11. For a discussion on the difficulties of coaling dredges in the gorge and the alternatives which were tried see McCraw, J. D. *Mountain Water and River Gold* 2000 Chapter 13.
12. *Alexandra Herald* 17 March 1937.
13. Robinson, Katie 1987 p.105.

10.

LEADING THE WORLD

—Dredging at Alexandra

The arrival of the steam gold dredge at Alexandra came in the nick of time, and may well have saved the place from becoming a ghost town. Central Otago was particularly badly affected by the nation-wide depression of the 1880s, as mining had practically petered out and there was little to replace it.

In the past, just when the fortunes of the little town had reached a low ebb, another gold discovery or a development in mining technique would assure its future for a few more years. By the end of the 1880s, however, the easily-won alluvial gold had long gone, the spoon dredges had been overwhelmed by the increasing gravel 'drift' and the current-wheel dredges had revealed severe limitations. The high hopes held for a sustainable dredging industry had received a further bad blow in the mid-1880s when the pioneer steam bucket dredge *Dunedin* had been removed to Coal Creek, leaving only two current-wheel dredges on the river.

Apart from some activity on the quartz reefs on the Old Man Range, the outlook for mining was bleak. People drifted away, and the population fell to fewer than 400. Houses remained empty and business was in the doldrums. Public meetings were held where responsible citizens cast about for a way of saving the town from oblivion. Then a dramatic change took place in the fortunes of Alexandra.

The short-lived gold dredging boom in the Wakatipu basin of 1889-1890 had not affected Alexandra directly, but ultimately the town reaped a huge benefit from it. Several citizens, prepared to take financial risks, bought four of the idle Wakatipu dredges, dismantled them and had them re-erected on the Clutha River between Alexandra and Clyde.

Small and under-powered as these early vessels were, the amount of gold they recovered encouraged others to build new dredges. Numbers increased steadily during the mid 1890s, culminating in a frenzy of construction at the turn of the century which resulted in an armada of nearly forty vessels by 1903.

Alexandra once again hummed with activity. The population increased to a level that would not be reached again for forty years. Almost everyone was devoted to servicing the dredges and the men who manned or supported them. Alexandra became the gold dredging centre, not only of

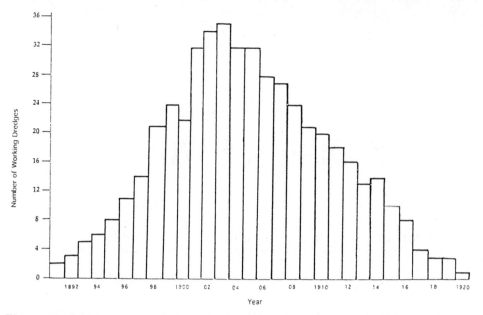

Figure 10.1. The number of dredges actually at work during each year peaked at 35 in 1903 then fell steadily until there was only one dredge left working in 1920 (*Earnscleugh No 3*).

Central Otago and New Zealand, but also of the world.

Boom and Bust

The high returns from the *Moa* and *Manuherikia* at Alexandra, together with the fantastic returns of the *Electric* and *Hartley and Riley* [1] dredges further up the river near Cromwell, triggered an unprecedented scramble to form gold dredging companies. For several months beginning in mid-1899 at least five new dredging companies were formed each day, and the buying and selling of their shares reached a frenzy. Alexandra itself was not immune to the fever and it has been estimated that citizens invested about £25,000 in dredge shares during the speculation boom. There was a corresponding rush to peg out claims on the rivers, and the Wardens' Courts were flooded with applications. For October 1899 alone there were 244.[2]

The madness did not last long. The decline in share speculation and company flotations began in April 1900. Only six new companies were registered in May compared with 33 in the previous February. In August there were only two. The speculation boom was over. Many companies had not even started, for various reasons, to build a dredge before the collapse. It must be said that some had never any intention of dredging, relying on rising share prices, and perhaps selling a river claim, to make a killing.

Construction Boom

Many companies had, however, ordered dredges during the height of the boom: so many in fact, that the engineering construction firms were overwhelmed. Most vessels had been ordered from firms in Dunedin, which had to rapidly increase staff to try to cope, but orders were also placed with firms in Christchurch, Invercargill and even in Melbourne. There were long delays but eventually trainloads of disassembled dredges began to leave the foundries for Central Otago. Such was the clutter at the railhead at Lawrence that appeals had to be made to clear the heaps of dredging machinery. Processions of big wagons, pulled by large teams of horses, laboriously hauled the heavy loads of steel and timber over the hilly roads to Alexandra and Clyde.

Figure 10.2. Parts for New Zealand dredges in the yard of the Austral Otis Engineering Works in Melbourne. *Hocken Library E1821/15*

Dredges were erected wherever there was access to suitable river beaches. Some were built in places where access was not so easy, as in the Alexandra gorge, where dredge materials had to be lowered down the slopes by ropes. Alexandra itself was one of the busiest dredge-erecting places on the river, often with several dredges under construction at the same time at the so-called 'Bendigo Dock' just upstream from the end of Dunorling Street.

A contractor and his team of skilled men who camped at the erection site built each set of big wooden pontoons on the beach. After the pontoons were launched, another team sent up by the foundry that had manufactured it, installed the machinery. Then followed a trial or running-in period, supervised by an engineer from the firm, and when everyone was satisfied with its perfomance, the dredge was handed over to the

Figure 10.3. A large boiler for *Earnscleugh No 3* dredge being hauled from Wedderburn to Alexandra.   *Hocken Library 6715/37*

dredgemaster and his crew.

Each dredge was in charge of a dredgemaster, often a man who had had experience at sea. The responsibility of his job was reflected in the respect he received from the community, and in his pay of up to £6 (equivalent to nearly $1,000 today) a week. With him was an engineer who operated the engine andsupervised repairs. The engineer was required to have a 'ticket' for operating a steam boilerand to have had experience with steam engines, either at sea or with stationary engines. Like the dredgemaster, he was on a weekly wage and not entitled to overtime. A winchman on 12 shillings a day, a fireman and one or two general hands completed the daytime crew. At night only two men would be on duty. Extra hands would be taken on when lines had to be moved and new anchors established.

Scores of men were employed on the fleet of dredges. They mainly camped in tents or crude huts near the dredge and when they came into town on Saturday night the place became quite lively. The dredges did not work on Sunday. That was devoted to essential maintenance and to housekeeping in the camp.

It was estimated that, in addition to the crew of six or seven, as many as 11 other men were provided with employment by each dredge. These included contractors, carters, blacksmiths, boat builders, wheelwrights and above all, coal miners. There were about as many men employed in the dozens of lignite mines that were hurriedly opened to supply the insatiable demand for coal, as there were working on the dredges themselves. Wheelwrights and wagon builders were busy meeting the demand for wagons to carry the huge quantities of coal required by the dredges;

Figure 10.4. Typical construction camp for those erecting a dredge. *Hocken Library 6715/38*

Figure 10.5. Dredges under construction in 1900 at Bendigo Dock in Alexandra. On the right is the current-wheeler *Golden Falls* and at least three other partly-built dredges are visible. *Hocken Library C16127*

farmers had to increase their acreage of oats to feed the horses and even a boat yard was established to build the necessary boats to service the dredges. Perhaps most important, a fully equipped engineering shop was developed which supplied hardware to the dredges and was capable of repairing and even manufacturing many dredge parts.[3]

Business in Alexandra boomed. The old corrugated iron and wood hotels were swept away and replaced by modern two-storied brick structures—the *Bendigo*, the *Criterion* and the *Caledonian*. Dozens of new businesses started up, including a newspaper full of advertisements for a wide range of goods and services. A reticulated high-pressure water supply was installed at great expense, and a well-equipped volunteer fire brigade established. The population climbed to over 1000 — a figure not reached again until after World War II.

Figure 10.6. B. Davis's boat-building yard in Dunorling Street.

Earnscleugh No 3, which started work in 1903, was by far the largest dredge constructed in Central Otago up to that time, but was also the last dredge to be built in the district for over thirty years. The construction boom was over.

Reality

When it came time to pay for their new dredges ordered during the boom, many shareholders were reluctant to, or couldn't, meet their calls. Some companies found that their claims proved, on inspection, to be impossible to dredge. Others who had managed to place dredges on their claims, found insufficient gold to pay their way, let alone pay dividends. Others again found their available ground was dredged more quickly than they had expected.

These companies went into liquidation, leaving half-completed, unused or little used dredges. The newspapers were full of advertisements offering dredges which had 'become available.' These were snapped up by established companies who wanted to acquire a larger, more modern vessel, or by newly formed companies who were able to buy second-hand vessels from liquidating companies at a fraction of the cost of new ones. New dredging companies continued to be formed over the next 10 years and most managed to acquire a dredge in this way. Dredges that had cost thousands of pounds were sold for a few hundred. The *Earnscleugh No 3*, which had cost no less than £24,000 was sold for £ 3,000. Groups of 'working men' were also able to buy the older and cheaper dredges and operate them as private companies. Scores of dredges were bought and sold.

Figure 10.7. *Earnscleugh No 3* was the longest dredge built during the boom period and the last to be constructed in the district for 35 years

The Swapping Game

With each change of ownership the name of the dredge was changed. Some dredges changed their names four or five times during their lifetimes and worked in several different, and often widely separated localities. Little wonder that there are often large discrepancies between the number of dredge names recorded and the actual number of vessels.

For instance, the early *Horseshoe Bend* dredge had been moved to Alexandra in 1894 and renamed *Enterprise*. Then the *Golden Point* was taken over by the same company in 1900 and renamed *Enterprise No 2*. In 1906 *Enterprise No 1* was sold and *Enterprise No 2* became simply *Enterprise*. The old No 1 dredge went to a group at Blacks and became the *Blacks Flat*. In 1909 it was brought back to the Manor Burn as the *Old Man* dredge.

Similarly when the Clyde Company, owners of the *Moa*, bought the *Golden Chain*, it became *Moa No 2* for about a month until the original dredge was scrapped, and then the new dredge reverted to *Moa*. Then in

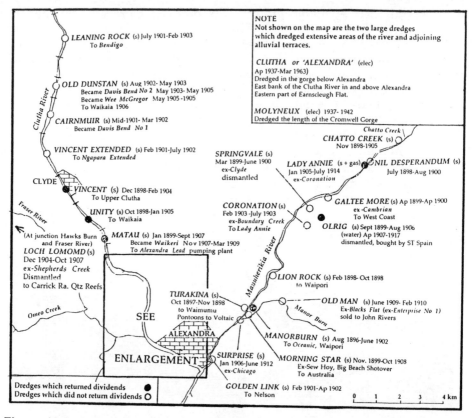

Figure 10.8. A, B and C. Set of maps with following data for each dredge that worked in the district:-

name and type (cw = current-wheel); s = steam); approximate location; length of time it worked; other names it worked under and time it worked under these names; eventual fate of the dredge where known, and whether or not the company which owned the dredge paid dividends.

A. Information about dredges which worked on the Clutha River near Clyde and on the Manuherikia River.

B. Information about dredges which worked in the vicinity of Alexandra.

C. Information about dredges which worked in the gorge below Alexandra.

1909 this new *Moa* became the *Island Basin*[4] and finally the *1911*, which sank bottom-up in the Alexandra gorge in 1912, bringing an end to the chain.

The Davis Bend Gold Dredging Company was registered in May 1900 and obtained a claim in the Alexandra gorge (its 'No 1 claim') but did not immediately build a dredge. Instead, in March 1903 the company bought the claim of the Cairnmuir Gold Dredging Company in the Cromwell Gorge along with its dredge. The Davis Bend Company referred to this new claim as 'No 2 claim.' The dredge continued working on the claim under its new owners.

The unoccupied claim in the Alexandra gorge was now 'attacked' and became the subject of an application for forfeiture on the grounds that it was not being worked. Although the company successfully defended itself against this attempt at 'claim-jumping,' it was strongly advised to put a dredge on the claim as soon as possible. So in May 1903 it bought the *Old Dunstan* dredge which, in the few weeks it had worked on its river claim a mile above Clyde, had already changed its name to *New Dunstan* as a result of restructuring of the company. The Davis Bend Company set its second purchase, now called *Davis Bend No 2*, to work on its No 2 claim in the Cromwell Gorge and began to move its original dredge, the old *Cairnmuir,* now *Davis Bend No 1*, down the river to its No 1 claim in the Alexandra gorge. This was a long job and involved a collision with the *Unity* dredge which resulted in a court case for damages. After a prolonged stop at Alexandra for an overhaul, it finally reached the company's gorge claim but it did not recover as much gold as expected. By December 1904 the dredge was up for sale and about to be taken up to Alexandra to be dismantled and shipped to Australia.

However, the nearby Sailor's Bend Company made a deal. It would take over *Davis Bend No 1* and send its own dredge to Australia in its place. So the original *Sailor's Bend* was dismantled, its machinery sent to Victoria and its pontoons taken over by a local coal mining company. *Davis Bend No 1* became the new *Sailor's Bend* and as such worked until 1919 when it was scrapped.

Meanwhile *Davis Bend No 2* was struggling to recover gold on the No 2 claim in the Cromwell Gorge. Shortly after the liquidation of the company in December 1904 it was sold to a syndicate of dredgemasters who renamed it *Wee McGregor*. Soon afterwards it was dismantled and sent to Waikaia, no doubt to assume a new identity.

It is hardly surprising that a list of names of dredges and dredge companies of Otago and Southland, no doubt far from complete, contains 859 names.

FATE OF DREDGES

As ruthless economics sorted the weak from the strong, more dredges 'became available' than could be sold in Central Otago, so some went to new dredging fields elsewhere. The *Manorburn* became the *Oceanic* at Waipori and the new dredging fields at Waikaia and Waikaka in Southland received *Unity, Victoria* and *Wee McGregor*. A number, including *Galtee More* and *Sandy Point* (formerly the *Glasgow*) went to the West Coast and a couple, *Golden Link* and *Bald Hill Flat*, were shipped to Nelson. Some, including *Bendigo* (built as *Leaning Rock*), *Morning Star* and the machinery of the original *Sailor's Bend,* went to Victoria, Australia.

Some met with disasters. The first *Bendigo* was destroyed by fire in the Island Basin in the Alexandra gorge and replaced by *Leaning Rock*. The *Fourteen Mile Beach* and *1911*[4] were wrecked in the same gorge, whereas *Enterprise No 2* mysteriously sank above Alexandra and could not be refloated.

However, the majority of worn-out, out-dated machines were dismantled.

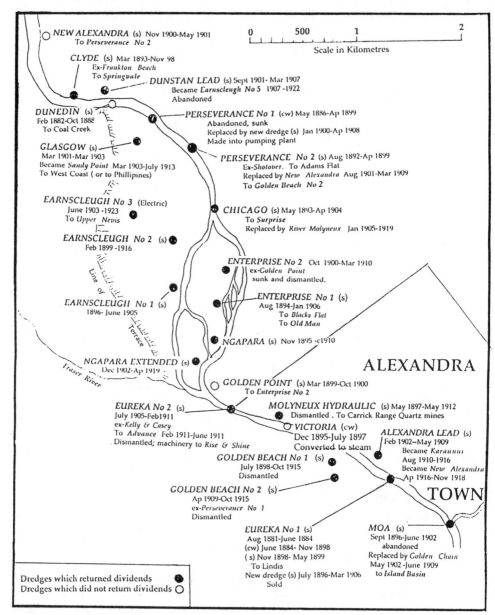

Figure 10. 8 Maps showing dredges & history

B

Engines and boilers were in demand for other industries. For example the mines on the Carrick Range bought *Loch Lomond* and *Molyneux Hydraulic*, and Central Otago Preserves Ltd took some of the machinery from *Olrig*. Timber from pontoons and hogposts (often kauri or bluegum) found its way into bridges and buildings, but most of the steel was recycled as scrap.

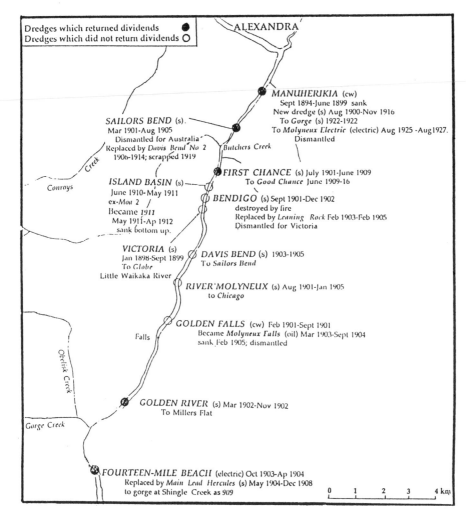

Figure 10. 8 Maps showing dredges & history
C.

A few dredges were simply abandoned. Until the waters of Lake Roxburgh covered them, the remains of the first *Moa* were visible at the mouth of the Manuherikia River. Air photos taken in 1948 clearly show the hull of a dredge, probably one of the early *Earnscleugh* vessels, lying in a pond close to the Clutha River on the Earnscleugh side, and another hull, almost certainly that of *Earnscleugh No 5,* (built as *Dunstan Lead*) lies in a pond a kilometre below Muttontown Gully. There are also reports of the remains of an, as yet, unidentified (dredge near the river at Galloway Flat.

Some delayed their inevitable fate. The steam dredge *Manuherikia*, which had replaced the earlier current-wheel vessel of the same name, began work in 1900 in the Alexandra gorge. It produced immense amounts of gold but finally closed down in 1916. It was then laid up in the gorge but was started up again in 1922 as the *Gorge*. This effort lasted only a month or so before the dredge was laid up again until 1925 when the steam engines were replaced by electric motors. But this, and the new name *Molyneux Electric*, didn't improve the gold returns and after a total of a few weeks' work over several winters the vessel was finally dismantled in 1927.

The big electric *Earnscleugh No 3* worked for 20 years and was then dismantled and carted with much effort into the Nevis Valley. Here it was re-erected in 1928 as the *Upper Nevis*. But there was insufficient water to generate the power required, so diesel engines were installed, and as the *Diesel-Electric*, the dredge struggled on until finally closing in 1934. It was dismantled in 1937.

As the dredges closed down one by one, the effect on the town was not as great as it might have been. Many dredge workers had been establishing fruit orchards during the time of high river flows when many of the dredges could not work. The arrival of the railway in 1906 opened city markets to Central Otago fruitgrowers and resulted in a great expansion of the industry. The 'cross-over' period when the fading dredging industry was overtaken in importance by fruitgrowing was in the period just before the Great War.

FINANCIAL RETURNS

There is wide variation in the calculations and estimates of the gold produced by dredges in the region. The reason is that early spoon dredges, the current-wheelers and the early steam bucket dredges were owned by private companies which did not make public their returns. Nine companies working between Clyde and Alexandra, (including the Clutha Gold Dredging Co) produced at least 10,750 kilograms[5] (345,182 oz) of gold, worth on present day values ($NZ 600 an oz), about $NZ 210 million. By way of comparison the Roxburgh basin produced 5,223 kg and the Cromwell area (including the big dredge at Lowburn) 3,115 kg.[6] But this list excludes the Clyde, Ngapara and post-1903 Golden Beach Companies — all prolific gold producers, as well as less productive companies such as Vincent, Unity, Dunstan Lead and Alexandra Lead.

The 58 dredges which worked in the district were owned by 46 companies and half of these companies returned a dividend.[7] Private companies such as the Ngapara Company, Lane's Golden Beach Company, and Fink's Lady Annie Company (not to be confused with the Lady Annie Company at Waikaia in Southland) did not publish their results. But it may be assumed from the fact that they continued operating for many years that they were paying their way.

Neither the total gold won nor the total dividend paid out is a measure of the success of a company, unless the capital that was outlaid and the time taken to achieve the result, are considered. To be successful a company must pay back the equivalent of the capital invested and then pay at least 20% on the capital annually. This is apparently the minimum return traditionally expected from risky mining ventures. When the company was finally liquidated any money raised from selling the dredge either as a going concern or for parts or scrap, would be regarded as a bonus.

Dividends won and return on Capital

Company Name	Capital	Total Dividends	Dividends less Capital	Years Worked	Return per Year
Clyde	4,000	24,500	20,500	11	46%
Enterprise	7,000	26,885	19,885	9	32%
Matau	7,000	15,225	8,225	10	12%
Perseverance	10,000	16,100	6,100	5	12%
Manuherikia	12,000	34,176	22,176	17	11%
Earnscleugh	11,000	30,250	19,250	23	8%
Chicago	5000	8,964	3,964	13	7%
Alexandra Eureka	12,000	18,900	6,900	11	5%
Molyneux Hydraulic	6,000	7,076	1,076	12	1%
Alexandra Lead	14,000	14,032	32	10	0.2%
Fourteen Mile Beach	6,000	5,991			
Lady Annie	4,200	4,200			
Sandy Point	8,000	7,197			
Vincent	5,500	4,811			
Manorburn	3,000	2,250			
Olrig	7,000	4,773	Capital not covered		
Golden Beach	13,000	8,125	by dividends		
Unity	10,500	6,100			
Sailors bend	8,000	3,587			
First Chance	7,000	3,150			
Dunstan Lead	14000	6118			
Golden River	8,000	1,000			
Turakina	4,000	200			
Electric	26,000	132,593	106,593	19	22%
Hartley & Riley	5,000	84,337	79,337	14	113%

Figure 10.9. Only about half the dredging companies in the district returned dividends and of these only 10 returned dividends equal to, or greater than, the capital invested. Only the Clyde and Enterprise companies returned more than 20% per year on invested capital, a figure regarded as the minimum acceptable for mining investment. The equivalent figures for the famous Electric Company and Hartley and Riley Company are included for comparison.

Generally a dredging company with a small capital investment will give better annual returns than one with large capital. And a company that produces gold quickly gives a better return than one that takes twice as long to produce the same amount of gold. Compare the returns of the famous Electric Company on the Kawarau River with those of the equally famous Hartley and Riley Company in the Cromwell Gorge (Figure 10.10). The Electric Company gave a yearly return of 22% on the money invested and although it produced a huge total dividend, it took a large amount of capital and 19 years to do it. The Hartley and Riley Company, on the other hand, produced total dividends that were not quite as large but were produced in a shorter time and with only a fifth of the capital, and so gave the very high annual return of 113%.

In the Clyde-Alexandra district only the Clyde Company and the Enterprise Company were able to better the 20% criterion, but eight other companies were able to give annual returns ranging from 12% down to 0.2% after returning the equivalent of the capital invested. Another 12 dredges were able to pay dividends but these did not reach the amount of invested capital. More than half of the dredges that worked in the district did not pay any dividends. As a columnist wrote in 1901:

> The history of Otago dredging is a reproach to human intelligence and serves only to illustrate the eternal truth that a fool and his money are easily parted.[8]

NOTES

1. Note the spelling 'Riley' used for the Hartley and Riley Beach Dredging Company Ltd (Burton 1900 p.80) is different from the usual spelling for the co-discoverer of the Dunstan Goldfield, Christopher Reilly (Pyke 1887 p.71).
2. Hearn, T. J. and Hargreaves, R. P. 1985 p.26.
3. See chapter 12.
4. The Inspector of Boilers mentions that the boiler and engine in the New Zealand Paper Mills at Woodhaugh, Dunedin were from the *Island Basin* dredge. But this dredge, renamed the *1911*, was wrecked in the gorge and was still lying bottom-up when the rising waters of Lake Roxburgh covered it. It would have been impossible to salvage a boiler from the wreck. Presumably there is some other explanation.
5. Robinson, K. 1988. pp.103-104.
6. Williams, G. J. 1974 p.82.
7. Hearn, T. J. and Hargreaves. R. P. 1985 pp.79-84.
8. *Otago Daily Times* 6 July 1901.

11.

BLACK GOLD

— Coal Mining

In the treeless landscape of early Central Otago the only firewood available was the thin branches of the prickly 'matagouri'[1] shrub. So Alexandra was fortunate in having, within a three kilometre radius of the settlement, large amounts of accessible coal. Seams were clearly visible on both banks of the Clutha River a couple of kilometres above the Manuherikia junction, and on the banks of the Manuherikia River a few kilometres above Alexandra.

Origin of the Coal

The coal, which is mainly rather poor quality lignite, was probably derived from thick layers of peat that formed on low-lying land some 25 million years ago. It is likely, judging from the remains of tree trunks and branches in the upper layers of the coal, that the bogs were surrounded by bush. Increasing earth movements interfered with land drainage so that a large fresh-water lake gradually covered the bogs. The weight of the sand and silt washed into the lake compacted the underlying peat[2] until lignite was formed.

The land was then lifted and tilted between faults to eventually form the parallel ranges and basins of Central Otago. The coal seams were tilted with the land and everywhere they now dip or slope downwards towards the centre of the valleys. Close to major faults, however, the sands and silts containing the coal ('coal measures') have been dragged upwards until they are standing nearly vertical. Debris from the rising ranges eventually filled the remnants of the lake and buried the underlying coal even more deeply.[3]

First Miner

In early 1863, George Telford began mining coal at a spot near the mouth of Letts Gully about three kilometres up the Manuherikia Valley from the settlement. Handed down through Telford's family[4] is a description of the frightful conditions under which he worked. George was forced to lie on his side in water as he picked the coal ahead of him and pushed the loosened coal behind him with hands and feet to where it was later bagged up. Little wonder Telford developed tuberculosis and died in 1867 aged only 36. The

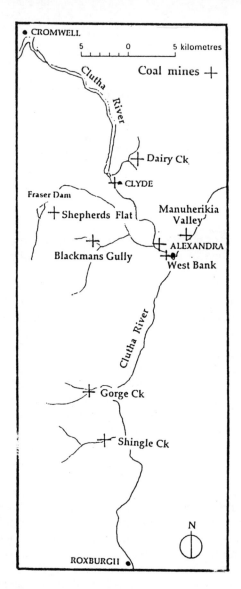

Figure 11.1. Coal mines in the Alexandra-Clyde district.

coal pit was sold to McKeenan and G. McDonald who later became a mayor of Alexandra.

BANKS OF THE CLUTHA RIVER

Coal was clearly visible close to water level on both banks of the Clutha River about two kilometres above the Manuherikia Junction. The early gold dredges established that the bed of the river itself, for a distance of 400 metres, was formed on coal.

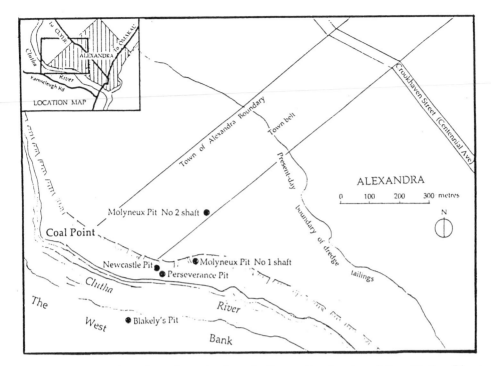

Figure 11.2. The location of coal mine shafts on the banks of the Clutha River near Alexandra.

In mid-1863, a coal mine was established by Blakely on the 'west bank of the Molyneux' [5] (Clutha River) midway between the mouth of the Fraser River and Chapmans Gully. A three metre-thick seam of good quality coal supplied Manuherikia Township at 40 shillings a ton. At first there was some difficulty with Hill, the ferry operator, over charges for taking coal across the river, but this was resolved by the coal miner paying a flat rate of 12 shillings a week.[6]

The mine was apparently[7] taken over in April 1864 by Edward Charnock, the blacksmith, who dug a shaft 6 metres deep, lining it with porter barrels with their tops and bottoms removed. It was reported that the roof of one drive, which ran out under the river, leaked rather badly. Little wonder with the river only a little over a metre above!

Charnock sold the mine late in 1864 to Jones who, on the 12 December 1864, was drowned in the river while unloading a boatload of sacks of coal near the punt. His foot tangled in a rope and he was thrown into the river.

Opposite, on the east side of the Clutha River, coal outcrops were visible along the low terrace (since dredged away) and the locality was promptly named 'Coal Point.' Although the outcrops were within the boundary of the soon-to-be-surveyed township of Alexandra, they were about 2 kilometres from the tiny settlement huddled on the terraces overlooking the river junction.

In July 1864 Carter sank a shaft at Coal Point. He reached a three metre-thick seam of coal of such good quality that it was described as 'Newcastle' coal and this gave the name to the mine. A horse-powered windlass drained the shaft, which went well below river level.

Within a year, the Newcastle mine was in the hands of Craven Paget and George Milne who made an agreement with the Borough Council, when it was formed in 1867, to supply coal at the pit head at 20 shillings a ton in return for a 14 year lease at 10 shillings a year.

Mining continued steadily for two years before things began to go wrong. First the partnership was dissolved and Milne became the sole owner, then the mine was flooded and the shaft collapsed. Both Alexandra and Clyde then had to rely on the poor lignite from McDonald's small pit in the Manuherikia Valley. It wasn't until August 1872 that Milne was able to complete a new shaft, but by this time he found it was all too much for him and he sold the pit to Edward Charnock.

Charnock had not long taken over when he met with a very serious accident. As he grasped the rope to descend the shaft he spoke to the horse to start turning the windlass, but in some way the rope jerked and Charnock was thrown down the shaft. He landed on the planks that covered the drainage well 15 metres below. His leg was broken in three places and it was feared it might have to be amputated which, in those days, was a life-threatening operation. It took him more than six months to recover but that was the end of his coal mining. He put the mine up for sale and returned to his trade of blacksmithing at Cromwell. There is no further record of the Newcastle mine.

The coming of the steam-powered gold dredge gave rise to an increased demand for coal. As each dredge used several tons each day, it was a major cost and owners of the early steam dredges thought they could make considerable saving by opening their own coal mines. One of these owners, Louis Gards, opened a mine at Coal Point in 1894 to supply his steam dredge *Perseverance II*.[8]

Gards' mine was just 50 metres back from the riverbank, and as the top of the coal seam was four metres below river level, the mine was very wet. Nevertheless, with Sam Cameron as manager, more than 3,000 tons of coal were raised over two years from the 'Perseverance' pit. Rather than sink a second shaft, which the Mines Inspector pointed out was necessary as a safety measure, Gards abandoned the pit.

Gards' decision was no doubt influenced by the fact that he had already sold his dredges to Robert Finlay. He had had his coal mine on the market for some time and had tried unsuccessfully to form a small company of dredge owners who would buy his pit. It wasn't until he pointed out to the March 1899 meeting of the newly formed Dredge Owners Association that the whole booming local dredging industry depended on two small coal mines in the Manuherikia Valley, that he got a response. Gards emphasised that flooding, or collapse, of these mines, or the petering out of coal, would bring 20 or more dredges to a standstill. It was agreed to form a coal mining company which, in spite of the fact that Gards was a principal shareholder, decided not to buy Gards' mine. Instead a new mine was to be

Figure 11.3. The Alexandra Coal Company's buildings. They had been rebuilt following the disastrous fire of 1906.

established at Coal Point with the entrance shaft to be sunk not on the flood plain, as had all earlier shafts, but on the terrace high above any possible flooding.

'Molyneux Pit'

Once the decision was made it was all action. A prospectus was to be drawn up for approval within a week, and an engineer was instructed to prepare plans for the mine. The following month the Alexandra Coal Company Ltd was registered and directors appointed. Contracts for sinking the steel-lined shaft were let in June and by mid-October it had reached a nine metre-thick seam of what was described as the best coal in the district. Coal was being produced by the end of 1899.

The Alexandra Coal Company's mine, generally known as the 'Molyneux pit,'[9] certainly did produce coal. At its peak in 1904 it produced 11,000 tons for the year — the largest output of any mine in the district. But the cost of pumping out water and the large labour force (29 at one time) meant practically no financial return to the shareholders. A major set back was the spectacular fire[10] in the mine in 1906. The entire population of Alexandra worked with the fire brigade, and miners from the surrounding district, to rescue four trapped men. After 18 hours of heroic effort they were brought safely to the surface.

The mine was sold to a private group in 1911 and closed down in 1914 after producing 130,000 tons of coal during its 15 year life.

MANUHERIKIA VALLEY

Apart from the big 'Molyneux' mine at Coal Point, coal mining activity became centred on a one kilometre-long stretch of the Manuherikia Valley between Gilligans Gully and Letts Gully.

William A. Thomson arrived in Alexandra in 1864 and after a few years of cutting water races and gold mining, he began in 1871 to mine coal in the Manuherikia Valley, a task that became his life's work. His pit was about 600 metres closer to Alexandra than Telford's original mine. Production at first was small and erratic, but by 1880 yearly output had settled down to 600-700 tons, and for some years his was the only mine in the district supplying domestic consumers.

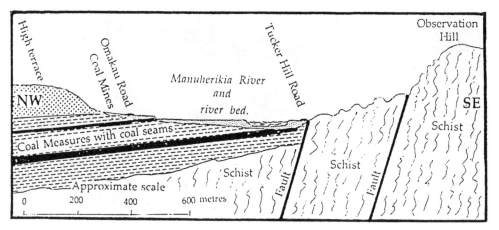

Figure 11.4. A diagrammatic cross-section across the Manuherikia River about two kilometres upstream from Alexandra. Several seams of coal, of different thicknesses and continuity, occur in clays and sands ('coal measures').

Thomas Jackson opened a mine in 1879 near Telford's old pit at the mouth of Letts Gully. He worked it in desultory fashion until 1884 when the mine was bought by the Dunedin Gold-dredging Company to supply coal to their new dredge, *Dunedin*, the first successful steam-powered bucket dredge on the river. Four years later the *Dunedin* moved down to Teviot and the mine, called 'McQueenville'[11] was sold to Robert Lett. So in 1886 the two main mines in the Alexandra district were the 'Alexandra' mine of W. A Thomson and the 'McQueenville' mine of Robert Lett. As the dredging boom developed many other mines started up but almost all had a short life.

'Alexandra' Mine.

As the number of steam dredges increased so did the output of Thomson's mine, until in 1899 it was producing 3,500 tons a year. After some initial argument, Thomson co-operated with the newly appointed Inspector of Mines, and did his best to meet requests that faults be remedied. The

Mines Department Annual Reports show that the inspector was always impressed with the working of the 'Alexandra' coal mine.

On one visit when the inspector and Thomson were at the coal face, they found that the ventilation was uncharacteristically poor. Thomson was at a loss to explain this until they climbed back to the surface and found that the outlet of the ventilation shaft had been covered with close-fitting boards held down by heavy stones. Under questioning the two Chinese workmen admitted that they had closed the shaft because they did not like working in the 'cold wind' caused by the circulating air in the mine.

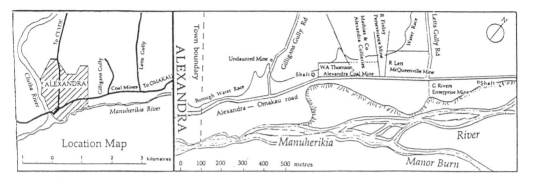

Figure 11.5. Location of the coal mines in the Manuherikia Valley.

Thomson continued as owner and operator, but latterly with a manager, until 1903 when the mine was sold to the Alexandra Coalmine Company of Mathias and party. Thomson died on 3 February 1906 aged 74.

'McQueenville' Mine.

Robert Lett, like William Thomson, and later Dan Mathias, became one of the well-known names associated with coal mining around Alexandra. Lett came to the district with the Dunstan Rush in 1862 and was a successful gold miner at Frenchmans Point and elsewhere before turning to coal mining. After the usual initial tussles with the Inspector of Mines over interpretation of regulations, Lett settled down to run a well-organised mine. At the height of the dredging boom the mine had 12 workmen and was turning out 7,000 tons of coal a year.

At about the time that Robert Lett died (mid-June 1903) and his son Sam, who already had a half share in the mine, took over, a series of unfortunate incidents began which eventually led to the abandonment of the mine. In early 1903 water and sand burst from the floor of the mine but was contained by building a concrete dam. While John Duncan, the deputy manager was inspecting this, his lamp exploded gas. It wasn't a serious explosion but was a warning of one of the main dangers in coal-mines. Worse was to come.

There was a sudden rush of water into the lower workings of the mine in April 1904, and in spite of the best efforts of the pumps, the water gained and filled the lower workings. Pillars of coal, left to support the roof, sagged

Figure 11.6. William A. Thomson and Mrs Thomson. Thomson was a pioneer coal miner in the Manuherikia Valley

and there was settlement of the surface over a considerable area above the mine. As the miners slowly withdrew in the face of the rising waters they salvaged what coal they could from pillars, but on 7 March 1905 the inspector finally ordered the men out. After the surface subsidence settled down the shafts were filled in, the surface levelled, and the mine formally abandoned in 1908.

The cause of the disaster seemed obvious to Lett. Running across the face of the terrace above the mine was the water race supplying much of Alexandra's water, and he was sure that leakage from the race must have been the source of the water. Lett sued the Borough Council for £1,000 for the loss of his mine.[12] But the Borough Council was upset too. When the mine collapsed it took the Borough race down with it. The council counter-sued for £240 damages for loss of revenue and damage sustained by the race.

The Warden hearing the case said he did not believe that the Borough race was responsible for the mine collapse but was unable to decide where the water came from. Lett was non-suited and the Borough Council awarded £8 11s with costs amounting to £62 1s.

Lett looked for a new site and in March 1905 he commenced to drive a tunnel into the hillside in Gemmels (Gilligans) Gully. He failed to find a

146

payable seam but instead found broken, faulted coal and running sand that flowed into the mine. By the end of the year Lett was bankrupt so he gave up coal mining and concentrated on carting coal to the dredges. He was killed when he fell under his wagon on 21 October 1918.

Coal Mining Boom.

Increasing dredging activity in the late 1890s meant an increasing demand for coal and a number of mines were opened up, worked for a short time and fizzled out. One of these, the 'Enterprise' or 'Light of Day' mine, was opened up by George Rivers in 1897 close to the Manuherikia River. It had been working for less than two years when one morning Rivers found it filled with water. There and then he gave up coal mining.

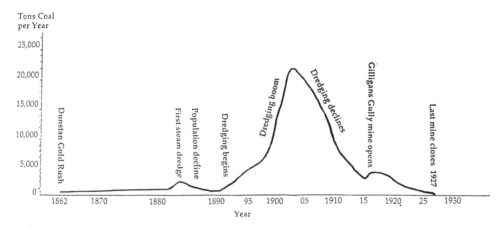

Figure 11.7. The rise and fall of coal production in the Alexandra district was clearly related to the rise and fall of the dredging industry.

Another mine was opened in 1897 by A. Bruce, Simpson and W. Theyers[13] who, with seven men, managed to extract 1,600 tons before it closed in 1900. Other failed attempts included a shaft put down by Louis Gards and C. P. Beck near Gemmels Gully and a mine opened by Mrs Drummey which had so much stone in the coal that it was practically unsaleable.

It looked as if a similar fate was in store for the mine opened in 1894 by R. M. Finlay and called the 'Perseverance' mine.[14] After extracting 724 tons over two years the mine stopped working, but in mid-1900 it began operating again with a new lease of life until April 1904, when it was taken over by the Mathias company.

A late comer was the 'Undaunted' mine in Gilligans Gully, then known as Gemmels Gully. Robert Ballantyne opened it as a one-man enterprise in late 1898.

The Mathias Company

The name 'Mathias' first appeared in August 1901 when Daniel H. Mathias took over the 'Undaunted' mine from Robert Ballantyne. He worked the mine for three years, but realising that it would require extensive redevelopment to make it profitable, he closed it down. Then in April 1904 he formed a private company comprised of the Mathias brothers (Dan and Gus); William Bowler, a coal merchant, and the mine manager, Andrew Hunter. As well as the 'Undaunted' mine, the Alexandra Coal-mine Company as the new company was called, took over Thomson's 'Alexandra' mine (and the name) and Finlay's 'Perseverance' mine. The Perseverance mine was closed and, after a short time, Thomson's original pit was closed also and a new mine opened up nearby.

With the collapse of Lett's McQueenville mine and the closing of the other mines, the only operating mine on the Manuherikia coal field after 1905 was that of the Alexandra Coal-mine Company. The workings became extensive and in October 1905, only a year after the new mine had opened up, the working face was 300 metres from the surface. Eleven men were employed in the mine and the same number above ground. Coal production was about 10,000 tons a year, rivalling that of the Alexandra Coal Company's mine at Coal Point. Production began to fall after fewer than 10 years as the mine was worked out, and it was finally closed in 1914.

Undaunted Coal Mining Co

To replace the worked out mine, early in 1915 Dan Mathias formed a small private company, the Undaunted Coal Mining Company, to reopen the old Undaunted mine in Gilligans Gully. The working partners were, Billy King and Les Churchill, who were survivors of the fire in the Molyneux pit, and Dan Mathias. With a total of nine men employed (eight of whom worked underground) it was necessary to have a Certified mine manager in charge. Fortuitously, Arthur Whittleston, the manager of the 'Molyneux' mine at Coal Point, had become available with the closing of that mine. He became the fourth partner of the Undaunted Company and was appointed manager.

For more than three years coal was extracted from a three metre-thick seam at the rate of more than 3,500 tons a year. A noteworthy feature was a large tree, completely converted to coal, nearly two metres in diameter and displaying perfect tree rings.[15] The main tunnel of the mine was driven along the length of this tree which was estimated to be more than 30 metres in length.

By 1920, in the face of falling demand and production, the work force dropped to six and Dan Mathias became manager again under the 'permit' system. The mine was put up for sale, but there were no takers at the time. With the main consumers of coal,the dredges, gone, Mathias continued to supply the domestic requirements for Alexandra and surrounding district with coal extracted from the pillars supporting the roof. It was always a 'lively' mine with the clay floor heaving and swelling so that constant work was required to keep the roadways open. Now, as the men worked their way back towards the mine entrance, mining the pillars as they went, pressure caused the clay floor to slowly rise and fill the mine.

The mine was finally sold to Joseph Robertson in 1925 who continued, with a couple of men, to supply a few hundred tons of coal extracted from the remaining pillars. The mine finally closed down in 1927.

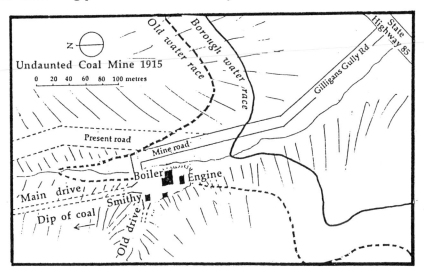

Figure 11.8. Sketch plan of the Undaunted mine in Gilligans Gully as it was in 1915.

Role of the Inspectors of Mines

From 1880 regular inspections of underground coal and gold mines were carried out by inspectors, and reports were sent to the Mines Department.[16] But by this time coal had been mined in Central Otago for more than 15 years and the mine owners thought they knew all there was to know about mining their coal. They resented these Government fellows snooping about finding faults.

The inspectors' job was a thankless one. Their task was to see that the various provisions of the Coal Mines Act were carried out, particularly when employed men worked underground. The inspector visited each mine at least once, and sometimes twice, a year, carefully pointing out faults and making helpful suggestions as to how the mines could be improved and brought within the regulations. Then they would go back to their office and put all their requirements in writing and send them to the owners. It must have been frustrating to find on the next visit that nothing had been done.

The inspectors persisted, however. They had no option. They selected the most co-operative owners and persuaded them to adopt safe practices and work within the framework of the regulations, and then used them as role models for the others. Slowly the inspectors made ground. After an initial period of confrontation, William Thomson, an early miner in the Manuherikia Valley, was regularly complimented in the inspector's Annual Report.

The inspectors let the small Central Otago mines off lightly. They did not insist that the owners produce up-to-date plans of their mines but they did insist that the owners have a copy of, and be familiar with, the Coal Mines

Act. One owner, when asked if he had a copy of 'the Act,' asked which Act the inspector was talking about! The most regular complaints were about the ladders in the shafts and the lack of fencing round the opening of shafts. To save labour and timber the vertical shafts down into the mine were made as small as possible — often only 3 feet by 2 ft 6 in (0.9 m x 0.77 m). Consequently the ladders by which the men climbed up and down were vertical, and this was illegal. They were supposed to be sloping and have landings every 9 metres, so that if a man did miss his footing he would not fall the 20 or so metres to the bottom of the shaft.

ALEXANDRA COAL MINES

NAME of MINE and Location	OWNER	PERIOD	TOTAL OUTPUT (Tons)
West Bank	Blakely E. Charncock Jones	1863-1864 1864 1864	unknown
'Newcastle' NW Town boundary	Carter Paget & Milne E. Charnock	1864-1864 1864-1872 1872-1872 (closed)	unknown unknown unknown
'Perseverance' NW Town boundary	L. Gards & S. Cameron	1894-1896 (closed)	3,128
'Molyneux Pit' NW Town boundary	Alexandra Coal Co W. Carson (mgr) J. Pollock (mgr) New Alex Coal Co J. Pollock (mgr) A. W. Whittleston	1899--1902 1903-1909 1909-1913 1913-1915	130,000
'Telfords' Manuherikia Rd	Telford, G McDonald & McKeewn	1863-1866 1866-(?)	unknown unknown
'Alexandra' Manuherikia Rd	Thomson, W. A. M. O'Connell (mgr)	1871-1901 1901-1903 (Mathias take over)	41,164
'Manuherikia' Manuherikia Rd 'McQueenville'	Thos Jackson Dunedin Dredging Co Robt Lett Sam Lett	1879-1884 (Dunedin Dredging Co takes over and renames) 1884-1888 1888-1901 1901-1905(Closed)	48, 607
'Enterprise' Manuherikia Rd	C. Rivers	1897-1898	700
'Bruces' Manuherikia Rd	W. Theyers, A. Bruce & Simpson	1897-1900	1,600
'Perseverance' Manuherikia Rd	R..M. Finlay J. Finlay (mgr)	1894-1904 (Mathias take over)	15,725
'Undaunted' Gilligans Gully	Robt Ballantyne	1899-1901 (Mathias take over)	122
'Alexandra' Manuherikia Rd	Alexandra Coal-mine Co (Mathias & Co) A. Hunter (mgr) G. Turner (mgr) A. E. Barnes (mgr) D. Mathais (mgr)	 1903-1908 1907-1908 1910-1911 1911-1914;	
'Undaunted ' Gilligans Gully	Undaunted Coal Mining Co A. Whittlestone (mrg) J. Robertson	 1915-25 1925-27 (closed)	110,915

Figure 11.9. A summary of the coal mining industry in the Alexandra district.

Figure 11.10. Coal wagon.

Time after time the owners promised to fix the problem — it almost always required a new and bigger shaft, but nothing would be done. So after years of cajoling, warning and finally threatening prosecution, Inspector Gow lost patience. He proceeded against Robert Lett.[17] The charge was that Lett had not fixed the ladder in his shaft in accordance with Section 33 of the Coal Mines Act of 1891. Similar charges were also brought against Louis Gards and George Rivers, but as these two both promised to sink new shafts within four months or close their pits, the inspector withdrew the charges. In the end they both chose to close their pits.

Lett was fined 10 shillings and 7 shillings costs. It wasn't much of a fine but the fact that Lett had been brought before the court was sufficient to bring other owners into line. This was the turning point. But it was also the time when mines were increasing in size and taking on more men to meet the needs of the booming dredging industry. Certified mine managers were being appointed and the old-time do-it-yourself owners were selling up or retiring. These new managers knew it was in their interests to co-operate with the inspectors, and the inspectors were in turn very helpful to the managers, often assisting them with surveying and in drawing up mine plans and so on.

It was largely owing to the vigilance of dedicated inspectors that Central Otago coal mines enjoyed such a low accident rate.

Delivering the Coal

During the gold dredging era, scores, if not hundreds, of men were employed in the coal business. Apart from the actual miners, large numbers of men were engaged in delivering the coal to the dredges. At least one wagonload of bagged coal was needed each day while a dredge was working. Most could be supplied by wagons using temporary roads cut down to the riverbank, and constantly relocated as the dredges moved. The heavy loads and rough roads needed teams of four to eight horses and the constant maintenance of wagons, harness and horses employed large numbers as wheelwrights, harness-makers and blacksmiths.

Dredges working in the gorge below Alexandra were particularly difficult to supply. Coal was brought to the lip of the gorge by wagon and then transferred to horse-drawn sledges. These followed rough, zigzag tracks down the steep walls of the gorge in the few places where it had been possible to find a route. In winter, when the dredges were best able to work owing to low river levels, the ground was frozen and sledging became dangerous. Sliding bags down a wire was tried but led to great loss of coal.

Once the coal was at the riverbank it was loaded into large coal boats and rowed down the river to the dredges. This was dangerous work but gave employment to a large number of hardy men. The supply of the specialised boats led to a flourishing boat-building yard in Alexandra.

Figure 11.11. The large Harley family was fortunate to escape without injury when their house fell into a hole which suddenly opened beneath it.

The Legacy

The coal mines are gone but they may not be forgotten. A network of water-filled tunnels with their roofs held up by decaying timber props, now lie under prosperous orchards. Already incidents have occurred which illustrate the danger hidden underground. About the time of Lett's mine collapse one of the Harley daughters had finished milking the family cow that was bailed up to a tree in a corner of the cow paddock. When she returned from taking the bucket of milk to the house she was amazed to find that the cow and the tree were in a hole five metres deep. In spite of valiant rescue efforts it is believed that the cow was lost in the depths of the water-filled hole.

Worse was to come. Shortly afterwards, Harley's house collapsed into a subsidence, fortunately with nothing more than bad fright for the large family.[18] As late as the 1960s the presence of old tunnels was dramatically demonstrated when a householder in Manuherikia Road decided to drain a persistent spring near his house. As he opened up the ground, a rush of water emerged which went on for some time. Shortly afterwards a crater suddenly formed near a house more than 100 metres distant.[19]

In these days of electric and oil heating there is little or no demand for coal. Almost all signs of the once extensive coal mining industry have gone. The mines at Coal Point were overrun by the gold dredges and now lie under a wasteland of tailings. Only in Gilligans Gully is it possible to trace signs of the old mine. Still visible are the old road leading to the mine, the flat top of the dump of mine waste and the slumped cut into the hillside, now filled with brambles and briar, which marked the entrance to a mine tunnel.

Until a few years ago the sites of the mines along the Manuherikia Road were marked by subsided ground and heaps of mining slag, but the ground has been levelled and planted with fruit trees. Every so often an orchardist may find a fruit tree in the bottom of a deep crater. It will be a reminder of the labyrinth of water-filled tunnels that lie beneath much of the Manuherikia Valley orchard land.

Figure 11.12. Briar and brambles now mark the site of a collapsed tunnel (perhaps that driven by Lett or Ballantyne) at the Undaunted Company's coal mine in Gilligans Gully.

NOTES

1. 'Matagouri' *(Discaria toumatou)* is an alteration of the Maori name Tumatakuru.

2. It is believed that 30 cm of peat are required to form 2.5 cm of lignite.

3. This is a very brief and much simplified version of these events. For a fuller account see McKellar *et al* 1967 or Williams 1974.

4. Peter Campbell (a grandson) taped by L. Thomson 1963.

5. For many years 'West Bank of the Molyneux' was an established address. It referred particularly to the stretch of river bank between Chapmans Gully and Clyde.

6. *Otago Daily Times* 21 September 1863.

7. There are several points of confusion. First, Charnock's mine was described (*Otago Daily Times* 11 July 1864) as being at Coal Point on the West Bank of the Clutha River. This Coal Point is not to be confused with the Coal Point at Dunstan (Clyde). But Coal Point at Alexandra was on the *east* bank of the river. Perhaps this mine should have been described as *opposite* Coal Point. Further confusion arises because Charnock apparently later moved across the river and took over another mine at the true Coal Point.

8. *Perseverance I* was a current-wheel dredge also owned and operated by Louis Gards.

9. Although 'Molyneux' mine or pit was an informal name it was used extensively by locals and will be used here to distinguish the mine of the Alexandra Coal Company Ltd at Coal Point in Alexandra from the 'Alexandra' mine of W. A. Thomson in Manuherikia Valley.

10. The history of the mine and the story of the fire is fully documented in McCraw, *Mine Fire* 1992.

11. Various spellings of this name are used in official reports including 'Macqueenville.' Presumably the mine was named after McQueen of Kincaid and McQueen, the firm which built the dredge and maintained a strong financial interest in it.

12. *Alexandra Herald* 29 September and 30 October 1904.

13. This may well have been the mine referred to as 'Ferris's mine' by Moore p.96. A. Bruce Snr lived on the property later acquired by Ferris.

14. Gards had sold the *Perseverance* dredges to Robert Finlay, a merchant who had been the first mayor of Alexandra and was Gards' partner in the dredging enterprise. The operator of the coal mine was James Finlay, a son of Robert Finlay. This mine was often referred to locally as 'Harley's mine' presumably because it was on Harley's property, but as far as is known, Harley had no connection with the mine other than possibly working in it and as a carrier carting coal from it.

15. Peter Campbell taped by L. Thomson 1963.

16. It was not until after the Brunner mine disaster on the West Coast in 1896 that separate, qualified inspectors were appointed to inspect coal mines.

17. *Dunstan Times* 19 June 1896.

18. Personal communication: Mrs Betty Wilson, Alexandra, a descendant of the Harley family.

19. Personal Communication: Mr N. H. Brent of Alexandra. a descendant of the Harley family.

12.

UP-COUNTRY INNOVATION

Louis Wilhelm Gards was a lucky man. He was one of the few survivors from a party of miners forced to retreat across the summit of the Old Man Range in a blinding snow storm after being starved out of diggings on the southern side of the range.

Perhaps Gards learnt something from this experience because he gave up prospecting and settled down in Alexandra, where, with John Mackersey as a partner, he bought out Beresford's wheelwright and carpentry business. Gards had followed the trade of wheelwright in Prussia, where he was born, and he came to New Zealand to take part in the early Otago gold rushes. Now that he was back in his old trade he soon extended his business to include general blacksmithing. Before long he had bought out Mackersey and so became sole owner of the business.[1]

It is not known when the substantial stone building lying between lower Tarbert and Mullingar (McDonald) Streets was built nor whether it was erected by Gards or had been taken over from Beresford. In addition to the main building there was a large store and stable on the other side of McDonald Street.

Gold was still in Gards' blood, however, and soon he was forming another partnership with Mackersey and George Spencer to build a current-wheel dredge. This led him into a career as the owner of a number of very successful dredges, and to have more time for his dredging interests he appointed James Kelman, in 1884, as manager of the blacksmithing business.

Kelman takes over.

James Kelman was a Scot born on Deeside and came to New Zealand with his parents in 1870 as a lad of 15. He learnt his blacksmithing in Riverton, and set up his own business in that town and later in Dunedin, before joining Louis Gards in Alexandra. Four years later, in 1889, he purchased the business from Gards.

Over the next ten years Kelman developed the simple blacksmithing business into a fully-fledged engineering shop. He was encouraged and supported, of course, by the gold dredging boom that began in 1890,

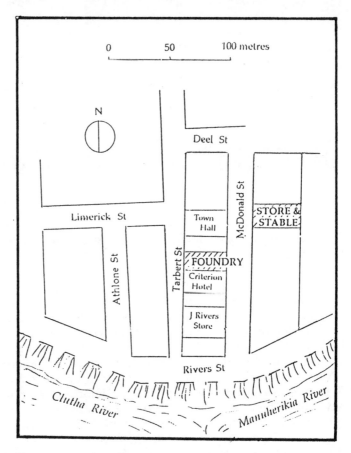

Figure 12.1. The Foundry was located immediately north of the Criterion Hotel.

wavered during the mid-1890s, and then took off towards the end of the century. Kelman's workshop was to play an extremely important part, not only in the constant repair work that was necessary to keep the dredges working, but also in the construction of large components for the dredges.

Kelman, like Gards before him, soon developed other interests. He was first elected to the Borough Council in 1888 and remained a member almost until he died. He became Mayor in 1897 and continued to hold this office during the turbulent period when the council was trying to decide on a permanent water supply. He had interests in a number of gold dredges, including the *Chicago* and was a major shareholder in the Earnscleugh Company. So when a Mr George Neill, representing the Tuapeka Foundry and Engineering Co, which proposed to open a foundry in Lawrence, appeared with a proposition that his company would be prepared to open a branch foundry in Alexandra, Kelman expressed some interest. In fact, he said at a public meeting called in 1897 to discuss the proposition, that while he was not at all anxious to part with his business, he agreed that an injection of capital was just what it needed.[2]

Figure 12.2. Foundry men:
Left: Louis Gards
Right: James Kelman

Otago Central Foundry and Engineering Company

It was not until 1899, however, that there was action. The Otago Central Foundry and Engineering Company was formed with James Kelman as principal shareholder. It was at this stage that the *Dunstan Times,* in an item about the forming of the company, reviewed the machines and facilities available in the former blacksmith's shop;

> Work can be done by the company from cutting the worm of a 2 in screw to welding a 6 in shaft and turning the same ready to go into position. In the blacksmithing shop there is a steam hammer, which strikes a blow equal to 3 cwt; a punching and shearing machine which will shear up to a 3/4 in plate of steel and which is extensively used for cutting and punching bucket lips; a screw-cutting lathe taking up to 4 ft 6 in. in diameter; a large vertical drill; a blower or fanner which supplies the draught to feed the smithy fires and the useful grindstone and emery wheels also find a place on the floor of the shop — all driven by steam[3].

The existing 4 hp steam engine was in fact proving too small for the job of driving all of these machines and had to be replaced by a larger engine. The manager (Mr Lindsay) also had plans for a cupola for melting metal for making small castings, but even though the business was known around the district as 'The Foundry,' foundry work was always on a limited scale and was confined to casting brass. In the yard at the rear of the premises, fluming and pipes were made, and there was a large bath for dipping these into hot tar. A large store stocked all sorts of engineering supplies and materials likely to be required by dredges. Altogether eight men were employed.

Figure 12.3. The 'Foundry'
Upper: In 1900 still bearing Kelman's name. Criterion Hotel on right.
Lower: 1905 now 'The Otago Central Foundry and Engineering Co, Ltd'

Figure 12.4 The Foundry was well equipped with heavy engineering tools.
Upper: The machine with the large flywheel is a punching and shearing machine. A lathe on the right.
Lower: More heavy machines.

As the number of dredges increased so did the amount and scope of the work. A drilling machine that could bore four holes at once was added in 1900, and a heavy punching and shearing machine that could handle 1 inch-thick steel plate was bought the following year. A planing machine, riveting machine and power hacksaw were added.

The largest jobs undertaken were the construction of bucket ladders for two dredges. That for the *Chatto Creek* dredge was some 13 metres long. It was made to Kelman's own design and was praised by the dredge master for combining strength and rigidity with lightness. As well as the ladder for the *Manorburn* dredge they made the complete set of buckets. In fact the firm made scores of dredge buckets of all sizes, and renewing the hardened steel cutting lips on buckets and making and rebuilding the large steel pins on which the buckets pivoted was never-ending work.

The manufacture of new pistons for the steam engines of dredges also kept the firm busy. Starting with a block of cast iron, Jack Coulson the turner, turned the pistons, cut the grooves for piston rings, made and fitted the rings and made the piston rods. One thing the foundry did not attempt was to make the very heavy gear wheels used on dredges.

Figure 12.5. This bucket ladder for the *Surprise* dredge was built at the Foundry. It was 21 metres long and weighed 10 tons. The Town Hall is on the right and the new Caledonian Hotel on the left.

Repair work was constant, and major overhauls and reconstruction were regular events as dredges were upgraded in the battle to dredge deeper and put more material over the gold-saving tables. The foundry played a vital part in these activities, and the advantages in having parts repaired or manufactured locally as against the long delay in obtaining them from

Dunedin was not lost on dredge owners. Some large repair jobs included the straightening of the ladder of the *Molyneux Hydraulic* dredge which was twisted when part of the high cliff of gravel under which the dredge was working, collapsed.

The Employees

Peter Campbell was employed at the works as a lad for some years during the first decade of the century. He distinguished himself in July 1906 on the occasion of the fire in the Alexandra Coal Company's pit by harnessing up the horse and dray belonging to the foundry, and using it to gather up all the picks and shovels from the stores in the town and from the railway construction camp on the outskirts. He delivered them to the mine where they were grabbed by men impatiently waiting to dig a ditch to bring water to the fire. The 400 metre-long water race was completed in an hour and was a crucial factor in the eventual rescue of four miners trapped underground.[4]

Campbell has left a picture[5] of the foundry during its busiest period and mentioned a few of the innovations that were necessary to carry out some of the awkward jobs that the foundry was confronted with. The large lathe, for instance, had a bed 3 metres long, which is large for a lathe but not nearly long enough to accommodate the main driving shaft of a dredge. One such, 12 metres long, was supported in the lathe at one end but it also had to be supported at several places along its length by improvised 'rests' slung from the ceiling by blocks and tackle.

Figure 12.6. In the yard at the rear of the Foundry pipes were made, and dipped in tar to preserve them.

Young Campbell's main job was to operate the steam hammer, but one day in 1910 he met with a serious accident when his clothing became entangled in the vertical drill he was using at the time. It was a large machine capable of taking a 75-mm diameter bit and powered by the steam engine, so when his coat was caught he was whirled round the drill with great force. Had his coat sleeve not torn off he would have suffered much more serious injuries than the broken arm with which he escaped.

Crankshafts for Cars

Perhaps the most innovative work of all, and which established a legendary reputation for the foundry, was the making of crankshafts for cars. It has been said that this was the only engineering shop in New Zealand where this was done, although the truth of this claim has not been established.

They were made during the Great War when spare parts were hard to obtain but, perhaps more important, when dredge work was falling away, so the firm was glad to take on all sorts of extraneous work to keep it occupied. As far as can be ascertained six crankshafts were made. Five were made for four-cylinder Buick cars and one for a two-cylinder Enfield.

Figure 12.7. After the Great War the building was converted to a motor garage for Alexandra Motors. A rather unusual repair job was to an aeroplane which damaged its landing gear when landing in 1939.

Great care was taken in marking out the initial block of chrome-nickel steel. Then the shape was cut out with the steam driven hacksaw, the necessary boring done and the whole thing forged with the steam hammer. Finally, Coulson turned the crankshaft to fine tolerances.

With the virtual demise of dredging during the Great War the work of the foundry fell away until the enterprise was no longer viable. On 10 September 1917 it was wound up voluntarily and the equipment was disposed of.

The building was sold in 1919 to Todd Bros of Dunedin who, as the agents for Fordson tractors, Massey Harris agricultural implements, etc. intended to convert it to a modern showroom. Instead they came to a deal with Henry Hesson who had bought a garage on the opposite side of the street the year before. Hesson and his two partners would move into the old foundry building and take over Todd Bros agencies. After renovations and modernising the move took place in November 1920. The partnership broke up in 1928 and Hesson went back to farming. The garage continued on until the business was sold to C. J. Rooney, a returned serviceman who established a new company, Alexandra Motors (1947) Ltd, which acquired the Ford agency. When this firm moved to a new building on a different site in the mid-1950s the old foundry building was let to various tenants, the last of whom was a panel beater. The building was demolished in the 1960s.

NOTES
1. *Dunstan Times* Obituary L. W. Gards 15 July 1908.
2. *Dunstan Times* 9 April 1897.
3. *Dunstan Times* 3 November 1899.
4. For a full description of this drama see McCraw, 1992.
5. Peter Campbell Tape 1963, Les. Thomson, Alexandra.

13.

THE YEARS OF SHAME

— Harassment of the Chinese

They first arrived at the Dunstan Township (Clyde). 'Ten interesting specimens of the Flowery Land' was the way the newspaper described them. Soon after their arrival they made their way down to the river beaches and began panning for gold. From then onwards, each coach arriving from Dunedin brought more Chinese to the Dunstan.

Much has been written about the industriousness and frugal lifestyle of the Chinese miners, who were perhaps at first regarded more as objects of curiosity than as any kind of threat. As their numbers grew, they continued to be welcomed by the business community but the attitudes of miners changed. The Chinese habit of leaving one member of a group to guard their river beach claim ('shepherding' it was called), instead of abandoning it during the summer high river period meant that when the river fell with the approach of winter, European miners were excluded from pegging out these lucrative claims. The Chinese ability to recover gold from previously worked-over ground caused some jealousy and resentment, and their lack of English led to misunderstandings and increased suspicions. Newspapers continued to refer to the Chinese in a patronising and sarcastic way as 'Our Celestial friends.'

It was evident that around Alexandra, where in 1890 they made up more than a third of the population, the Chinese were tolerated up to a point. That point was reached when they were seen to be threatening European jobs. But at the same time there were Europeans, including the magistrates and wardens (often the same people) and leaders of the community, who, no matter what their private thoughts, or their motives, were prepared to defend the Chinese in public.

James Rivers, a prominent local storekeeper, was one of these. A public spirited man with influence in the town and strong financial interests in a number of mining claims, he often represented the Chinese in the Warden's Court. By so doing he earned the opprobrium of Europeans but, at the same time, he earned the gratitude of the Chinese miners which was, no doubt, tangibly expressed by their patronage. The businessmen of the town went out of their way to befriend the Chinese in these times of depression, and tried to outbid each other in offering terms of credit and other inducements that were not available to European miners.

John Magnus

From the late 1880s, however, a new and disturbing element entered the relationship between the Chinese and Europeans in Alexandra. There was an outbreak of 'Chinese bashing.' It was led by a group of larrikins who made life miserable for the Chinese for about 10 years. James Ng[1] attributes this to a combination of factors including: a general upsurge of anti-Chinese feeling throughout the country; increasing unemployment as the long depression deepened; lack of a strong Chinese leader in the town; weak men in the local police force who did not seem to know how to handle the situation, and finally, to the arrival of John Magnus.

Johannes (John) Magnus, a man of 31 with a great deal of worldly experience, arrived in Alexandra in November 1887 to join his brothers Olof[2] and August. John, like his brothers, was born in Sweden, but he was brought up and educated in England, serving for two years in the Hull Police force and later with the police in the International Settlement in Shanghai, China. Then for several years he sailed the world as a ship's carpenter.

Figure 13.1. John Magnus (1856-1939)

In later life Magnus used to show a scar across the palm of his hand which he said was the result of grabbing at the blade of a sword wielded by an attacking Chinese in Shanghai. He also claimed to have a knowledge of the Cantonese dialect. Whatever the truth of these claims, John Magnus apparently had a deep-seated hatred of the Chinese. He seemed to assume that this gave him and his mates the licence to bully and harass Chinese whenever he wished.

Only nine months after his arrival Magnus was up before the Magistrate's Court for tipping a bucket of urine over the head of a Chinese storekeeper. It cost him £1 with costs £4 10s. or seven days in Clyde gaol.

It was from late 1893 onwards that Magnus and his mates, based at their gold mine at Butchers Point about four kilometres down the river from Alexandra, began to seriously harass the local Chinese. This harassment may have begun as a series of impulsive, unrelated incidents, but soon developed into an organised campaign to get rid of the Chinese from the business section of Alexandra.

John Magnus was annoyed that 'a crowd of grinning, jabbering Chinese' regularly blocked the footpaths outside the Chinese boarding houses in Tarbert Street so that he and his wife had to step out into the road to pass. He claimed he understood sufficient Cantonese to pick up the remarks the crowd made about his wife. He went to the mayor (James Simmonds) who was sympathetic but pointed out that there was no by-law to deal with the matter, and, according to Magnus, said something like "You were a policeman — you must have some ideas." Then Magnus went to the lone policeman, Constable Pratt, who pointed out that he couldn't spend all day standing at the boarding house doors ordering the Chinese off the footpath. So Magnus apparently decided to take the law into his own hands and get rid of the Chinese from the main street.[3]

Campaign Begins

The campaign began in the early hours of the morning of 25 November 1893, with assaults on Chinese in the street and the breaking of windows in the Chinese premises in Tarbert Street. Several men were charged over the incident, including Bill Noble, Steve Spain and John Magnus himself.

John Magnus's version of events, as recorded in his *Reminiscences*[4] tells of a party of 15 young fellows drinking in the Caledonian Hotel and discussing the five candidates for the forthcoming election.[5] Suddenly a crowd of Chinese, armed with picks, shovels and axes, burst into the hotel through a rear door, demanding Bill Noble — 'Killim him' was the cry. Magnus shouted to Noble, who was in the hotel, to clear out, and he escaped through a side door, flattening a couple of Chinese on the way. Noble was a fleet runner and made it across the bridge. The remaining 14 of the hotel party armed themselves with empty bottles 'to wollop the Chows with' and went after the Chinese. They caught up with them in the middle of the bridge where the Chinese were milling about, fearful to venture further out into the darkness of the countryside. By this time the constable had turned up wanting to know what the fuss was about.

Shortly after Magnus and party returned to the hotel to celebrate Noble's escape they heard a great noise outside and on investigation they found
> . . . that there had been something like an earthquake for the Chinese windows and doors had all fallen in.

Noble, who was charged with assault on Chow Cat, was able, with the help of his friends, to prove an alibi and the case was dismissed.

According to Magnus, Steve Spain was convicted when a Chinese witness swore he recognised him because of his rather bandy walk and the witness gave a good imitation of it in front of the magistrate. Spain, who was charged with breaking a window, was fined £2 with damages and costs — 'fined for not walking straight' as Magnus put it.

The poor constable had to walk down to Butchers Point to deliver a summons to Magnus and to inform him that a special court session had been arranged for him at Clyde, at the request of the Chinese. Magnus was charged with 'malicious injury to Chinese property' — in other words breaking the window of a Chinese store by throwing a large rock through it. Evidence was given that about 3 o'clock in the morning Jay Cooe had been sitting in his house writing, when a stone came through his window and broke his lamp. Another struck Chow Kee who was sleeping. They slipped out the back entrance and arrived on the street in time to see John Magnus pick up a stone and throw it through Jay Cooe's window. Many other Chinese said they saw Magnus throwing the stones. The defence was an alibi, a defence that was to become all too familiar. Three citizens swore that Magnus was in bed during the disturbance and only got up after it was all over.

According to Magnus, it took the strength of three Chinese to roll a rock into the Courtroom — the rock he was supposed to have thrown through the window. And when Magnus's lawyer asked them to demonstrate how it was thrown, not one of them could lift it.

According to the Magistrate, however, it was another unsatisfactory case. He said the Chinese had given clear and apparently very truthful evidence, but on the other hand several other witnesses swore that Magnus could not have been at the scene. As his liberty was at stake, Magnus had to get the benefit of the doubt. Case dismissed.[6]

Although the assault charge against Noble had been dismissed, the police brought him back into court early in the New Year charged with breaking Chin She's windows during the same incident. The familiar defence was offered. His mates all swore that Noble had never left the sitting room of the Caledonian Hotel. But Chin and three or four other Chinese swore that they had clearly seen Noble standing in the middle of the street, throw stones through the windows of Chin's place, and then run off. The magistrate found the evidence not conclusive and dismissed the case, whereupon the police, presumably discouraged by this outcome, withdrew the cases of a 'similar nature' against four others. There may be some significance in the fact that William Noble, with others, left Alexandra for Coolgardie in Western Australia shortly after the hearing and did not return until the following year.

Incidents in the Gorge

During most of 1894 and early 1895 Magnus was apparently too busy mining to worry about Chinese except for a couple of incidents.[7] Magnus tells of problems his family had with Chinese while living at Butchers Point, a rather isolated place down the gorge from Alexandra. One day three Chinese came to the house asking for food. Mrs Magnus was alone so she told them she had none. Obviously not believing her, one pushed his way into the house and the others made to follow. Louisa Magnus pulled a revolver, which she always carried at John's insistence, and fired a shot over their heads. They left smartly.

John Magnus employed a servant girl at Butchers Point but when it was necessary for the girl or Mrs Magnus to go up to Alexandra for supplies, a Chinese miner on the opposite bank

> . . . would undress and expose his person in the most disgraceful and shameful manner and would run along the side of the river calling on the women. . .

After putting up with this behaviour for some time Magnus decided to teach the exhibitionist a lesson. He got a pot of coal tar and 'put a little nitric acid in it to make it hot' and a bag of feathers from one of his wife's pillows. As his wife prepared for her next trip to Alexandra, John crossed the river with his workmen whom he wanted with him as witnesses.

Sure enough the man began his performance and Magnus approached and asked him what he was up to. 'Me no savee' was the only answer he got. Magnus said that he would make him 'savee.' The operation didn't take long. The victim got a good coating of tar followed by the feathers. Magnus thought he looked a pretty sight and would do well at a show. Apparently the poor fellow lay in his cave for a week and then went to the police. But he got no sympathy there. Constable Pratt told him bluntly that he got what he deserved and that he was lucky he didn't end up in the river. He was advised to leave town at once and he did just that.

Violence Restarted

The campaign against the Chinese in Alexandra was then restarted in August 1895 with even more violence. John Magnus, John Rainham, Oscar Johnson and Harry Redman attacked Wong Sing while he was cooking his supper in his cave in the gorge below Alexandra. They tied him up with rope and then set fire to his bed. The man managed to wriggle out of the cave but was not released until another Chinese found him next morning. In spite of a spirited defence by their lawyer and their insistence that they were nowhere near the cave that night, the four were found guilty by the three Justices of the Peace on the bench.[8] They were fined £1 each together with substantial damages and costs. Further charges were withdrawn provided the quartet entered into recognisances of £25 each as a guarantee that they would keep the peace. But still the harassment went on.

An old Chinese working his cradle was asked by several men to show them his gold. When he refused, they cut off his queue ('pig-tail') close to his scalp with a pocket knife. Another Chinese came back from a prospecting trip to find his few belongings, bedding, clothing, etc, worth about £5, completely destroyed by fire. Others had come back to their caves to find they had been entered and all the contents smashed or burnt, and others again had been fired on while in their caves.

Then the pace quickened. While Magnus kept the constable busy in his office with the payment of fines for his recent convictions, what sounded like two shots rang out. Magnus remarked to the constable that someone was out shooting rabbits by moonlight. A Chinese came running shouting that a hut belonging to Fon Yim, in what is now McDonald Street, had been blown up with one end and the roof destroyed.

Another night all the chimneys in the Chinese boarding houses were mysteriously blocked but not before a good quantity of 'cyan' (cayenne pepper?) had been emptied down on to the fires below and the doors fastened on the outside. Magnus tells of half-choked Chinese scrambling out through windows, and even the constable, who rushed to the scene and into the building, beat a very hasty retreat.

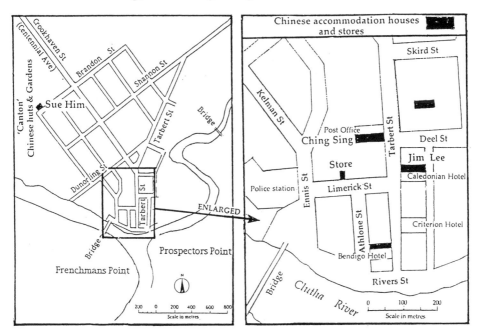

Figure 13.2. The probable location of the Chinese accommodation houses in Alexandra in Magnus's time.

The climax came on 3 October while the policeman was in the police cell attending to a prisoner. Unfortunately the constable had left the key in the lock on the outside. Suddenly the door was slammed shut and locked. At least, as Magnus remarked, the constable had the prisoner for company. In the time it took for the policeman's wife to respond to his calls for help, and for her to find someone to break open the door, three of the Chinese boarding houses had been attacked. A mob of 20 to 30 Europeans throwing stones and wielding shovels had smashed the doors and windows. According to Magnus, explosives were placed so that the Chinese buildings were showered with rocks that took out the windows and doors. Then, shortly afterwards a flume carrying the Caledonian water race to a party of Chinese sluicing in Chapmans Gully, was also blown up, causing £20 worth of damage.

At this stage a newspaper letter[9] from 'Fairplay' expressed horror at the damage done to Chinese property by the vandals. 'Now, when things like this happen in a civilised community it is time that larrikinism was put down,' the correspondent wrote and called for stronger action and for more police. It was responded to by 'Reform' who was probably John Magnus, judging by the venomous sentiments expressed:[10]

> The time appears to be fast approaching when the Chinaman will have to be rooted out of our main street at any price. A pretty 'civilised community' sir, when a lady, passing along our streets is subject to the insolent, insinuating leers of these abominable creatures, who stand in half-dozens in front of their dens. Even grown girls must bear the unspeakable horror on their way to school of passing these dens under the loathsome gaze of these hideous jabbering heathens. 'Civilised community' indeed! . . . while our footpaths are cursed by gambling, putrid celestials loafing everywhere; let no man have the hardihood to call *this* a 'civilised community.'

In the middle of all this a Chinese went missing. According to the newspaper,[11] Kong Wah Jun had come into town and intended to go out to Butchers Gully to collect money owing to him before returning to China. He set out on foot on 2 October and nothing further was heard from him. Ah Wye, a prominent Chinese storekeeper, offered a £20 reward along with a fairly detailed description of the man and the clothes he was wearing. This was all too much of a temptation for John Magnus and his mates at Butchers Point — they decided that they would find the missing Chinese.

The story of how they manufactured a body from parts of a sheep and a goat carcass, is well known.[12] The finding of the body, on a river beach, dressed in clothes similar to those described for the missing man, was duly reported in Alexandra by an excited prospector. It was taken up river in a boat obligingly supplied by Magnus and company (for a fee of £5), and a Coroner's Inquest and *post-mortem* examination was conducted in the stable behind the Bendigo Hotel. The solemnity of the occasion was interrupted now and then by the perpetrators of the hoax who could not contain themselves. Probing of the body exposed the terrible truth, whereupon the whole show broke up and adjourned to the neighbouring pub.

The whole business was reported in a very restrained manner by the *Dunstan Times*[13] which referred to 'the perpetration of a ghastly hoax' but did comment that 'The *post mortem* inquiry broke up in most admired confusion.' It added that the discoverer of the body considered himself badly treated because the £20 reward had not yet been paid to him. Unfortunately, in the same issue an article contributed by 'Two to One' began:

> One of the most amusing things that has ever taken place in New Zealand, or perhaps in the world, took place in our little mining township of Alexandra last Monday.

This attitude, which probably reflected the view of the majority of the population, set the pattern that was maintained until recently. John Magnus cashed in by writing up the story for the *Alexandra Herald* in 1928 which then reprinted it as a booklet entitled *The Lost Chinaman* with a subheading *The World's Best Practical Joke*. There is a photo in existence of

John Magnus taken in old age showing him standing in front of a sign proclaiming 'Champion Practical Joker of the World'. As late as 1958 a musical production, called *The Image of Ju Lye*, was based on the 'Lost Chinaman' incident and produced as part of the annual Blossom Festival activities. It was so popular in Alexandra that it was taken on tour and then replayed some years later.

In his later years Magnus became increasingly proud of this episode and, by and large, the European population thought, with one or two notable exceptions, that it was a good joke. Magnus himself said it was not intended to hoax either the doctors or the police but they were 'merely out to play a lark on the Chinese beachcombers.' In the light of Magnus's notorious record of crimes against the Chinese, there can be little doubt that it was racially motivated.

Finale

The final act in this particularly turbulent period in Alexandra's history took place on 27 November 1895 when John Rainham attacked a Chinese, Ah Que, in his hut in the Gorge. The sack door of the hut was set alight and the burning material thrown into the hut followed by a bottle of kerosene. While the Chinese was trying to put the fire out, a bag was thrown over him and doused in kerosene. He was badly burnt and lost all his possessions including his store of rice.

In court Rainham put forward the usual defence of completely denying

Figure 13.3. Sue Him, a respected Chinese orchardist and storekeeper, built a combined house and store in Brandon Street The building was subsequently used as a fruit packing shed.

that he was anywhere near the hut at the time. His mates, Redman and Johnson, as expected, backed him up but now Alexandra had a new policeman who was not one to be put off, and also there was a magistrate rather than Justices on the Bench. Rainham was given the maximum penalty — two months hard labour in Dunedin's prison.[14]

This effectively put an end to the period of violent harassment that had plagued Alexandra for more than a year. Magnus claimed success for his campaign in that the Chinese did leave the boarding houses (or 'dens' as he called them) in the main street, and re-established themselves near the river bank in the north-west outskirts of the township. Here they erected huts and a few substantial buildings in a village that the Europeans called 'Canton.' Remnants of the Chinese camp and the market gardens were still in existence during the 1920s and 30 years later the remains of a few huts were still scattered about the orchards that occupied the area until recently.

Reaction
The Reverend Alex Don, the Chinese Missioner for the Presbyterian Church, in his report[15] on his tour of duty through Central Otago, waded

Figure 13.4. Rev. Alexander Don (1857-1934).

into the European population of Alexandra for their apathy during the whole shameful period. There were fewer than 10 ringleaders, he said, and public opinion could easily have dealt with them, but in Alexandra public protest had been feeble or lacking. While the actions of these louts were perhaps not actively encouraged, they had certainly not been discouraged.

Don was particularly wrathful over the 'Lost Chinaman' hoax and was disappointed with the fact that a leading newspaper in the district — 'a wretched rag' he called it — had published a comic poem about the whole episode. How would the European population have reacted, he asked, if the roles had been reversed? What would have happened if a respected European citizen had gone missing and the Chinese had rigged up a body out of half-rotten animal remains? Don was surprised that the Chinese did not retaliate. He was sure men of any other race would not have tolerated the treatment dished out to the Chinese without some sort of reprisal.

Poor Policeman Pratt

Constable Pratt was in sole charge of Alexandra Police Station during the 'troubles' and was the butt of many of the larrikins' pranks. Pratt was not the brightest member of the Force and had had a turbulent career which had its climax in his asking to appear before the Royal Commission set up in 1898[16] to inquire into conditions in the Police Force. He had a whole series of complaints to lay before the Commission, ranging from excessive transfers and lack of promotion to black marks entered on his record without his knowledge. His cross-examination covered many pages of the voluminous report and disclosed an incompetent and perhaps lazy officer who had been the subject of numerous complaints by the public and his superior officers.

Pratt had joined the Force in Dunedin in 1875 after serving for 16 years in the Artillery in Britain, and was posted to no fewer than 10 police stations in Otago and Southland over the next 15 years. He was transferred to Alexandra, a sole constable station, in 1890. The transfer was much against his will but he was given no option. His Inspector had already commented that he did not know what to do with this man — a man, who had already petitioned Parliament about his 'harassment,' as he called it, in the Police Force. For some reason the Commissioner of Police was not prepared to dismiss Pratt, perhaps because he had a family of 10 children. But Alexandra apparently was his last chance.

Most of the 12 printed pages of minutes of Pratt's interview by the Royal Commissioners deal with Pratt's complaints and one part in particular bears on his time in Alexandra. Describing his difficulties dealing with the larrikins he said:

> . . . it is well known there was no man living that could cope with Alexandra. It was notorious for years before I went there as a hotbed of larrikins doing outrageous things. The department will say I could not cope with the crimes committed there; but I say it was impossible for any man single-handed to cope with the crime there. The crimes committed were something awful. For instance, tying a Chinaman up, and setting fire to his place, and leaving him to roast. . . You never heard, I suppose, of any such things being

done in any part of the world. I had these men up several times, and if I had a dozen witnesses to prove the charges they would have twenty to prove they were in bed. . . I have been out till 3 and 4 o'clock in the morning in all sorts of disguises to try to catch them. Of course they were watching me. The fact was I was simply laughed at—no support in any one way or another. Had I the Magistrate that is there now, larrikinism would have been stamped out long before it was.

It was disclosed that a public meeting had been held in Alexandra to discuss the ineffectiveness of the police in controlling the larrikinism during which a suggestion was made that police be brought from the North Island to clean the town up.[17]

Pratt had been replaced in November 1895 and his successor, Constable Chisholm, almost immediately arrested John Rainham for setting fire to Ah Que. The subsequent gaoling of this man marked the end of the period of larrikinism.

A job had been found for Pratt as gaoler at Clyde. It was a sinecure. Under examination, he agreed with the Commissioner that he received £156 per year — more than the pay of a first-class constable. In addition he also got sixpence a day extra, plus one shilling a day long-service allowance, together with free quarters, fuel and light. And if he had to look after one prisoner a month he thought he was hard-worked!

NOTES

1. Personal communication from Dr James Ng, the foremost authority on the Chinese in Otago.
2. Olof Magnus appears in the 1884 Electoral Roll so presumably arrived in Alexandra at least a year earlier. There is variation in the spelling of his forename. 'Olof' rather than 'Olaf' is used by the family.
3. The Yellow Agony in Tarbert Street Thirty-Five Years ago. *Alexandra Herald* 3 October 1928.
4. *Chows After Killing W. Noble.* Magnus, J. in *Reminiscences.* 1928.
5. This would be the 1893 Parliamentary election to be held in December for which four candidates were standing for the Mt Ida electorate (which included Alexandra). Vincent Pyke won by a large majority.
6. *Dunstan Times* 8 and 22 December 1893.
7. *Tar and Feathers.* Magnus, J. in *Reminiscences* 1928.
8 *Dunstan Times* 6 September 1895.
9. *Dunstan Times* 4 October 1895.
10. *Dunstan Times* 11 October 1895.
11. *Dunstan Times* 11 October 1895.
12. *Dunstan Times* 18 October 1895.
13. *Alexandra Herald* 22 August 1928 and issued in pamphlet form 1928 by Alexandra Herald Company.
14. *Dunstan Times* 6 & 20 December 1895.
15. *Christian Outlook* 5 June 1897.
16. Commission on the Police Force. 1898.
17. No report of this public meeting has been found.

14.

GOOD AND BAD

—The Saga of John Magnus

The publicity given to the harassment of the Chinese, and especially to the 'Lost Chinaman' affair, has overshadowed the fact that John Magnus and his two brothers played an important part in the gold mining history of Central Otago.

They were hard-working, skilled men who all held, at various times, important mining jobs. But John had an unfortunate streak of larrikinism in his make-up, which, exacerbated by over-indulgence in alcohol, led him into constant conflict with the law. He also made great use of the law in that he was regularly in the Warden's Court as a lead player in mining disputes.[1] He is remembered as one of the 'hard cases' of the later part of the gold mining era and it is perhaps only fair that a brief record of his achievements should be set beside his better-known lawless escapades.

Figure 14.1. The Magnus brothers. Olof (left) dredge owner, August (Gus) (middle) dredgemaster and alluvial miner, John (right) mine manager.

After his arrival in Alexandra in 1887 Magnus worked for a time in alluvial mines and on current-wheel dredges, but then took employment in the big Hercules mine at Roxburgh owned by Bedford Butler. He married the owner's daughter Louisa, in May 1889 and managed the mine for a year or so. In November 1892 he was appointed as working manager of the newly established Molyneux Hydraulic Elevating and Sluicing Company at Alexandra. Eight months later a new manager was appointed. It is not known for certain that Magnus was dismissed, but if he were, he was only the first of a series of managers to suffer the same fate. The claim was almost impossible to work because of flooding from the Clutha River, and the company's directors all thought they knew better than the managers how it should be mined.

Butchers Point

John Magnus now began his own mining venture. With a partner, John Everitt, he took over a claim, probably James Coleman's, at Butchers Point, about four kilometres down the gorge from Alexandra. The plan was to mine by hydraulic elevating, a method which requires large amounts of water at high pressure. Application was made for eight heads[2] of water from Butchers Creek, a stream which entered the Clutha River opposite the claim. Nicholas Anderson, however, already held the water right and Magnus had to prove in the Warden's Court that the water race had not been used for some time and so was liable to forfeiture. This he was able to do readily enough as Anderson had not used the water right since the 1878 flood had destroyed his flume across the river. Magnus had to build a dam across the gorge of Butchers Creek, and construct a water race from it around vertical cliffs to a point high above the river. A pipeline was laid down the hillside, across the river suspended on wire ropes, and then back up into a race. This took the water to the intake of another pipeline leading to the elevator. All in all, it took something over £1000 and more than a year's work to develop the claim.

Magnus and Everitt formed the Butchers Point Hydraulic Company and were granted a claim of 10 acres. However, large boulders in the gravels made it difficult to excavate down to the gold-bearing 'wash,' especially during the winter when the water in Butchers Creek was insufficient to work the elevator. This was not helped by a mining company at Bald Hill Flat drawing off some of his water from the headwaters of Butchers Creek. Magnus sued the Bald Hill Sluicing Company for damages, and in a case that dragged on for nearly a year, and included a Supreme Court hearing and several appeals, he finally won.

Nine men were employed on the Butchers Point claim but it wasn't until April 1895 that they reached the 'wash.' Gold, however proved elusive. Shortage of water, boulders, increasing seepage from the river, and 'bottom' as it sloped down below the river, worked against their success.

Poverty Beach

With foresight, John and his brothers formed the Golden Beach Hydraulic

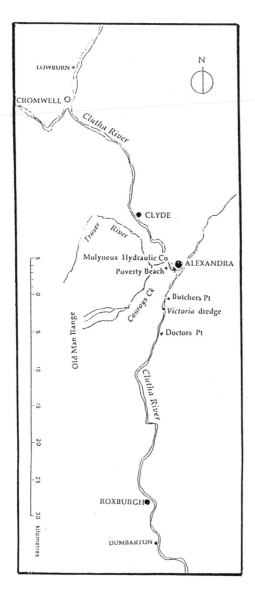

Figure 14.2. Map with places connected with John Magnus.

Gold Mining Company with a 50 acre (20 h) claim at Poverty Beach, just over a kilometre above Alexandra on the Earnscleugh side of the Clutha River. By 1 May 1896 the Butchers Point operation was closed down and the elevator shifted to Poverty Beach where John was appointed manager of the new company.

Olof Magnus had already purchased the Caledonian water race that brought two heads of water from the headwaters of Butchers Creek. This proved insufficient to work the elevator, especially when it was discovered that it was not a first right and some water had to be allowed to flow past

177

the intake for people with prior rights further down the stream. A campaign to secure more water was begun. John was soon in strife with a former employee, Michael McCarthy, now mining in his own right, who accused Magnus of illegally diverting the north and middle branches of Conroys Creek into the Golden Beach race. McCarthy sued Magnus for damages and applied for an injunction to prevent further theft of water. McCarthy won the case.

Figure 14.3. The gorge below Alexandra. Butchers Point protrudes into the river (centre) with Colmans Gully behind.

In spite of every scheme Magnus could dream up, he could not produce sufficient water to run the elevator efficiently, particularly when so much barren overburden had to be removed to reach the thin layer of gold-bearing 'wash.' Mining came to a standstill while the future of the claim was debated. It was decided that the only way to work the claim successfully would be by dredging, so in August 1897 a new company, the Golden Beach Hydraulic and Elevating and Dredging Co Ltd, was formed. There was no place for a conventional mine manager on a dredging claim so John resigned but remained a shareholder in the new company.

At a Loose End
Magnus spent some time mining at Blackmans Gully. He then began boating coal down the gorge to the *Victoria* dredge, but soon realised that there were less dangerous ways of making a living. So in 1898 he pegged out a claim on a small section of land that was almost surrounded by the Golden Beach Company's claim. Unfortunately for John, the land was

already occupied by John Pattison who was not only mining the section but living on it. He promptly charged Magnus with trespass. Pattison won damages and an injunction to keep Magnus off his claim. Then in April 1898 the newspaper reported[3] that he was mining in Chapmans Gully under an arrangement with the Golden Beach company to use their pipeline and water for his elevator.The enterprise must have been short-lived as Magnus's application was withdrawn before it had come before the Court.

Like many Central Otago miners, John Magnus dabbled in gold dredging shares during the boom years. As well as his shareholding in the Golden Beach Company he had financial interests in other dredges, including the *Gold Queen* at Dumbarton and the *Maori King* on the West Coast, where he was a director of the company. Although his entry in the *Cyclopedia of New Zealand* [4] (probably written by himself) describes him as a 'former dredge owner' no other evidence can be found of John owning a dredge or acting as a dredgemaster. His brothers Olof and August (Gus) were owners or part owners of dredges and were both dredgemasters.

Unable to settle to mining, John Magnus decided to try a different lifestyle. He took over the Wheatsheaf Hotel at Teddington, a small place at the head of Lyttleton Harbour. This would seem a most inappropriate occupation for a person of John's habits. Sure enough, he was back in Central Otago within two years. After his return in 1906, Magnus worked as a carpenter and dredge hand until January 1909 when John and his brother Gus won the contract for the construction of the new Borough reservoir on Bridge Hill.

Doctors Point
While they were building this reservoir, the Magnus brothers were developing a gold mine at Doctors Point, about 10 kilometres down the gorge below Alexandra. An old race was repaired to bring water to the claim from nearby Shanty Creek. Soon the partners were on rich gold, but it was too good to last. In May 1909 Arnold Nordmeyer[5] was granted a claim directly below Magnus's that effectively prevented the Magnus party from getting rid of their tailings, and virtually brought their mining to a halt.

They had seen no sign of Nordmeyer working his claim so the partners decided to take a risk. They continued mining and discharging their tailings through his claim. As might have been expected, Nordmeyer turned up almost immediately and took John Magnus to the Warden's Court to answer a 'Plaint' of trespass, and to ask for an injunction to prevent it happening again. The Warden refused to issue an injunction but fined John £2 10s and costs.

This added to John Magnus's woes. His personal financial affairs were going from bad to worse. The cost of the Butchers Point mine and other unsuccessful ventures, including speculation in dredging shares, coupled with his drinking habit, kept him poor. The Nordmeyer affair had meant that the mine had produced little gold so far, and the destruction by fire of his house in Alexandra did not help. In December John was declared bankrupt. His only asset was a quarter share in the Doctors Point claim

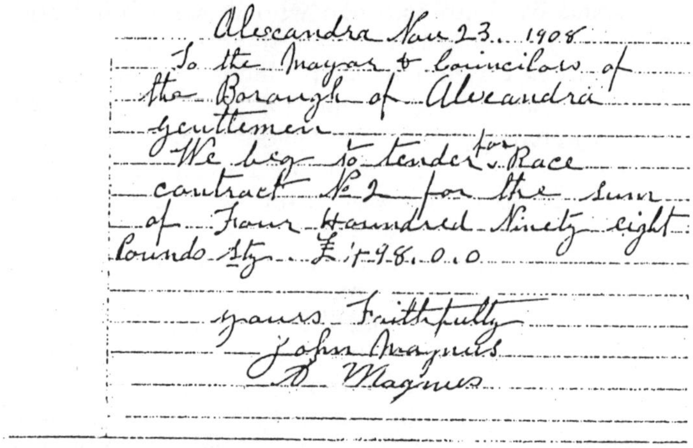

Alexandra Nov 23. 1908

To the Mayor & Councilors of the Borough of Alexandra

Gentlemen

We beg to tender for Race contract No 2 for the sum of Four Hundred Ninety eight Pounds stg £498.0.0

Yours Faithfully
John Magnus
A. Magnus

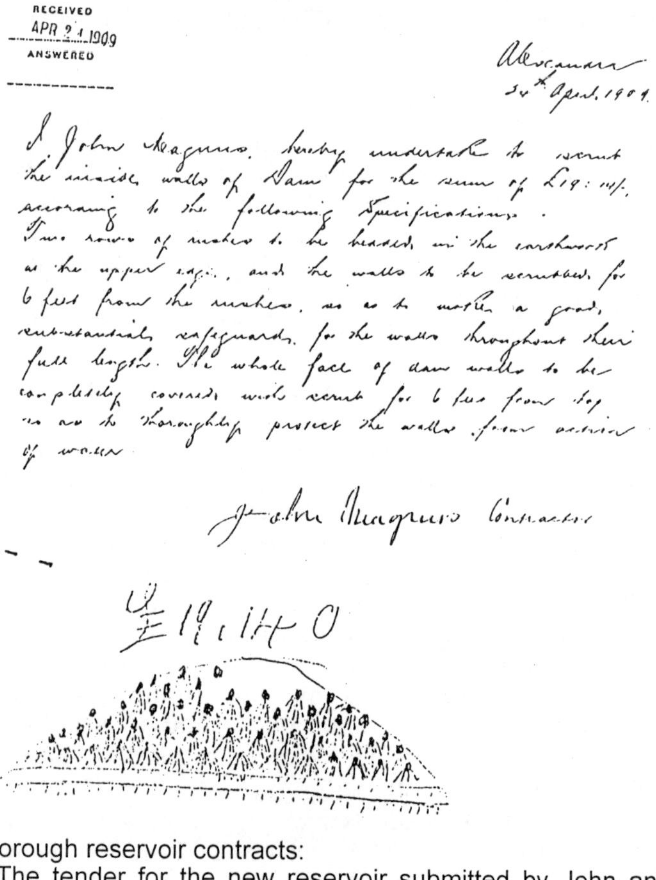

RECEIVED
APR 2 1 1909
ANSWERED

Alexandra
30th April 1909

I, John Magnus, hereby undertake to scrub the inside walls of Dam for the sum of £19:14/-, according to the following Specifications.

Two rows of rushes to be headed in the earthworks at the upper edge, and the walls to be scrubbed for 6 feet from the rushes, so as to make a good, substantial safeguard, for the walls throughout their full length. The whole face of dam walls to be completely covered with scrub for 6 feet from top, so as to thoroughly protect the walls from action of water.

John Magnus Contractor

£19.14. 0

Figure 14.4. Borough reservoir contracts:
Upper: The tender for the new reservoir submitted by John and August Magnus.
Lower: John Magnus's offer to 'scrub' the Borough reservoir. This offer, complete with sketch attached by a rusty pin, was signed, but not written, by John Magnus.

Figure 14.5. Borough Reservoir on Bridge Hill was built by Gus and John Magnus in 1909.

which would, of course, be sold. And everyone thought that was the end of John Magnus's mining activities at Doctors Point.

Gus Magnus and partner Lewis Cameron were able to acquire Nordmeyer's claim and so solve the tailings problem, but another cropped up. In April 1910 an application was lodged for three heads of water out of Shanty Creek and for a six-acre claim which included the southern part of their own claim. The applicant was Laura Selma Magnus, the 17 year-old daughter of the bankrupt John Magnus. The girl's name was obviously being used by her father to obtain the water right and claim which, as a bankrupt, he could not himself own. Although the application was granted, no work was ever done on Laura's claim and it was soon forfeited to Gus Magnus.

Contractor

Doctors Point was, as far as is known, John Magnus's last 'hands-on' mining venture. Tired of the hard, uncomfortable work, he chose the easier life of a jobbing carpenter, painter and paperhanger. But he was now drinking heavily with occasional binges.

It was during one of these that he broke into the magazine of the Antimony Mining Company and stole 50 lbs of gelignite and three boxes of detonators with a total value of £5. A tolerant magistrate realised that drink was the problem and ordered Magnus to return the goods, pay £6 costs and take out a six-month Prohibition Order. But only three months later he was up before the court and fined £2 with costs for breaking this Order.

Figure 14.6. The claim of Magnus and party at Doctors Point (highest workings, on the right).

Such was John's reputation for misdeeds, that he found it necessary to write to the paper in 1913 denying that he had stolen produce from a church 'bring and buy' stall. He said he had heard that the police were looking for him over the incident, but he assured the ladies concerned that he was not the culprit. 1914 was a bad year for Magnus. He was arrested for stealing a goose worth 5 shillings. It cost him a £2 fine or 7 days in gaol. Then the Acclimatisation Society prosecuted both John and his son Olaf for using explosives to catch fish in the Manor Burn on 4 March. It cost John a total of £13 and his son £5.

On 3 April he was charged with being drunk in Kenmare Street at 11 am on Sunday and with committing an indecent act. He was sentenced to a total of six weeks gaol on the two charges. This was the first time in his turbulent career that he was actually gaoled.

One of Magnus's mates was James Halpine, who was also a noted drinker and also had a Prohibition Order taken out against him. On two occasions during October John Magnus supplied Halpine with liquor, with the result that they were both fined, one for supplying and the other for procuring. However, they were both slow learners, as exactly a year later they were both up again on the same charges. When Magnus appeared, the magistrate remarked "I don't know what to do with this man." He was fined £2 and costs.

The Island

The magistrate warned Magnus when he appeared at the end of July 1917 on a charge of drunkenness that he was on the verge of being sent to 'the island' — the Inebriates' Institution on Rotoroa Island near Auckland.[6] But only a week later he was arrested in Mullingar (McDonald) Street in a helplessly drunken state and still clutching a partly full bottle of whisky. The climax came at the court sitting on 9 August 1917 when Magnus was charged with 'being a person against whom a Prohibition Order was in force, did procure liquor'. William Bodkin, the lawyer, did his best, pointing out that John was a widower who lived alone. It was obvious that drink was his failing, but with the fruit season coming on Bodkin suggested that John would be too busy in his orchard to drink excessively. He hoped a fine might meet the case.

Figure 14.7. John Magnus and his children about 1907. From left Zella, Olof and Laura

It was a forlorn hope. The magistrate didn't need to look at John's record — he knew it by heart. Magnus had been warned the last time he appeared and now he was for it. Sentence: one year on Rotoroa Island. He was given a few days to get his affairs in order before being taken away.

Within a week of returning to Alexandra in August 1918 after his 'holiday,' John was fined 5 shillings for drunkenness and warned that if he came up again he would go straight back to 'the island.'

For several years there were no court appearances. Perhaps John had got the message at last, or more likely, the police had given up on him. He apparently worked quietly at his business, with regular advertisements in the *Alexandra Herald*. Occasionally he wrote a letter to the newspapers about such things as the Borough race overflowing in Ngapara Street, or overgrown shrubs obstructing the footpath in upper Tarbert Street.

It wasn't until June 1921 that Magnus was back in court[7] to face an application by the police for a renewal of a Prohibition Order against him. Constable Murphy pointed out that a previous Order had expired on 12 April and John had been seen the worse for liquor several times since. The constable considered another Order necessary. The lawyer, William Bodkin, who appeared for Magnus, pointed out that for the Court to issue a Prohibition Order, it had to be shown that the victim had wasted all his estate on drink or had greatly injured his health or had acted detrimentally against the peace and happiness of his family.

In evidence Magnus said that as a builder he paid his way, but had no money to spend on drink during April and May because progress payments on work done had not come through. He enjoyed good health and produced a medical certificate to say so. He was a widower and lived by himself so had no one dependent on him. He made the point that an order would prevent him from doing work in hotels or entering an hotel to have a meal when working away from home. Yes, it was probably correct that 10 Prohibition Orders had been issued against him over the last 20 years. The magistrate decided that it was a border line case but he would give Magnus another chance, so he refused the application.

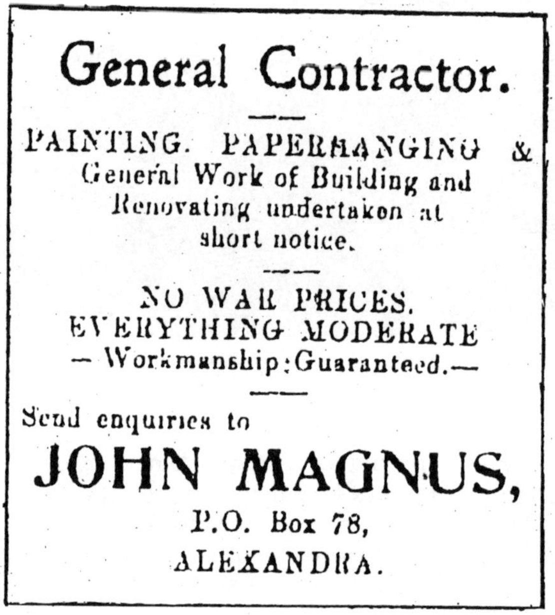

General Contractor.

PAINTING. PAPERHANGING & General Work of Building and Renovating undertaken at short notice.

NO WAR PRICES. EVERYTHING MODERATE — Workmanship:Guaranteed.—

Send enquiries to

JOHN MAGNUS,

P.O. Box 78,

ALEXANDRA.

Figure 14.8. John Magnus advertised in each issue of the *Alexandra Herald*.

In spite of his statement in court that he paid his way, John Magnus was apparently not always able to do so. More than once he had been sued by firms for money outstanding and now, in February 1923, Cardogan, the timber merchant, sued him for £31 for building materials supplied. With court costs, solicitor's fees and witness's expenses, John was up for £40 and he could not pay it, so in March for the second time in his life, he was bankrupted. It was noted that his assets comprised a four-roomed house on a 1 acre 27 pole section in Ngapara Street.

Boat Journey

The man was apparently irrepressible. At the age of 71 he undertook to bring a large coal boat single-handed down the Clutha River from Lowburn to Alexandra, a feat that was thought not to have been accomplished previously.[8] We are not told why it was necessary to bring this boat to Alexandra, but as the old *Manuherikia* dredge, which had lain idle in the gorge for many years, was being overhauled and recommissioned as the *Gorge* by John's brother, Gus, it is likely that the two events were connected.

John left Lowburn at noon with an inflated inner tube from a car wrapped round him as a lifebelt, and had no trouble until halfway to Cromwell where the river current was set towards the sunken *Rise and Shine* dredge. He had considerable trouble avoiding the wreck, but then found himself in the swift rapids just above Cromwell. The boat spun round and went down through the rip backwards. The worst part of the journey through the Cromwell Gorge was at the old Halfway House Hotel where the boat nosed through three large standing waves and took aboard a considerable amount of water. Again the boat finished up going through the rapids backwards. Much bailing was required but finally the calmer water below Clyde was reached and the remainder of the journey to Alexandra was routine. The whole trip took Magnus 4 hours 20 minutes of actual floating time for the 45 kilometres.

A fair amount of the old excitement was generated by the prospect of a dredge beginning work again in the vicinity of the town, and the favoured sites in the gorge around the mouth of the Manuherikia River, and as far up the river as the Shaky Bridge were pegged out. Among the Special Dredging Claims applied for was one by John Magnus at Butlers Point. The possibility of rich gold here was freely discussed by the old timers who were certain that Bedford Butler (John's father-in-law) had been forced to stop work by floods when he was on good gold.

Unfortunately Gus Magnus's dredging scheme never got off the ground and his company was liquidated. A new company converted the dredge to electricity and renamed it *Molyneux Electric*, but worked for only a few months in the gorge before closing down. John Magnus's claim at Butlers Point is still undredged.

Magnus the Author

John Magnus's command of written English, as demonstrated by a hand-written manuscript held by the Turnbull Library, was by no means perfect, so his published articles, including 'letters to the editor,' were of necessity heavily edited, presumably by the newspaper.

An article appeared in the *Alexandra Herald* in 1913 under the heading *Goldfield Tales: The Story of the lost Chinaman and how he became a Sheep (As told by John Magnus) Instigator of the Famous Fake.*[9] Although there had been suspicions from the outset that John Magnus had been associated with the affair, this was the first time he had publicly declared that he was the instigator. In the article he told the story, in detail, of the manufacture of the 'body,' and of the events at the subsequent Coroner's

Figure 14.9. At the age of 71 John Magnus, single-handed, brought a heavy coal boat down the Clutha River from Lowburn to Alexandra, a distance of about 46 kilometres.
Upper: The boat passing down the rapids at Halfway House, Cromwell Gorge. *Hocken Library E6497/12*
Lower: John Magnus and the boat after the journey. Magnus is still wearing the inner tube he wore as a lifebelt during the trip.

Inquest. He admitted, too, that the episode was designed to play a lark on the Chinese beachcombers.

In July 1928 the *Alexandra Herald* published a summary of the 1895 newspaper reports on the Lost Chinaman hoax as part of its feature, *A Glimpse into Yesterday*. Magnus, without doubt, began to enjoy the notoriety he gained from the publicity, and either offered or was asked, to write a full account of the event. This was run in the *Alexandra Herald* over three issues in 1928.[10] The newspaper then published the articles as a booklet which retailed at six pence, but demand was such that it had to be reprinted a number of times, and sold at an increased price of one shilling.

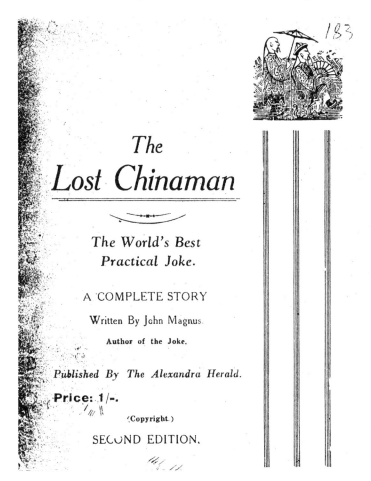

The

Lost Chinaman

The World's Best
Practical Joke.

A COMPLETE STORY

Written By John Magnus.

Author of the Joke.

Published By The Alexandra Herald.

Price: 1/-.

(Copyright.)

SECOND EDITION.

Figure 14.10 A second edition (1928) of John Magnus's account of the infamous hoax he instigated.

James Ng[11] is of the opinion that it was the publication of this article that prompted Magnus to set down in long-hand, in his peculiar version of English spelling, a number of stories about aspects of his life.[12] They include 'The Gold Nuget,' 'The Lost Chinaman,' 'Civis Otago Daily Times,'

'Mr Choke Tared and Feathered,' 'A Glimps of the Town of Alexandra in the year 1889,' 'Chows After Killing W. Noble,' 'Mothers Goose,' and 'Tobaco Smuglin.' This manuscript is preserved in the Turnbull Library. A copy donated by the Magnus family to George Griffiths of Dunedin is now in the Hocken Library.

As late as 1934, Magnus wrote a letter to the newspaper[13] which told of an encounter he had had with a monster in the Clutha River while working on a dredge. It was obviously engendered by the interest, current at the time, in the Loch Ness monster. The editor remarked in a footnote that 'For this record of our early history our correspondent deserves the grateful thanks of the County.'

Finale

In his latter years John Magnus lived alone in his house in Ngapara Street, Alexandra, but in the mid-1930s he left to live with his daughter, Laura, in Christchurch. He died on 25 June 1939. His body was brought back to Alexandra to be buried beside that of his wife who had predeceased him by 32 years. The obituary, which spoke of his good fellowship, enterprise and boundless energy, referred to the large cortege as evidence of the esteem in which John was held by the people of Alexandra.

Good or bad, John Magnus was certainly a colourful Central Otago personality.

Figure 14.11. The Magnus headstone in Alexandra's cemetery.

NOTES

1. Dr Ng (1999 p.29-30) lists 13 appearances of John Magnus in the Warden's Court between September 1893 and the end of 1897. His brothers also appeared more than a dozen times during the same period.
2. A commonly used miner's term, 'head' is short for 'sluice-head,' which was

defined as water flowing at the rate of one cubic foot (2.4 litres) per second.

3. *Dunstan Times* 22 April 1898.

4. *Cyclopedia of New Zealand, Volume 4:* p 717.

5. Father of A. H. Nordmeyer, the future Labour Member of Parliament for Oamaru Electorate 1935-49 and Island Bay Electorate 1951-69. He was Leader of the Opposition from 1963-65.

6. Rotoroa Island is in the Hauraki Gulf three kilometres off the east coast of Waiheke Island. An institution was set up for 'drying out' and rehabilitation of alcoholics by the Salvation Army under the Inebriates Institutions Act 1909. It is still in operation. Being sent to 'the Island' was the ultimate threat for alcoholics.

7. *Alexandra Herald* 15 June 1921.

8. *Alexandra Herald* 27 May 1925.

9. *Alexandra Herald* 17 September 1913

10. *Alexandra Herald* 22 August; 29 August; 5 September 1928.

11. Ng, J, *Windows on a Chinese Past* Vol 3 1999. p.28.

12. Magnus, J. 1928 *Reminiscences of John Magnus of Alexandra or Early Central Otago, 1887-1897*

13. *Alexandra Herald* 1 August 1934.

15.

'AN UNHEALTHY PLACE'

—Outbreak of Typhoid

Alexandra in the early years of the 20th Century could not be described as a sanitary town, but it was perhaps no better or worse than many other country villages of the time. In spite of the bracing winter climate and the warm dry conditions in summer, illnesses caused by tummy bugs were common. Diphtheria and the odd case of typhoid were not unknown.

When we look at the conditions prevailing in 1909 and compare them with our efficient sewerage and water supply systems, to say nothing of our modern standards of personal hygiene, it would seem that the odds were stacked against people reaching mature adulthood. And yet the majority did survive.

Take the water supply for instance. Since December 1903 residents in the most closely settled part of the township had enjoyed, spasmodically, the convenience of high pressure water piped into houses. Those on the outskirts still dipped into one of the distributaries of the town water race that brought water from Chatto Creek. It wound its way for more than 30 kilometres through rabbit-infested farm land, and then through the suburbs of the town before finally flowing down the gutters of the main street.

Those on piped supply were not too concerned where the water came from as long as it flowed from their taps. Few bothered to climb up the steep hillside behind the town to the large, open, concrete tank at the head of the pipeline that supplied the town. The water race from Mt Campbell Creek which discharged into this tank, had also wended its way for 30 kilometres or more across rabbit-infested farm lands. Heavy rains washed the loose soil, along with the abundant rabbit and sheep dung, into the race that carried it to the reservoir. Every so often the debris had to be shovelled out of the tank to prevent the outlet pipe becoming choked.

Because of shortage of water in the creek, or breaks and leaks in the race or even deliberate diversion of water for mining purposes, the supply provided by the Mt Campbell race was most unreliable. For frequent and sometimes long periods there was no water available from the reservoir, and the town had to be supplied from the polluted Chatto Creek race, or by barrels of water carted from the river.

Then there was the problem of disposing of household wastes in a town with no sewerage system. Once a week the nightman emptied the outside dunnies, his noisome activities mercifully hidden by darkness punctuated only here and there by a few, largely ineffective, kerosene street lamps. And how did he get rid of the night's collection? He tipped it over the river bank at the Earnscleugh end of the main bridge. Had the bulk of his cargo reached the river it would have been swept away to be diluted to the point of innocuousness by the mighty torrent. But most remained on the banks and beach giving rise to such an appalling stench that the crew of the *Manuherikia* dredge, when it was brought up the river to work off Frenchmans Point, demanded that the mess be cleaned up and the dumping zone shifted elsewhere, or they would stop work.

Figure 15.1. The main street of Alexandra in 1905, four years before the outbreak of typhoid. The building in the left foreground is the Fire Station in Skird Street.

Then there were household 'slops.' These included what we now call 'grey water' — dish washing water, washing water, bath water and so on. Fluids were not allowed to be included with nightsoil, so in the town this soiled water was run out to the gutters, These were supposed to be flushed constantly by water from the town race — when it was available. Certainly the replacement of the filthy, weed-choked ditches by smooth concreted gutters was hailed as a great improvement. In the suburbs the 'slops' were thrown out on to open ground and no doubt some found their way back into the town water race, to be recycled further along its course.

There were numerous letters to the editor about the insanitary conditions of the place, about the smell in the main street and about the need to flush the gutters thoroughly and regularly, but it all came back to lack of money on the part of the Borough Council.

Trouble Ahead

The first intimation of trouble ahead was a small item[1] in the newspaper on 5 May 1909 about three cases of infectious diseases that had occurred in the town — one each identified as enteric fever, typhoid and diphtheria. Dr Gregg, the local doctor, was sufficiently concerned to ask the Regional Health Officer, Dr Ogston, to visit Alexandra and investigate the cause of the outbreaks.

The following week[2] saw a very strong editorial delivering a blast at the Health Officer who had turned up as requested and inspected the homes of the three victims. Then he had had a quick look at one of the dairies[3] that supplied milk to the town, before he left next morning for Palmerston where he was to look at the site of a proposed sanatorium. "Which is more important," the paper asked, "an outbreak of typhoid or the inspection of a sanatorium site?" There were now five typhoid victims.

The *Herald* went on to speculate that contaminated milk was a possible cause of the disease, and asked for more rigorous inspections of dairies by surprise visits. No mercy should be shown to the unscrupulous milk sellers who were prepared to dilute their milk with water from the nearest stream or water race. And the Borough Council also was castigated for allowing the disgraceful dumping of 'refuse' into the river.

Figure 15.2. The only available photograph of Dr Gregg, local medical practitioner, and recently elected mayor. He is seen here (fourth from left) with his councillors in front of the Town hall on the occasion of the Memorial Service for King Edward VII on 20 May 1910.

A fortnight after the first case of typhoid had been recognised, the situation was very serious. William Muir, aged only 32, and the first to be taken ill, had died and there were 10 other cases. The paper was full of notices of cancellation of meetings; the school was to be closed for a fortnight; the Anglican Church social; the Caledonian Society's social; the brass band concert — all were cancelled. And people began to leave Alexandra to stay with relatives in healthier places.

The Borough Council held a special meeting every evening, and at the one held on 15 May, councillors met Mr Gladstone, the Inspector of Public Health who had been sent up from Dunedin. It was decided that next day he should inspect all dairies and other places that were suspected of being sources of the disease.

Gladstone made his verbal report to the council on the following evening. He was of the opinion that the dairy that had first been suspected was indeed the cause of the outbreak. All of the houses where typhoid had broken out drew their milk from this particular farm. He described in detail the filthy conditions of the dairy and of the cows, and when he gave instruction about the washing of the cows he was horrified to see that the water was taken from a cesspool in the paddock. He didn't close the place down but insisted that, under his supervision, all milking buckets and milk cans be scalded, that a man and a boy working in the place be removed until they had scrubbed up and changed their clothes, and the whole surrounds liberally treated with quicklime.

Apparently it came as a surprise to the Borough Council when Gladstone informed it that it was the body responsible for all matters pertaining to public health. Some members insisted on studying the relevant Act before they would believe it. Once the information had sunk in, however, the council acted with commendable speed in issuing instructions for cleaning and flushing the town water race, and attending to other sanitary defects that had been pointed out by the inspector.

The newspaper also printed[4] a copy of a leaflet issued by the Department of Health which, it was suggested, should be cut out for display in a prominent place in the home. The paper pointed out that typhoid fever is infectious, and that it had been demonstrated many times that it was a disease to which people who lived in dirty surroundings were especially susceptible. Foul privies and cesspits, polluted soils, dirty yards and badly made drains were often found around houses where the disease had broken out. The article went on to describe at length precautions that should be taken, especially as regards the handling of milk and water and the use of disinfectants around the house.

By the end of the third week the local doctor thought the epidemic was on the wane, but was confounded when four more cases were reported. By the end of the following week a total of eighteen had been reported, one of whom had to be transferred to Dunedin Hospital.

The Borough Council now had Mr Gladstone's written report in front of it and quickly instructed Charles Murphy, its own Sanitary Inspector, to visit all the places mentioned and see that the defects listed were remedied. It was perhaps ironic that Mr Gladstone, who had done a good job investigating the causes of the epidemic, had been transferred, almost immediately on his return to Dunedin, to the office of the Registrar of Births, Deaths and Marriages. This was the result, it was said, of reorganisation in the face of Government retrenchment.

Figure 15.3. Charles Murphy was the Borough's Sanitary Inspector. When a second outbreak of typhoid occurred, Murphy now a councillor, volunteered to act as unpaid Sanitary Inspector again.

Aftermath

Thanks to the work of the Health Department officers and the Borough Council, together with the co-operation of the citizens, the epidemic was halted and no further cases of typhoid were reported. But the repercussions were to be felt for some time.

At the regular monthly meeting of the Trustees of the Dunstan District Hospital, for instance, held on 8 June, it became clear that while the Borough Council was trying to contain the epidemic in the town, the hospital had been struggling to cope with the victims. For a small institution, used to having two or three patients at a time, an influx of 18 people, each requiring 22 days of quarantine, just about overwhelmed the place. An old hospital building used as wardsman's quarters and storeroom was hastily converted into a ward. Partitions were knocked out, two coats of lime wash given to walls and ceilings, linoleum laid on the floor and an old range renovated as a heating unit. Five convalescing patients along with the wardsman were installed in the renovated building. But this was not all. Large quantities of extra blankets, sheets, waterproof sheeting and beds had to be bought, and two extra nurses and a servant were engaged.

All of this cost money, and the Trustees found themselves in debt to the tune of £160. One or two local people, with the encouragement of the *Alexandra Herald,* organised a special public appeal. Collectors went from door to door shaking boxes to the backdrop of the brass band out in the streets. Apparently the result was 'gratifying.'

Figure 15.4. Dunstan Hospital as it was in 1910.

It was not until December that the Borough Council received the formal report from the Minister of Internal Affairs on the cause of the typhoid outbreak. In fact the council got two reports from the Minister, and they flatly contradicted each other. The first said that the Health Officers were unable to trace the cause of the epidemic, but the second letter clearly stated the source from which the fever emanated.[5] Council members were, not unnaturally, very unhappy about these reports and suggested placing the matter in the hands of the Member for the district.

Although the typhoid epidemic was over, the disease constantly lurked in the background. For instance, there is a report in April 1910 that enteric fever was more prevalent than usual over the whole of New Zealand. Otago was no exception, with 28 cases reported. Then on 11 May 1910, in an issue taken up with the death of King Edward, the *Alexandra Herald* found room to report that a young man had been admitted to Dunstan Hospital with typhoid. The following week the paper published an article[6] about the 'typhoid fly' which turned out to be the common house fly, but recent research in America had shown the role of this insect in spreading typhoid. The article advocated a campaign against flies:

> It is the duty of every community, through its Board of Health, to spend money in the warfare against this enemy of mankind. The duty is as

195

pronounced as though the community were attacked by bands of ravenous wolves.

Nevertheless it was announced in mid-June that typhoid seemed to have disappeared from Otago, and certainly few cases were reported over the next 12 months. But they spoke too soon.

Second Epidemic

In the Autumn of 1911, typhoid was back in Alexandra and a second epidemic swept the town. This time the Borough Council took action immediately, and Charles Murphy, now a councillor, offered his services as sanitary inspector, free of charge, to carry out an inspection of all properties within the borough. He was to pay particular attention to an area in Fastnet Street, where no fewer than six cases of typhoid had occurred within the last two years. As a result, the drains on a property were disinfected at the expense of the owner the following day.

Once again the *Alexandra Herald* blasted the Health Department for claiming to have carried out 'a rigid inspection of all possible infection,' when the inspector had actually been in the district for only 24 hours. The town was fortunate in that it now had Dr Barr as the local doctor. He was a specialist in Public Health, and had spent some time in Germany working in that field. Dr Barr immediately sent off for vaccines and began inoculation of those at risk.

Figure 15.5. Councillor Archibald Ashworth was not pleased when he received a letter from the council informing him that the sanitary arrangements on his property were unsatisfactory.

As was not uncommon in local body affairs in Alexandra, the outbreak led to a row in the Borough Council. A regular meeting of the council proceeded normally until the Town Clerk read out copies of letters which had been sent to a number of property owners. In these cases, sanitary conditions were such that immediate attention was required. At once Councillor Ashworth wanted to know who gave permission for these letters to go out. "They were sent out by the Clerk as a result of Inspector Murphy's report and I approved them," said the Mayor. Ashworth held that a special meeting of Council should have been convened to approve the letters. Notwithstanding that both the Town Clerk (who consulted the relevant Act) and the Mayor declared the notices legal, Ashworth continued his opposition. After Inspector (unpaid) Murphy offered to resign, not only from the inspectorate, but also from his council seat as well, a resolution was passed, with two voting against, that the notices be approved and Inspector Murphy thanked for his efforts to improve the sanitary conditions of the town.

What was all this about? It turned out that Ashworth had received one of the letters and had not only taken umbrage, but also asserted that he was being harassed. It was all to do with disposal of nightsoil from his property. He had some private arrangement with the contractor,[7] but as the mayor pointed out, a typhoid case had occurred just below Ashworth's property and was no doubt the reason for his letter.

The second epidemic was nipped in the bud, and the whole episode ended with Dr Barr giving a well-prepared and well-presented lecture on Public Health to a full Town Hall. In easily understood language, according to the published account, he gave a very good coverage of the kinds of infectious diseases, their causes, methods of spreading and measures for their prevention.[8]

Perhaps the message was finally driven home, as Alexandra has never again experienced a typhoid epidemic.

NOTES

1. *Alexandra Herald* 5 May 1909.
2. *Alexandra Herald* 12 May 1909.
3. The 'dairy' of this period had no connection with the modern 'corner dairy.' It was a small building attached to a milking shed where the milk was cooled and stored before being poured into large milk cans. These were carried by horse-drawn cart around the streets, and milk ladled into the householder's 'billy' left at the gate.
4. *Alexandra Herald* 19 May 1909.
5. The source was not revealed in the report of the council meeting and neither of these letters can now be found.
6. *Alexandra Herald* 18 May 1910.
7. A fellow councillor remarked that Ashworth had confessed to breaking the law. Perhaps he had arranged to have the nightsoil buried in his orchard.
8. *Alexandra Herald* 5 July 1911.

16.

SWIMMING IN CONTROVERSY

—From Coronation Baths to Centennial Pool

The death of King Edward VII in 1910 and the subsequent Coronation[1] of King George V was fortuitous for Alexandra. It so happened that the Alexandra School Committee had received, early in 1911, bequests totalling £250 from Mrs Isobel McDonald, who was the widow of a former mayor, and Mr James Cunningham for the purpose of building swimming baths. They were concerned that children should not only be taught to swim but should also have somewhere to swim safely. To help the project along, Billy Theyers, the 'Grand Old Man of Alexandra,' donated[2] the section on the corner of Tarbert and Walton Streets and this was accepted with grateful thanks.

Figure 16.1. Mrs Isobel McDonald (above) and James Cunningham left money to the Alexandra School Committee to provide swimming baths.

The Subsidy

When it became known that the Government was prepared to grant £ for £ subsidies to Local Bodies for approved projects to mark the Coronation of King George V, the School Committee decided to hand over the money and land to the Borough Council. The condition was that the council agreed that the baths should be the town's Coronation project and so become eligible for an application for the subsidy. The arrangement suited both parties. The School Committee on the one hand, saw this as a way for the school to have the use of baths without being responsible for the upkeep. On the other hand the council saw it as an opportunity to acquire a swimming pool at no cost to the ratepayers, so had no difficulty in supporting the project and in applying[3] for the subsidy. Word that the subsidy had been granted came through the day before the Coronation.[4] Shortly afterwards, a set of conditions that had to be met also arrived but apparently Council had no difficulty with them.

Now it was all action. It was decided that, if at all possible, the baths should be ready for the coming summer, and it was already June. A Committee of Council was set up and promptly invited Thomas Wilkinson,

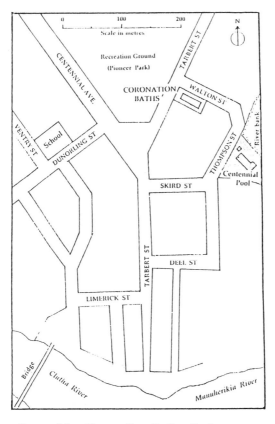

Figure 16.2. The locations of the Coronation Baths, their successor, the Centennial Pool and the Alexandra school.

a well-known contractor and bridge builder of Clyde, to inspect the site and draw up plans and specifications. Within a week he laid the documents on Council's table and, after a few minor alterations, it was decided to call separate tenders for the excavation and construction of the pool and for the fencing and buildings, which included a gymnasium. The School Committee handed over the money and a couple of councillors were appointed as Trustees of the fund.

There was disappointment when the tenders were opened on the evening of 31 July. The lowest tender exceeded the available funds by a considerable amount. The gymnasium was promptly cancelled and councillors went home to think about what else could be done.

At a special meeting the following week the councillors were full of ideas. It was agreed for instance, that as males and females would be using the baths at different times, only one dressing-shed would be necessary. So they accepted Noble Ruff's tender of £173 3s. 6d. for the building and fencing. But the tenders for the construction work of the pool itself were rejected, and it was decided the work would be done instead by day labour under the charge of the Borough dayman, George Hannay. There and then Council arranged to call tenders for earth material for filling the site, for gravel and clean sand for concrete and for plastering work. Then, in a fit of generosity Hannay's wages were raised to 12 shillings a day for the period he was working on the baths. No doubt the councillors went home feeling that they had done a good evening's work.

Indeed they had. It was a good decision to use George Hannay to supervise the project. He was a skilled bricklayer and plasterer[5] who had worked on many large buildings in Clyde and Alexandra, including the building of the Bendigo Hotel, before becoming dayman for the Borough.

Figure 16.3. George Hannay, a master bricklayer and plasterer, built the baths.

Construction

The excavation of the site was not the formidable task it may have seemed. The section was mostly occupied by a gully, formed in the early days by sluicing, which extended from Tarbert Street down to the bank of the

Manuherikia River. The lower part of the same gully was to become a source of gravel for the Borough and later it became the Borough storage yard. Later still it became the site of Alexandra Museum.

Little excavation was actually required. In fact, 300 cubic yards of gravel were dumped into the gully and used to provide the sloping floor for the new pool. While construction was going on, a formal agreement with the School Committee about the use of the funds and pool was signed and sealed by the Borough Council. A small hitch occurred when Mr Ruff asked to be relieved of his contract to build the changing shed and fence. Presumably the building of these was then organised by Hannay.

Meanwhile the concrete sides of the pool had been completed, and councillors expressed satisfaction with the progress and quality of the work. But before the large expanse of concrete for the floor could be poured, the Borough Council had to apply to the Warden's Court for permission to run what was quaintly described as a 'dry' water race, in other words a pipeline, from the baths down to the river for draining the pool. By the end of October, only three months after work started, water was run in for a trial and the pool was found to be watertight. The jarrah fence posts were put in during a slight delay caused by the late arrival of the timber and iron for the changing room, but otherwise everything was on schedule.

Building the changing room, finishing the galvanised iron fence round the whole section, installing seating around the fence, concreting the surrounds of the pool and other details occupied November. One detail was an inscribed brass plate, prepared by J. Swan & Co of Dunedin at a cost of £5, which was attached to the lintel over the main entrance gate. This stated:

> **ALEXANDRA CORONATION SWIMMING BATHS[6]**
> These baths were established to commemorate the
> Coronation of King George V 22nd June, 1911 and
> were constructed with funds provided under the wills of
> the late Mrs I. McDonald and the late James Cunningham.
> The site was presented by Wm Theyers E^{sq}
>
> Edward Marslin, Mayor   Mostyn A. Fleming, Town Clerk

Finally, everything was ready, and the opening was held on 21 December 1911 with the inevitable speeches and mutual congratulations for a job well and speedily done. Swimming sports for the children and a social evening in the Town Hall followed afternoon tea ('Ladies are specially requested to bring baskets').

Trouble

Then the trouble started. One clause in the Baths Rules and Regulations, which were under discussion by the council, stated that all children attending the Alexandra public school were entitled to use the baths free of charge, and an hour each day was set aside for their exclusive use. This clause was one put forward by the School Committee as part of its

Figure 16.4. When the baths were demolished the brass commemorative plate vanished, but it was found in storage nearly 40 years later.

agreement with the council. Perhaps it was a condition of the original bequests, or perhaps it was inserted by the School Committee on the grounds that its school should have priority as it had provided half the money. But the clause overlooked the fact that a private Catholic school was about to begin teaching in Alexandra, and the condition effectively excluded the children of this institution from free use of the baths. When the rules came up for approval, Councillor Murphy moved to have this clause changed to include 'every child of 14 years and under residing within the Borough of Alexandra,' but he found no support.

Perhaps councillors had had time to think about it over Christmas, because at a special meeting of the council held in January 1912, it was moved that the troublesome clause be rescinded. During the ensuing discussion the copy of the letter sent to the Minister of Internal Affairs the previous June requesting a subsidy, was read to the meeting. There was no mention of any restrictions and indeed, as Councillor Murphy pointed out, if there had been any, it was doubtful whether a subsidy would have been granted. The meeting broke up without agreement being reached.

The editor of the *Alexandra Herald* quoted the words of Lincoln:-

> "With malice towards none, with charity towards all, with firmness in the right . . . let us carry on the work we have begun." Would that some of our public (?) men could follow this principle and imitate the spirit of Lincoln in preference to assuming the role of Cain.[7]

There followed in the next week's[8] issue a strong letter accusing members of the council of bigotry. The difficulty was that half the council members, including the mayor, were members of the School Committee,[9] and in spite of their protestations about their unbiased approach to borough affairs there is no doubt that they were in a difficult position.

Finally, at its next meeting, Council reached a compromise. The clause was amended to allow all children under the age of 11 years to have the use of the baths free. When it was pointed out that this would cover children from outside the Borough as well, the mayor agreed and said it would include visiting groups of children from Dunedin and elsewhere. The amended rules were sent to the School Committee and at its next meeting were approved by 6 votes to 3.

Final Days

The Coronation Baths served two generations of Alexandra people, particularly the children, well enough. In the blistering hot days of Central Otago summers, it was refreshing to lower oneself into a small area of somewhat murky water visible between some of the scores of bodies that practically hid the pool surface. Swimming was out of the question on busy days, and you were lucky if you could splash about a bit before striking someone. But lack of space wasn't the only problem.

Figure 16.5. For a small country town the opening of the Baths was a festive occasion. The umbrellas are for protection against the summer sun.

Cracks began to develop in the walls, caused no doubt, by the settling of the fill that George Hannay had carefully placed in the old gully 40 years before. As water penetrated through the cracks into the fill behind, it began to exert pressure, and whole sections of the walls — particularly towards the deep end of the pool, began to lean inwards. And the cracks widened alarmingly.

There was of course no filtration or chlorination, and the practice was to drain, sweep out and refill the baths each week during the summer, with 'pure' mountain water from the Borough mains. Even when freshly filled, the water in the pool had a brownish tinge derived from organic matter of one sort or another picked up in its long journey through open water races. During the week the colour steadily darkened until there was a real possibility of some unfortunate body lying on the bottom, and not being discovered until someone stepped on it or until the baths were drained. It is said that school teachers in charge of parties of children, held a head count before leaving the baths to make sure everyone was accounted for.

There was a near fatality in January 1940 when a 13-year-old boy was seen floating face down in the water. A schoolgirl, Joy Russell, who was only 11 years old, dived in and pulled the boy to the side of the pool. But she was too exhausted, and the boy too heavy, for her to pull him from the water. Luckily schoolboy Lunn rushed to help her, and between them they managed to get the unconscious lad out of the baths. Then young Lunn used artificial respiration techniques he had been taught at school to revive the youngster. Joy Russell was sent a letter of thanks and congratulations by the Borough Council and she was awarded a Certificate to mark the occasion.[10]

Figure 16.6. Shortly after the Centennial Pool was opened in 1962 the Coronation Baths were demolished. The badly cracked wall on the right collapsed with vibration of the bulldozer.

As the flow through the cracks in the walls increased, water had to be constantly admitted to restore the level, and whereas this did something towards keeping the water in the pool reasonably fresh, it did little for the over-stretched Borough water supply. In fact as the population increased, and there were yearly water supply crises, it was decided to supply the baths from a borehole specially drilled on the alluvial river bank terrace below the baths.

An electric pump was fitted and there was great satisfaction when a strong, steady flow of clear, sparkling water poured into the freshly cleaned pool. Bystanders remarked that they could actually see the bottom over the whole pool. But imagine the surprise of the same bystanders when they discovered next morning that the water was a rather striking bottle-green colour, and in a few days the colour deepened as the water became thick with algae. Apparently these microscopic plants were lurking in the cold bore-water, and the heating of the water in the strong sun, which drenched the pool, caused them to propagate with prodigious rapidity. So the bore-water was used for irrigating Pioneer Park where the algae could do no harm, and the baths were refilled again from the Borough mains.

Water leakage was such that the pool half-emptied over night and water could be heard trickling underground. The walls leaned further and further until they threatened to collapse inwards. The days of the baths were clearly numbered, but it was not until the Centennial Pool was opened in 1962 that the old Coronation baths could be filled in and the section converted, first to a car dealer's yard and then to a site for a modern building. They had served the people of Alexandra for just over 50 years.

The Centennial Pool

A new pool to replace the Coronation Baths had been talked about by successive Borough Councils for years. It was, however, the organising of a Blossom Festival by the local Chapter of the Jaycees in 1957, with the promise that money raised would go towards a new pool, that gave hope of material progress. As money from the yearly Festival accumulated, Council began to discuss the type of pool required and its location. When a largely new council was elected in 1959, sufficient money had already been raised to allow planning to start. A committee of council members,[11] set up to oversee the designing and construction, understood that the previous council had in mind that the pool would be large, have separate diving and learners' pools, use treated water and be located in Pioneer Park.

The committee was not happy about the Pioneer Park location. Over the years there had been many proposals to erect public buildings of one kind or another on the park. The attraction, of course, was the central location and the free land. Under a *nom de plume*, the Convenor of the committee wrote a tongue-in-cheek letter to the local paper, emphasising the advantages of putting the new pool in Pioneer Park, and suggesting that this was the only location worth considering. He was delighted with the six or seven replies condemning the proposal and pointing out other possible sites.

Eventually eleven other possible sites were inspected. Each was given a points rating based on such factors as availability of land, cost of development, closeness to schools, closeness to utilities, shelter, parking, traffic hazards to children, and so on. In the end the site in Thompson

Figure 16.7. The site of the former Coronation Baths is now occupied by a modern office building.

Street, recently vacated by a Ministry of Works storage yard, gained a high score. The Borough owned the land and the site seemed suitable in most respects.

One disadvantage was that the site had been a gully sluiced out in the early days and refilled with schist rock debris from the blasting of building sites in the town. Another was that the site was rather small for the extensive layout planned, but this problem was largely solved when the occupier of the adjacent land, Mr Alex Taylor, promised to donate an area of his orchard. The possibility of future flooding was investigated. Certainly the 'Old Man' flood of 1878 had almost reached the proposed site. But it had not been included in the land taken for 'Water power development' by the Government, as was other land regarded as liable to flooding after the formation of the lake behind Roxburgh Dam. Nevertheless, the engineer in charge of construction of the new pool was careful to point out that if there were any threat of flooding, the pools must be kept filled with water to prevent them floating out of the ground.

An architect was commissioned to design the pools but his preliminary sketches costed out far above the most optimistic estimate of the money likely to be available. He was recompensed for his trouble. Council was pleased and grateful when the retired Resident Engineer of Ministry of Works, Mr J. D. Watt, volunteered to design the pools and supervise their construction. The design adopted was based on that developed by the New Zealand Portland Cement Association and had been used with success at Wellington East Girls' College and elsewhere. The walls were to be pre-cast

Figure 16.8. The site chosen for the new pool had been, like that of its predecessor, a gully sluiced out in the early days. It had been filled with schist rock debris from excavated building sites.

in 3 metre-wide panels on the floor of the pool. After curing, they were raised into place, with the base grouted into a slot in the floor, and the vertical joints sealed with bitumen filler.

Mr Russell Ball, draughtsman with the Otago Central Electric Power Board, volunteered to draw detailed plans for the building and surrounds. These were based on a general design sketched out by Mr Bruce Russell, a young architect, while on a short visit to his parents in Alexandra. The Alexandra Swimming Club, which was consulted in the design of the whole concept, built, largely by voluntary labour, a Club meeting room that was incorporated into the complex.

Before construction could commence, many truckloads of sand were dumped on the rock debris filling the old gully, and this was washed into the gaps between the rocks by water jets from hoses lent by the Fire Brigade. Construction was started in May 1961 by Breen Construction Company and the completed pool was opened by the Minister of Internal Affairs, The Hon F. L. A. Gotz, on 29 September 1962. It was named the 'Centennial Pool' to commemorate the centennial of the Dunstan Gold Rush which had taken place in August 1862.

The pool, which is 33 1/3 metres long and 15 metres wide with depth ranging from 1 metre to 1.2 metres, was painted with polyurethane resin. Water, which constantly enters through outlets in the floor of the pool from the filtration/treatment plant, overflows through peripheral gratings into 'scum' channels. The 12 by 9 metre diving pool is 3.5 metres deep and equipped with one-metre and three-metre boards.

Figure 16.9. The Centennial Pool.

The total cost was about £22,000, a third of which came from a subsidy from the Lottery Fund administered by the Department of Internal Affairs. The remainder came from profits of successive Blossom Festivals.

With a professional coach employed, 'Learn to Swim' classes became popular and the standard of competitive swimming was raised, but the greatest benefit was to the public who flocked to the new facility to enjoy the spaciousness of the pool, the clean water and the pleasant, sheltered surroundings.

It was unfortunate that in the mid-1990s Alexandra was subject to two devastating floods. Neither carried the volume of water of the 1878 flood but in both the water reached considerably higher. This was because the water level had been permanently raised when the river backed up behind Roxburgh Dam. The flooding was made worse by the deposition of sand and gravel that had begun at the head of the lake (several kilometres above Alexandra), and had moved progressively downstream to Alexandra.

The Centennial Pool was inundated twice and on the last occasion the advice about making sure that the pools were kept full of water was forgotten. The diving pool was pumped out while the flood waters were still high. The result was that the diving pool began to rise out of the ground.

A site on the outskirts of the town, far above possible floods, has been selected for a new pool. However, many people would like to see the old pool retained if it is at all possible.

NOTES.

1. The Coronation was on 22 June 1911.
2. *Alexandra Herald* 5 May 1911.
3. Application was made on 17 June 1911.
4. *Alexandra Herald* 21 June 1911.
5. Forty years later, in the early 1950s, George Hannay, then a man in his eighties, showed the author how to plaster and roughcast a mud brick house the author was building.
6. The word 'Pool' as in 'swimming pool' or 'Pool complex' was apparently not in use at this time. The swimming pool was always referred to as the 'baths.'
7. *Alexandra Herald* 17 January 1912.
8. *Alexandra Herald* 24 January 1912.
9. Members of Council on the School Committee were: the Mayor Edward Marslin (Chairman of the School Committee), Jack Coulson, George Campbell and A. Ashworth.
10. Recorded in Minutes of the meeting of 4 March 1940. Other details supplied by Mrs Gill Grant, a cousin of Joy Russell.
11. The committee comprised the Mayor, K. W. Blackmore. the Chairman of the Works Committee of Council, R. Lopdell and the Convenor J. D. McCraw.
12. With the old gully filled with rock debris providing a very permeable passage for water it is difficult to see how any kind of flood-protection walls could be made effective. Perhaps it would be possible to encase the pumping and treatment machinery in a watertight building and allow the pool to be inundated during very infrequent high floods.

17.

SAVING THE ORCHARDS

The years just before the Great War were to see great changes in Alexandra. Gold dredging had steadily declined from its peak at the turn of the century, and now there was only a handful of the vessels left. Luckily, a booming new industry was taking its place. Fruitgrowing had, from the early beginnings of Feraud, Dawson, Iversen and Noble, slowly expanded as the decline of mining freed up water for irrigation. The industry got a boost when it was found practical to transport fruit by wagon to the railhead at Lawrence, and later to Oturehua and then Ida Valley as the Otago Central railway line crept closer. No longer were sales confined to the limited local market.

From their own experience and with the encouragement of Government experts, fruitgrowers decided to concentrate on growing stone fruit, particularly apricots, which found the free draining soils and climate of the Alexandra district to their liking.

It was the arrival, at long last, of the railway in Alexandra in 1906 that really brought the industry alive. And it was not only the locals who were planting orchards. Business men from Dunedin, no longer finding mining shares attractive, were looking elsewhere for investment opportunities. In the years immediately after the coming of the railway, a number of syndicates began to develop or plan large-scale orchards. Among these were the Central Otago Fruitlands Company, the Ripponvale Company, the Terrace Orchard Company and the Alexandra Development Company.

Public attitudes had changed with the decline of mining. Citizens began to realise that the extraction of a single crop of gold led to only short-term benefit. Active opposition, particularly to dredging with its wholesale destruction of land, strengthened. The opposition was particularly strong when deep fertile soils suitable for fruitgrowing were threatened.

Nevertheless, the dredges still had the Mining Act on their side. Alternate or better use of land was not a factor that had to be taken into account when a dredging licence was to be issued. If the land was unalienated Crown Land, there was little to stop the issue of a licence. '

'Unalienated' did not necessarily mean 'unoccupied.' In fact it was common in the early days for a miner to apply for a 'Residence Area' of one acre on which he could build a house, and then go ahead and farm or plant fruit trees on the surrounding land which would be part of a sheep run. The miner/orchardist would have no title whatever to the land and may or may not have had the permission of the runholder to use it.

These 'squatters' had no protection against a dredging company which might apply for a licence to dredge the unalienated Crown Land, even if it were planted in flourishing orchards.

The most famous example was that of William Noble who had lived on a block of land at the mouth of Chapmans Gully for 40 years, and had established a flourishing orchard there, only to have it ruined by a gold dredging company. The company claimed the right to dredge through the orchard because, legally, it was unalienated Crown land and thus, in a Mining District, available for mining. Many other blocks of fertile land had been destroyed or threatened with destruction.

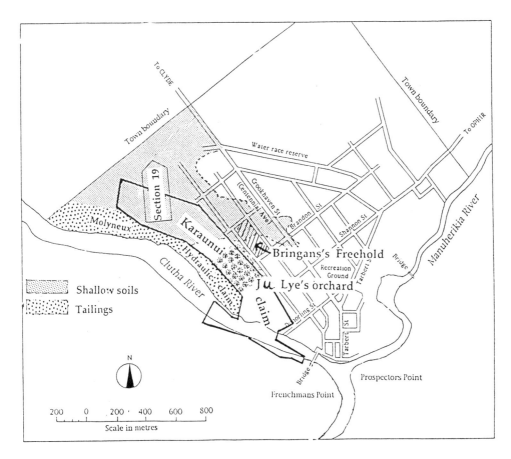

Figure 17.1 The claim of the Karaunui Gold Dredging Company, Bringans' freehold property, and Ju Lye's orchard which Bringans bought. Also shown is Block 19 with its readily identified outline.

211

One such block was on the western side of Alexandra township. There was a substantial strip of unalienated Crown land between the most westerly street (Blaskett, now Bringans Street), and the wasteland of tailings along the river produced by the recently closed-down dredge of the Molyneux Hydraulic Company. About 16 acres (6.5 h) of this strip of Crown land had deep fertile soils suitable for fruitgrowing. By 1912 a number of Chinese had established a settlement in the vicinity and had planted much of it in orchards and market gardens.

About 12 acres (4.8 h) of this fertile Crown land was included in a large area licensed, ten years before, to the Alexandra Lead Gold Dredging Company. The land could be dredged without any regard to the rights of the occupiers. In 1909 the company went into liquidation and a new company, the Karaunui Gold Dredging Company took over the dredge and claim. But still no conditions were placed on their mining licence regarding compensation to those already occupying the land.

Part of an orchard originally planted on this land by Chinese, now owned by Sam Cameron, had already been destroyed and now another orchard was threatened by the approaching *Karaunui*.[1] This time, however, one of the orchardists, Bill Bringans, was prepared to do something about it.

Figure 17.2. William Bringans MBE, 1870-1962. Miner, dredgemaster, orchardist, long-serving Borough Councillor and Mayor (1915-1940), Hospital Board member (20 years) and Otago Central Power Board member (37 years — 30 as Chairman).

Bill Bringans buys an orchard

By 1908 the gold dredging boom was well and truly over. There were still a number of dredges on the river between Alexandra and Clyde, but no new ones were being built and there was a surplus of dredgemasters. Some went to take command of dredges on the West Coast, others went overseas to Africa and other places where dredging was developing. Others came ashore and began farming or growing fruit. Bill Bringans was one of these. Dredgemaster of a number of dredges, including the *Golden Beach* between 1903 and 1905, Bill bought Ah Wye's garden in Conroys Gully in 1908 and settled to the life of an orchardist. But it was an isolated locality, and soon he had his eye on land closer to the railway and to the amenities of the town. He anticipated a future move into town[2] by buying the 6 acre (2.4 h) orchard of Ju Lye between Blasket Street and the dredge tailings flanking the river. When Bringans finally moved into Alexandra in 1912, he bought the freehold of the whole 6 acre (2.4 h) block between Ventry and Blasket (now Bringans) Streets, and Matau and Brandon Streets. One third was the orchard of Sue Him and the remainder was the farmland of Mrs Deady. His neighbours to the south, also orchardists, were Sam Cameron and Thomas W. Brown.

Figure 17.3.. After Bringans moved into town in 1912 he acquired the property of Sue Him.

Most of Bringans' new purchase was ideal orchard land. The soil, except in the most north-western part, was deep and fertile; there was irrigation water available from the town water race, and the orchards were only a short distance from the main street and the railway station. But there was one serious difficulty: the land on which Ju Lye had developed his orchard was still Crown Land, and most of it was included in the land to be dredged by the *Karaunui*. Ju Lye did not have a title to the land and nor did Bringans, who had merely bought the improvements.

Why did Bill Bringans, an astute man who knew what he was doing, purchase an orchard on land that was already licensed to a dredging company? He would know that he could not obtain a title to such land, and would be well aware of its approaching fate. We can only surmise that he gambled. As a fruitgrower he would recognise the potential of the land,

and no doubt the much lower price paid for it compared with freehold land of similar potential, would be a factor. From his knowledge of dredging he would perhaps interpret the published figures of declining gold returns to mean that the *Karaunui* dredge had only a limited life.[3]

Although the dredge employed 11 men and contributed about £200 annually to the Borough Council by way of rent for the use of the Borough water race, it was recognised by almost everyone that mining was no longer the mainstay of the town. The support given to William Noble in his battle with the Golden Beach Company, showed that the people's attitude had turned against the destruction of valuable horticultural land. They could see that mining was in decline and fruitgrowing was the coming industry.

Figure 17.4. The Karaunui Gold Dredging Company took over the *Alexandra Lead* In June 1909 and renamed it *Karaunui* in May 1914. It was a large dredge for the time.

Exchange Proposed

Nevertheless, Bringans thought it wise to acquire a title to Ju Lye's orchard as soon as possible. So he approached the Karaunui Company to see if it would surrender the part of its claim with the orchards on it so he could apply for a title. Not unexpectedly, it refused. A little time went by while Bringans considered his options. Then he had an idea.

Nearby was Block 19, comprising 16 acres of land which had been vested in the Borough Council 40 years before, when the council was interested in the site for a future town reservoir. The block, shaped like a Gothic church window, stood out on all maps of the town as the only surveyed block in a large area of blank paper representing the unsurveyed, and undeveloped, outlying parts of the township. More than half of Block 19 was already included in the Karaunui Company's claim, but as the block was owned by the Borough, it could not be dredged without the Borough's consent and that would mean negotiation and payment of compensation.

Bringans, who had no doubt already informally discussed his ideas with Borough Councillors, approached the directors of the Karaunui Company about the possibility of exchanging the whole of this block for the area with the orchards. The company directors showed interest in the proposal, so Bringans went off to see his lawyer, William A. Bodkin, who was also the Borough Solicitor and a man who knew a great deal about land and mining law.

Difficulties in Proposed Exchange

In March 1913 Bodkin appeared before the Borough Council to ask its consent to begin negotiating on Bringans' behalf. He pointed out to Council that the transfer would benefit the Borough in that it would, at no cost to the ratepayers, relinquish a block of sandy wasteland and gain an area of much more fertile land. All of the councillors, including Councillor Murphy, agreed that the exchange seemed a good proposition for the Borough. One potential difficulty was resolved when Mr Terry agreed to relinquish his lease on Block 19.

Figure 17.5. Edward Marslin was the mayor during the exchange of land with the Karaunui Company.

On the face of it, there should not have been much difficulty in negotiating a settlement between the dredging company, the Borough Council and the orchardists when all three parties were in favour of the proposal, but like many other propositions which seem simple in the beginning, it rapidly became complicated.

One problem was that if the orchard land were vested in the council, all Bringans' improvements, including his fruit trees and any buildings, became the property of the Borough Council. The council recognised this as unfair but had no power to offer compensation.[4] Moreover if the council

215

wished to offer the land for lease, it would be forced, under the Municipal Corporations Act, to either sell the leases at auction or call for tenders for them. But whoever got the lease would not be obliged to pay compensation to Bringans. The Borough Council was in a bind. Much as it wanted to, it could not pay compensation to Bringans, nor could it lease the land to him without calling for public tenders. Bringans would have to take steps himself to protect his improvements in the advent of the exchange taking place. This would mean attempting to outbid any competitors when the lease was put up for auction.

The Agreements

As a first step, Council set up a committee, which included Councillor Murphy, to meet the directors of the Karaunui Company. Agreement was reached, but as a condition, the company wanted £100 from Bringans to cover its costs. Bringans, however, would not commit himself to paying this sum until he had come to a satisfactory arrangement with the council.

Bodkin, as Borough Solicitor, was asked to draw up several documents. One was a straightforward agreement between the council and the Karaunui Gold Dredging Company to exchange the two blocks. The second agreement was between the Borough Council and William Bringans. It consisted of two clauses and, in view of later developments, is worth presenting (in simplified form):[5]

> 1) The Corporation, in the light of the agreement between the Karaunui Company and Council, shall make application to exchange Block 19 for the land described; and shall also make application to Parliament to pass an Empowering Bill, enabling the Corporation to lease the land occupied by William Bringans, subject to the payment to Bringans of reasonable compensation for any buildings or improvements belonging to William Bringans which may be on the said land.
>
> 2) If the Corporation is successful in having the Enabling Bill passed and is authorised by Parliament to lease the area of land occupied by William Bringans subject to paying compensation, then William Bringans shall pay to the Karaunui Company the sum of one hundred pounds, and no portion of the costs of the exchange shall be paid by the Company.

It will be noted that this agreement does not say that William Bringans will be granted a lease — only that land occupied by Bringans could be leased, but compensation for improvements was to be paid. However, it was abundantly clear that Council wanted the orchard occupied by Bringans to be leased to him. Later Bodkin, referring to the June 1913 council meeting at which agreements were signed, wrote:

> The council at the same time intimated that it would grant to Mr Bringans a lease without competition if an Empowering Bill could be put through Parliament giving them power to do so.

Before the exchange and leasing could be legalised, the Borough Council required the authority of an Act of Parliament. This was not as difficult as it might at first appear. Parliament passed an Act each year to take care of the scores of requests from Local Bodies for alterations to the status of land under their care. So, along with the other agreements, Bodkin was asked to draw up the draft of a Section to be included in the next annual Bill, giving the council authority to carry out the various steps of the exchange.

Bringans was not happy with the draft of the proposed Section of the Bill. It did not give him what he wanted, which was the lease of his orchard. So an extra clause was drafted for inclusion in the Bill which gave the council the authority to lease the orchards to the present occupiers 'without competition'. This apparently satisfied Bringans and he then paid the Karaunui Company the £100 thus allowing the exchange of land to go ahead.

The two agreements, together with the draft Section of the Bill and the additional clause, were presented to Council for approval and signing at the June meeting. There was a word of caution from Councillor McClintock who, noting that only four out of eight councillors were present, thought that the signing should be delayed until a full muster was present.[6] But the mayor was worried that delay would prejudice the passing of the Bill through Parliament, and asked that the signing be completed. So the documents were signed and received the Borough seal.

The Act

The Reserves and other Lands Disposal and Public Bodies Empowering Act 1913[7] appeared early in the New Year. Sure enough, Section 116 began:

> **116** (1) Whereas Block XIX of the Town of Alexandra in the Otago Land District, containing sixteen acres one rood twenty-nine perches, is vested in the Corporation of the Borough of Alexandra as a site for a reservoir, but is not required for the said purpose: . . .

The essence of each of the four clauses in the Section was:
1. Authorised the council to transfer Block 19 back to the Crown.
2. Vested the 16 acre orchard block in the Borough Corporation.
3. Authorised the council to lease the orchard land to the occupiers.
4. Fixed the leases at 21 years, renewable.

As soon as the Act became law the Borough Council called a special meeting to arrange the leases. At this meeting, held on 28 January 1914,[8] the mayor pointed out that it was not necessary to call for public tenders, as the Empowering Act gave the council power to lease the land to the occupiers. This set Councillor Murphy off.

Murphy Questions Agreements

Councillor Charlie Murphy was a passionate believer in 'transparent government.' He saw himself as the watchdog for the ratepayers and the voice of the common man. No slick businessmen or big property owners were going to pull a fast one while he was on the Alexandra Borough Council.

In truth Charlie was something of a dog in a manger, in that he opposed almost everything that cost money. The editor of the *Alexandra Herald* had, on a number of occasions, taken him to task editorially, pointing out that he was really a bit of a nuisance on the council and wasted a lot of time. Murphy would be well advised, the editor said, not to open his mouth until he understood something of the matter under discussion.

The townspeople, however, admired Councillor Murphy. They could count on him to ask the sort of questions that they wanted to ask. If the truth be known, other councillors would probably have liked to ask the same questions too but were afraid to do so in case they were made to look foolish. Even the newspaper conceded that council meetings would be pretty boring without the fireworks Murphy provided. And he had earned the gratitude of councillors and townspeople alike by volunteering to carry out a sanitary inspection of the town, free of charge, during the typhoid epidemic a few years before.

Now, in February 1914, Murphy was sure that a secret deal was being jacked up between the mayor and the Borough solicitor to give Bill Bringans preferential treatment in the leasing of the new block from the Borough. Murphy went on the warpath. He questioned the mayor and wasn't satisfied with the answers. In fact, he thought he was being given the run-around. Words, and then insults, were traded.

"Is it not a fact" he asked the mayor "that there is an agreement between Council and Mr Bringans giving him prior right to lease?"

The mayor said he knew of no such agreement. But Murphy insisted that he had seen the agreement, which was signed by the mayor and Councillor Munro, and he wanted to know if such an agreement had been sanctioned by Council, as he for one knew nothing of such an agreement being passed by the Council.

Murphy thought that he was on to something illegal — the signing of a document by the mayor which had not been brought before council. This was the kind of behind-the-scenes activity that Murphy was constantly on the lookout for. He thought he saw the Old-Boy-Network in action and he had reacted accordingly.

The Mayor was right, of course, but was being deliberately obtuse. The presence, before the Empowering Act came into force, of a written agreement giving Bringans the right to lease his land would have been most unlikely as it was illegal. And yet there was in existence a document, destined to be added to the Empowering Bill as Clause 3, which stated clearly that the occupiers would get a lease on their land once council had authority to issue one. Presumably this is what Murphy was referring to.

But what upset the mayor was the implication that he had signed an agreement that had not been seen and approved by the council. At the next ordinary meeting of council, held five days later, he made a statement about the remarks made by Councillor Murphy.[9] The mayor said he took great umbrage at the implication that he and Councillor Munro had signed an agreement that had not been sanctioned by council. He admitted that there was an 'agreement' but council had sanctioned it before it was signed. It had come before council 'at a time when Councillor Murphy was not a councillor' — in other words not present at the council table.

Murphy was apparently not alone in his ignorance of this 'agreement' that had now surfaced. Under questioning by those other councillors, who also, apparently, had not heard anything of the agreement that Murphy was talking about, the Town Clerk explained that the 'agreement' was to insert the clause in the Empowering Bill. This gave Council the right to lease to the present occupiers. He was asked to read the minutes of the relevant meeting — the meeting at which half the councillors, including Councillor Murphy, were absent.

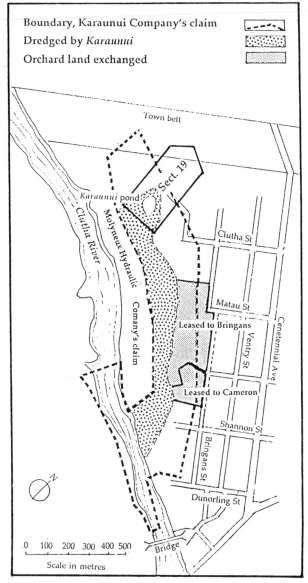

Figure 17.6. The final arrangement. The previously unalienated Crown land, was transferred to the Borough and leased to Bringans, Cameron and others.

When things settled down and the meeting was able to proceed, it was agreed that the newly acquired orchard land be cut into four blocks; the small section of T. Brown; Sam Cameron's section; Bringans' much larger section and a top section of about five acres of poor sandy soil. The mayor then moved that the annual rent be 10 shillings per acre. Murphy tried to amend this to 30 shillings per acre for Bringans, but could not get support.

Murphy Criticised

The editor of the *Alexandra Herald,* in the next issue,[10] waded into Councillor Murphy. His editorial said, 'It would have been a piece of impudent extortion had the Council been guided by Councillor Murphy with his demand for a rent of 30 shillings per acre for Bringans' land.' Ten shillings per acre was, in the editor's opinion, a fair rent. The editorial went on

> Cr Murphy sometimes fills a useful position in that he probes matters to the bottom but his influence would be greater were he more careful to be sure of his facts before speaking. For instance, the agreement about which he made such a fuss, and in connection with which, he by implication, threw a stigma upon the Mayor and a councillor, had not only been adopted by council, but was in addition absolutely necessary to protect the improvements on the land Mr Bringans occupied. It was not, as Cr Murphy asserted, an agreement to give any right of priority but an undertaking that Mr Bringans' improvements would not be commandeered when the council became the owners of the land upon which they stood. A man occupying a responsible position should not make charges based on hearsay evidence. .

Murphy was normally quite insensitive to criticism, but this time he was upset, and at the March meeting[11] he rose to refer to the article in the local paper. However he was pulled up by a Point of Order raised by Councillor Black, who pointed out that the council was not obliged to discuss what appeared in the press. Murphy was called to order.

But he wasn't finished. He next rose to refer to an agreement between the council and Mr Bringans giving Bringans prior rights of lease. He was stopped in his tracks by the mayor jumping up and demanding that Murphy sit down.

> Words got fast and furious as Cr Murphy insisted on pressing his explanation, and the Mayor refused to allow him to proceed. The matter had been dealt with by the council and he would not stand for Mr Murphy wasting the time of the council going back on the matter.[12]

At last Cr Murphy resumed his seat and peace was restored. Perhaps someone took him aside, and explained to him in simple language, that he was not at the council meeting at which the agreements, the draft Section of the Bill, and the additional clause for the Bill, had all been approved and signed.

That should have been the end of the matter, but apparently the 'secret deal' was being widely discussed in the town. Bringans felt he had to clear the matter up once and for all, so he instructed Bodkin to publish the whole story as an 'open letter' in the newspaper. The letter began:[13]

> Mr Bringans would like the circumstances to be generally known because of an impression that appears to have gained ground of late — ie. that he got an undue preference from the council in getting a lease of this land without competition.

Figure 17.7. An air photograph taken in 1949 shows the Bringans' property
Between Ventry Street and the dredge tailings flanking the Clutha River.
The business area, and the old bridge are in the middle of the photograph.

After the publication of the very full history of the saga, Mr Murphy could find nothing more to say and that was the end of the matter.

Oddly enough the local newpaper's attitude underwent a gradual change towards Councillor Murphy. Some time later it published an editorial extolling his virtues with phases such as 'we need more men on council like him,' and 'as long as he is on council we ratepayers can be sure our interests are being looked after.'

NOTES

1. An appropriate name. It means 'Big dredge.'
2. Bringans bought Ju Lye's property in 1910 according to a summary of the affair written by W. A. Bodkin in the *Alexandra Herald* 13 May 1914.
3. In fact the company went into liquidation before the land deal was completed.
4. Although private citizens may legally do what they want to unless there is a law which prevents them, local bodies can only do what is permitted by Act.
5. *Alexandra Herald* 13 May 1914.
6. *Alexandra Herald* 11 June 1913.
7. The full title of the Act (15 December 1913) was *An Act to provide for the Exchange, Sale, Reservation, and other Disposition of certain Reserves, Crown Lands, and other lands, and Endowments, and to confer certain powers on certain Public Bodies.*
8. *Alexandra Herald* 4 February 1914.

9. Referring to the meeting of 2 June 1913 when Councillor Murphy was absent.

10. *Alexandra Herald* 11 February 1914.

11. *Alexandra Herald* 7 March 1914.

12. *Alexandra Herald* 11 March 1914.

13. *Alexandra Herald* 13 May 1914.

18.

LIBRARY SCAPEGOAT

Like most Scots, William Fraser, the town blacksmith, believed in education for himself and others. He was an avid reader and was a regular patron of the Alexandra library. This library, such as it was, stood alongside the town hall in lower Tarbert Street directly opposite Limerick Street, where it shared an old wooden building with the Borough Council office.

Figure 18.1 At present this is the only known photograph of the old library building.

Andrew Carnegie

Fraser had read about the generosity of Andrew Carnegie, a fellow Scot, who had emigrated to America as a boy of 13, and in a short time had worked his way up from bobbin-boy in a cotton mill to Divisional Controller of the Pennsylvania Railroad. Trading in oil and steel shares proved profitable, and before long Carnegie controlled not only a steel works but coal and iron fields, a line of lake steamships and nearly 800 kilometres of railway. In 1901 he sold his companies to J. P. Morgan, who merged them into the giant U. S. Steel Corporation, and Carnegie retired back to his native Scotland. From here he planned to oversee the administration of the numerous charitable trusts he had set up and which controlled, in all, about £450 million.

One trust was devoted to setting up libraries[1] throughout America, Britain and the Dominions, and it was this one that caught the eye of William Fraser.

Fraser visits Carnegie

Fraser longed to see 'the old country' again before he passed on, and in March 1909 he set out on his nostalgic journey. Before he left Alexandra he was given a public farewell, chaired by the mayor of the town, with many speeches and toasts as was the custom of the time. But there was no hint that this trip to Scotland was anything more than a private holiday. It was only when a note appeared in the newspaper[2] to the effect that the mayor had received a letter from Fraser saying that he had visited Mr Carnegie at Skibo Castle, and that Carnegie had agreed to establish a library in Alexandra, that the citizens realised there was more to Billy Fraser's Scottish visit than a holiday.

Skibo Castle is on the northern shore of the Firth of Dornoch on the East Coast of Sutherland County in northern Scotland (now part of Highland District). The estate embraced 13,000 hectares of heather-covered moorland and farmland lying between the Evelix and Shin Rivers. Carnegie had bought the decrepit property for £85,000 in 1897, and spent $US1,000,000 on the restoration of the streams, forests and tenant farms, and on the renovation and extension of the castle. It is a huge edifice in the traditional Scottish-baronial style of architecture.

It was to this great house, to meet perhaps the wealthiest and one of the most influential men in the world, that our village blacksmith was invited. This in itself was quite an achievement. Thousands of letters deluged the castle each year, and hundreds of people called personally to ask for money for one purpose or another, but very few ever met Carnegie. How had Fraser managed to pull off such a coup?

In his letter to the mayor,[3] Fraser explained that he had had to wait an opportune time as Mr Carnegie was in indifferent health, but finally he had been ushered into the presence on 24 June 1909. Carnegie was apparently intrigued with this man who had come back to Scotland from the other side of the world, and in whom he perhaps recognised a kindred spirit. Fraser too, had started with nothing, and through hard work was now the largest property owner in Alexandra. But that was not all. Fraser came

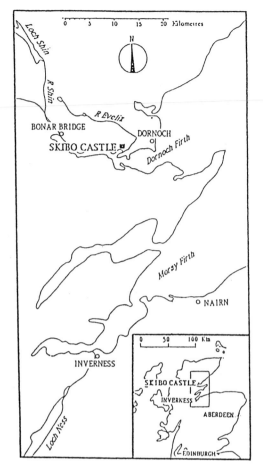

Figure 18.2. Skibo Castle, the Scottish home of Andrew Carnegie, is in Sutherlandshire (now Highland District) in the north of Scotland.

originally from Dornoch, only a few kilometres from Skibo, and this apparently was the factor that took Carnegie's attention.

Fraser put the case for a library for Alexandra to the great man, who questioned him closely about the number of people in the town and their ability to support a library. He agreed that the requested sum of £750 to £800 'was not excessive,' and promised that if an application were made he would see that it got a fair hearing.

Carnegie was at pains to explain to Fraser the conditions that applied to all of his library grants. First, the library had to be free and secondly, he required the town authorities to spend the equivalent of 10% of the grant each year on the upkeep of the library. In several of his early library grants, Carnegie had included an endowment for the acquisition of books and for maintenance of the library. But he found that the town had then contributed nothing further, in the belief that the library was set up for all time. He now felt that unless a community was prepared to tax itself to maintain a library, it obviously did not appreciate it and perhaps did not deserve to have one. Lastly, Carnegie made it known:

> . . .that there should be placed over the entrance to the libraries I build a representation of the rays of a rising sun, and above LET THERE BE LIGHT and I hope you can have this on the building.

Not all communities complied with this request.[4]

Fraser left Skibo with a warm invitation to return for another visit before he finally left Scotland, and came away much impressed with Carnegie's courtesy and kindness to him.

Fraser had outlined Carnegie's conditions in his letter to the mayor, including the need for a special rate to cover the cost of upkeep. Believing, as indeed a good blacksmith must, in striking while the iron was hot, Fraser collected an application form from Skibo and sent it with his letter.

The letter caused a great deal of discussion at the September 1909 meeting of the Borough Council and the conditions attached to the grant were studied carefully. It was obvious that a special rate would be required to meet Carnegie's conditions, and it was resolved then and there to make it 2d in the £:

> . . . for the purpose of the upkeep and maintenance of the Free Public

Figure 18.3. Andrew Carnegie spent over a million dollars restoring the estate and reconstructing the castle. It is a very large building in the Scottish baronial style.

Library presented to the inhabitants of Alexandra by Andrew Carnegie, Esquire.[5]

Fraser returned to Alexandra on the last day of 1909 and was quickly interviewed by the local newspaper.[6] He expressed some surprise that the money from Carnegie had not yet arrived. He should have known better than to expect such rapid decision-making from a local body. Perhaps with the idea of speeding things up he stood again as a candidate for the council at a by-election in early February, and was elected by the rather slim margin of two votes.

Figure 18.4. Andrew Carnegie, the ultimate example of the local boy making good, was a Scot who emigrated to America and made a vast fortune from railways and steel.

Shortly afterwards a letter arrived from Carnegie's secretary setting out more conditions. Yes, Mr Carnegie would be glad to give £800 to erect a library in Alexandra but only if the maximum levy allowed under the 'Free Public Libraries Act' was adopted. This Act was a new one to the council and a thorough search by the town clerk and borough solicitor confirmed that no such Act existed. But to satisfy Carnegie's condition and to keep up the momentum, Councillor Fraser's first motion at his first council meeting was that the special rate be increased to 3 pence in the pound.[8] This was hardly the way to make friends, either inside or outside the council, but nevertheless Fraser's motion was passed.[9] Furthermore, fellow councillors made eulogistic references to the good work he had done and accorded him a hearty vote of thanks.

Carnegie was not satisfied with the rough sketch of the proposed library that had been sent — he wanted proper plans and specifications drawn up by an architect. Alexandra Borough Councillors were not used to all this red tape, and there were mutterings from some that they doubted if Carnegie's conditions could be fulfilled. Nevertheless a committee was appointed to discuss plans and specifications with Tom Wilkinson, the well-known builder of Clyde. He inspected the proposed site and promised a set of plans gratis which, after approval by council, were duly sent off.

Application for a Grant

Early in February 1911,[5] the council received a reply from Carnegie's secretary informing it that Mr Carnegie had asked his cashier, R. A. Franks of New Jersey, to authorise progress payments of up to a total of £800 as work progressed.. Some councillors were enthusiastic to start the building at once but others were more cautious.

Their problem was still the conditions attached to the grant, particularly those which stipulated that the library had to be free, but at the same time a sum equal to 10% of the grant had to be expended each year in upkeep. This amounted to £80 a year, whereas only £35 was being spent on the existing library. It was the special rate necessary to cover the difference that worried some councillors. But Fraser was a persuasive speaker and finally managed to have the council resolve to call tenders for the erection and furnishing of the building.

Fraser Rejected

There were repercussions, however. Apparently some citizens and perhaps councillors too, thought that Fraser had taken liberties in approaching Carnegie on his own initiative for money for a library, and then foisting this expensive luxury on to the ratepayers. In their view Fraser needed cutting down to size and they did it at the election held in April 1911. Poor Fraser, after all his efforts on behalf of the town, was defeated.

The mayor, who almost certainly had a guilty conscience, felt it necessary at the first meeting of the new council to make some explanations about Fraser's role in approaching Carnegie.

Explanations

He regretted, said the mayor, that ratepayers had been under some misapprehension regarding Mr Fraser's connection with the proposed Carnegie library, reports of which had been maliciously spread and had seriously affected Mr Fraser's candidature for the council. What they didn't realise, the mayor explained,[11] too late to do Fraser any good, was that Fraser was merely acting as an agent for the Borough Council in visiting Carnegie. At councillors' request, the town clerk read the following letter which Fraser had taken with him:-

> Andrew Carnegie
> 23 March, 1909
> Skibo Castle, Scotland
> Dear Sir,
> The bearer, Mr William Fraser, is one of the oldest and most highly

respected residents of Alexandra, and a native of your country and immediate neighbourhood. For the past 40 years he has been closely identified with the interests of this borough having credibly filled, at various intervals, a seat in the council. We have requested Mr Fraser to approach you with a view to enlisting your sympathy in the matter of providing a new library for this town, the present building being unsuitable for this purpose. Knowing the great interest you take in matters Colonial, we commend Mr Fraser to your notice, as we know of no person more thoroughly conversant in all matters relating to the conditions — past and present — of the Central Otago goldfields, of which Alexandra is the centre. We are, dear sir, your obedient servants,

Henry Schaumann (mayor), M. A. Fleming (town clerk).

There was no doubt that this was an official letter from the Borough Council and the old hands on the council immediately began to remember what a good and upright citizen their former colleague was. But more significantly, the new councillors said that they and the ratepayers generally were completely unaware that Billy Fraser had conveyed such a letter to Carnegie.

Nevertheless, now that Fraser was no longer on council to push for the new library, the conservatives gained the upper hand and saw that the subject was quietly dropped. It was not until more than a year later that Cr Ashworth was game to ask what they intended to do about the Carnegie grant. If they did not intend to use it, he said, then Mr Carnegie should be thanked for his offer and that would be that. The mayor pointed out nothing had changed — the borough still could not afford the sum required for upkeep under the terms of the grant, but it was decided that the whole matter would be thrashed out at a special meeting to be held in the following month.

When, at this meeting, it was disclosed that, for some reason, council had not received a reply to a letter it had sent to Carnegie's secretary about the grant, this gave some councillors the excuse they wanted — it was moved that the Carnegie grant be declined. In an effort to save the grant, a number of amendments were proposed: that the amount asked for be lowered to £600; that it be requested that the percentage for upkeep be changed to 7%, and that a public meeting be called to discuss the whole matter. But none was adopted. Instead, at the August 1912 meeting all resolutions concerning the requesting of a grant from Carnegie were rescinded.

The Fire
That would have been the end of the matter if the old public library and council rooms had not caught fire at 3 am on 15 October 1913. In spite of hard work on the part of the fire brigade, daylight revealed only a blackened shell.

Six months later a special meeting of council was held to discuss the question of a new library.[12] An offer had been received from John Rivers to sell to the council for £265, a two-storied building adjacent to the site of the burnt-out library. There was also an estimate from Mr Kofoed, a builder of Clyde, for a new building on the old site. He was asked for a firm price for a building 9 metres long and 8 metres wide but only rough-finished inside. The meeting ended with the mayor promising that he would call a public meeting when all the information was to hand.

Public Meeting

The meeting was held on 19 June 1914.[13] The mayor announced that the council had received tenders ranging from £149-16s. to £615 and now he was looking for suggestions as to how to proceed. The meeting first confirmed that a library and reading room were required, and Mr W. A. Bodkin, the local lawyer, then suggested that Carnegie be approached again. A Library Committee was set up and granted £50 by Council to buy books to replace those lost in the fire.

A deputation was elected to discuss the whole matter of the library with the Borough Council. Finally Bodkin proposed that a vote of appreciation for William Fraser's efforts be recorded and passed to him.

Figure 18.5. William Fraser was born in Dornoch, Scotland in 1843 or 1844 He died in 1925. He stands (on the right) in front of his Shoeing Forge in Tarbert St with employees and customers.

The deputation duly met the council and formally requested that the matter of the Carnegie grant be reopened. At a subsequent special meeting of council[14] the question of reapplying for a Carnegie grant was fully discussed. Some councillors brought up the old concern about the cost of upkeep, but now council had £280 in hand from insurances on the old library, and this made a difference to its thinking.. One, who obviously believed in the principle of 'user pays,' suggested seriously that those who wanted to read books should pay for the library. Council was still not prepared to commit itself, and a motion that a fresh application be made to Carnegie for £800 was defeated. But in the end even the opponents agreed that a poll of ratepayers be held to decide the matter once and for all.

Now the newspapers weighed in. An editorial[15] in the *Alexandra Herald* accused some councillors of selfishness and others of an over-zealous concern about money. A library, the editor said, should be in the same class as a school or a hospital and should command support and pride from the citizens.

There was an interesting little sideshow in the same issue when the previous editor of the *Alexandra Herald*, Thomas Cahill, took umbrage at a report that the townspeople had not been informed about Fraser's visit to Carnegie on behalf of the council. In what was described by the incumbent editor as a 'somewhat peppery' letter, Cahill said the report implied that he had failed in his job of keeping the people informed.[16] This he vigorously denied, but it all helped to arouse the public interest in the cause and the results of the poll of ratepayers gave a clear indication that the citizens wanted a library, and wanted the council to reapply for the Carnegie grant.

Second Application
Council did so in August 1914 and a 'very satisfactory letter' was received[17] from Mr R. A. Franks, Treasurer of the Carnegie Corporation of New York. He affirmed that the offer of £800 was still open and suggested that Council could get on with the erection of the building without further delay. A special meeting, held on 25 January 1915, accepted the offer and at the same time called for plans from architects. There was still some public controversy about where the library should be built, and a public petition asking that it be placed on the old site next to the town hall was received. But the council decided that the new library would be sited on William Fraser's paddock at the corner of the main street and Skird St, which he had offered for £35. Meanwhile Fraser offered the use of his office as a temporary library.

Plans Prepared
Edward Anscombe, a Dunedin architect, was asked to prepare plans, but took so long to finalise them, that the mayor was heard to remark that it was 'a pity he didn't show the alacrity that he demonstrated in getting the work in the first place.' It was not until October that council was able to consider the tenders which had been received for the building, and the tender of A. A. Auburn for £661-9s. accepted. There was more delay, but once excavation for the foundations began in February 1916, progress was very rapid, so rapid in fact that council thought it wise to apply for two progress payments at once.

Dentist Electrician
It was decided that the building should be lit by electricity, and there was much discussion about how this could be done and how much it would

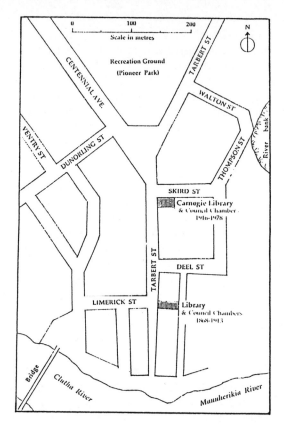

Figure 18.6. Map showing location of the old library and the Carnegie Library.

cost. The problem was that the town was not reticulated with power, so any lighting had to come from a special generator for the building. Councillor O'Kane, the local dentist, came to the rescue and offered to install electric lighting provided he could have the help of the borough dayman, George Hannay, for four days. This was a generous offer quickly taken up. O'Kane already had his own premises lit by electricity from a dynamo. It was powered by a small pelton wheel run by water from the borough mains. He installed a similar system in the library and it worked well until mains supplies arrived in the town in 1925.

Opening — Fraser Vindicated

At the opening ceremony[18] on 30 November 1916, the mayor, Archie Ashworth, after outlining the history of the negotiations for the library, addressed the assembled school children. Ashworth was shortly to stand for Parliament as the Labour candidate for Otago Central and his liberal thinking showed through in his address. The theme was the need for more education. He quoted Frederick the Great who, in reviewing his troops said, "If only these people would think — I would not have one of them in my army." Ashworth was sure that there would come a time when people

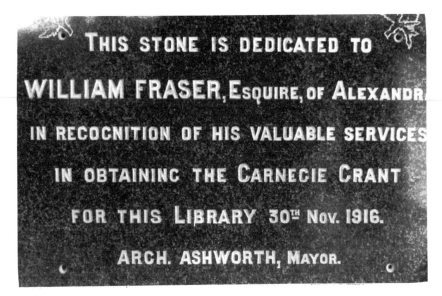

Figure 18.7. The tablet in the Carnegie Library commemorating the contribution of William Fraser.

were sufficiently educated to refuse to follow their leaders into the sort of holocaust that was engulfing the world at that time. It was wrong to send 14 or 15-year-old youngsters out from school, with minimal education, to face the world. He made a strong plea for what we call these days 'continuing education,' and he was sure libraries such as the one they were opening would play an important role in this.

The highlight came when the mayor unveiled a tablet which read:-

> This stone is dedicated to William Fraser, Esquire, in recognition of his valuable services in obtaining the Carnegie grant for this library, 30th Nov. 1916 — Arch. Ashworth, Mayor.

The Carnegie library was a rather handsome building that lent a certain elegance to a street that was a little short of that particular commodity. The interior was somewhat stark but along the back wall were several glass-doored cases with a reasonable selection of books. In the middle of the room stood a reading stand on which were local and provincial newspapers. High on one wall hung a large, framed, coloured portrait of a bewhiskered man which carried a brass plate proclaiming:-

> Andrew Carnegie 1835-1919. Presented by the
> Carnegie Corporation of New York, 1935.[19]

The building was dreadfully cold in the chilly Central Otago winters, but on Friday nights it became quite a social centre, with the regulars meeting as they changed their books and enjoyed the heat from a small kerosene heater specially provided for this weekly occasion. A meeting room for the Borough Council and a small office for the town clerk were also incorporated into the building. However, it was all hopelessly inadequate to serve a population that rapidly increased after World War II, and the Carnegie-Fraser library was demolished in 1978 to make way for a new civic building, incorporating a large modern library.

NOTES

1. Carnegie paid for a total of 2,505 libraries costing $50,364,808. 18 are in New Zealand.
2. *Alexandra Herald* 11 August 1909.
3. *Alexandra Herald* 18 August 1909.
4. Alexandra was one of the communities that did not comply.
5. Resolution passed at the meeting 6 September and a public notice appeared *Alexandra Herald* 15 September 1909.
6. *Alexandra Herald* 5 January 1910.
7. William Fraser was no stranger to the Borough Council table. He had been a member of Council from 1879 to 1885 and again from 1899 to 1902.
8. *Alexandra Herald* 9 February 1910. In spite of the fact that this special rate was approved and advertised formally in the newspapers there is no evidence that it was ever collected.
9. Notice *Alexandra Herald* 16 February 1910.
10. *Alexandra Herald* 8 February 1911.
11. *Alexandra Herald* 3 May 1911.
12. *Alexandra Herald* 18 March 1914.
13. *Alexandra Herald* 24 June 1914.
14. *Alexandra Herald* 1 July 1914.
15. *Alexandra Herald* 8 July 1914.
16. *Alexandra Herald* 15 July 1914. Careful perusal of the *Alexandra Herald* confirms that the first public announcement that Fraser was acting on behalf of the Borough Council was the reading, at the meeting of 1 May 1911, of the council's letter to Carnegie. This was nearly two years after Fraser's visit to Carnegie.
17. *Alexandra Herald* 20 January 1915.
18. *Alexandra Herald* 6 December 1916.
19. Presumably these prints were presented to all Carnegie libraries on the centenary of Carnegie's birth. The print was salvaged before the building was demolished and now hangs in the new Civic building.

Figure 18.8. Alexandra's Carnegie Library was a well-designed and rather elegant building. It was demolished in 1978.

19.

THE MONUMENT

Ask anyone in Alexandra to point out the War Memorial and they will direct you to 'the Monument' standing in the middle of the busy intersection of Tarbert Street and Centennial Avenue. The fact that less than 100 metres away[1] stands a Community Centre proudly announcing in large letters that it is the 'Alexandra District War Memorial' is overlooked by the majority of citizens. The Monument is where the annual Anzac parade assembles, where the wreaths are laid and the melancholy notes of the 'Last Post' are sounded.

Alexandra people are proud of their 'Monument.' It is the centrepiece of the town — an easily recognisable point of reference and an obvious starting point for directing strangers to outlying parts of the district.

Figure 19.1. The Alexandra War Memorial stands at the junction of Tarbert Street and Centennial Avenue.

It consists of a life-sized figure of a New Zealand soldier, sculptured from white marble, standing on a columnar pedestal of grey marble about three metres high, on which are engraved the names of those killed in the Great War and the Second World War. This pedestal rests on an octagonal concrete platform some two metres above street level and is reached by a set of concrete steps. It is on this platform that wreaths are laid during Anzac Day services. Below the platform a sloping flower garden is contained by a low wall capped by an ornamental low iron rail. The whole memorial is surrounded by a concrete footpath.

According to Maclean and Phillips,[2] New Zealand developed the memorial-erecting habit after the South African War of 1899-1902. So it was not surprising that even before the Great War had ended, some communities were discussing suitable memorials to honour those who had died in the latest conflict. War memorials of all shapes and sizes were erected in scores of towns all over the country, to commemorate those who had been killed and to record their names.

With its flower garden, rather elegant marble pedestal, realistic, if stereotyped sculpture and generally satisfying proportions, the Alexandra monument ranks among the more interesting of those erected in the smaller communities.

Patriotic Committees

Within two weeks of the declaration of war in 1914 the mayor of Alexandra had called a public meeting to discuss ways and means of raising funds to assist the war effort. A Patriotic Committee, comprised of most of the prominent male citizens, was elected with the mayor as chairman. A month later the mayoress, in response to a nation-wide appeal from Lady Liverpool, the Governor-General's wife, had formed a women's committee — the Alexandra Women's Patriotic Association, to send food and comforts to the troops.

These committees, soon known as the 'Men's Committee' and the 'Women's Committee,' and consisting in total of about 40 people, quickly got into their stride. Garden fetes at the big sheep stations and a Queen Carnival were among the first fund-raising projects. Aid was dispersed to whatever need seemed most urgent — the Belgian Relief Fund; a Soldiers' Room in Wellington for those on leave from Trentham Camp; help for families of sailors lost in battles in the North Sea, and other good causes.

The Women's Committee was asked for help in hand-knitting the top of machine-knitted socks, then to supply cakes for a big sale of produce at the Dunedin Winter Show, followed by requests for donations of jam, or sugar for jam-making and so on. It was not long before this Committee was organising fund-raising bazaars, card evenings and raffles which resulted in a steady stream of food parcels flowing overseas to local soldiers.

All through the War these committees laboured at their good works. The Women's Committee, for example, raised £646 over the four and a half year period and with it had bought food for parcels to the value of £250. It had also sent money to a host of organisations, among which were the Salvation Army, the Red Cross, Nurse Cavell Fund, and Aid to Prisoners of

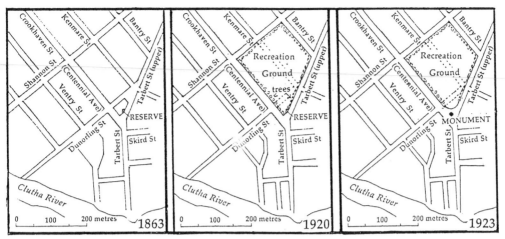

Figure 19.2. Plans showing how the intersection of Tarbert Street and Centennial Avenue was laid out by surveyor Connell in 1863; how it developed in practice, and then was modified to make room for the monument.

War.

Although the Women's Committee still had money in hand at the end of the War, it was quickly dispersed in organising 'Welcome home' functions for returning soldiers. The Patriotic Committee, however, did have surplus money from the activities of the Men's Committee and this was handed over to Trustees appointed to administer the funds.

Monument Approved

A public meeting was held[3] on 8 April 1920 to discuss the whole question of a war memorial. The Mayor at the time, William Black, mentioned that a sum of £430 was available, but depending on the type of memorial, it was very likely that more would be required.

Archie Ashworth, a Borough Councillor and ex-Mayor, thought that a building to serve the recreational needs of the young people of the district would be most appropriate. This found favour with a number, including W. A. Bodkin, the lawyer, but in the end it was decided that the memorial would take the form of a monument. Within a week the Returned Soldiers Association had endorsed the proposal and pledged full support.

A deputation was appointed by the meeting to approach the Borough Council about selecting a site and to ask the council to take charge of the monument when it was erected. Finally, a Fallen Soldiers' Memorial Committee was elected, with the Mayor as Chairman and the Town Clerk, C. M. Burgess, as secretary. Members were mainly from the Patriotic Committees and the Returned Soldiers Association.

Design Selected

The committee got down to work immediately. It wrote to a number of well-known monumental masons in Dunedin and Invercargill for their suggestions as to the kind of monument Alexandra might be able to erect

Figure 19. 3. A 1962 photograph shows the monument at the intersection of major streets between Pioneer Park and the business area (middle right). The old suspension bridge (lower left) has been replaced by a steel arch bridge but not yet demolished.

for about £500. Replies came flooding in, often accompanied by photographs or sketches of monuments the firms had already erected.[4]

One firm had, however, stolen a march on all the others. W. Parkinson and Company[5] of Victoria Street West in Auckland, had the year before sent out scores of albums of photos and sketches of suggested monuments to local bodies. It was particularly energetic in pushing New Zealand marble as a construction material. The Alexandra committee was impressed with a design referred to in the album as the 'Anzac' design. It was of a figure of a New Zealand soldier carved in white Italian marble standing on a pedestal of greyish Nelson marble.

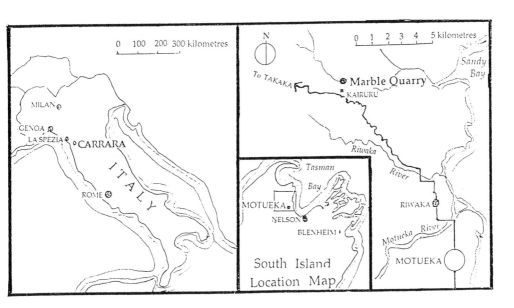

Figure 19.4. Sources of the marble: Carrara and Kairuru.

There was much correspondence with Parkinson & Co. The firm advised that the price for the marble pedestal and figure would be £600, landed in Dunedin. The figure would be carved in Italy where the firm had its own representative who would keep an eye on the work. By June 1920 the Committee had practically decided on the 'Anzac' design, but was worried that it was not large enough. Before coming to a final decision, the committee wrote to Parkinson & Co:

> The town is surrounded by high hills and mountains and the committee are (sic) afraid that the Anzac design would appear dwarfed by the surroundings. Have you anything of a more imposing type of design. . .

The reply was predictable. Yes, of course you can have a larger version. We can increase the figure to 7 ft 6 in high but it will cost more — over £800. That was the end of that suggestion.

Taking into account the fact that Parkinson's quote of £600 was for the upper part of the monument only, it was obvious that much more money

239

would be required.

Over the next three months a steady trickle of money came in as various organisations held functions to aid the cause, but it was not until £300 was raised by a monster bazaar (the town was given a half holiday) arranged by the Women's Committee, that the project became viable.[6] The committee judged it now had sufficient money on hand for a monument.

Early August 1920 saw the project make important progress, although it was threatened by diversions. The Women's Committee asked the Borough Council to rename the streets so that each street would bear the name of a fallen soldier. The local newspaper came out against the proposal, taking the view that the proposed monument was sufficient. A deputation approached Council with the scheme but, predictably, Council decided it 'could not see its way clear' to agree to the request.

A set of 38 photographs of war memorial designs, selected from a large collection assembled by the Christchurch architect Hurst Seager, was sent to the mayor for public display by the Department of Internal Affairs. Accompanying the exhibition was a pamphlet written by Seager[7] setting out his view on the types of monuments that were most appropriate, and the settings in which they should be located. He had assembled the exhibition in an attempt to raise the standard of proposed war memorials. Throughout the week beginning 15 August it was on display in the Town Clerk's office. But the committee had already made up its mind.

Contract with Parkinson & Co.

A subcommittee was appointed to draw up the terms of a contract with W. Parkinson and Company. It was a straight-forward agreement in which the company promised to deliver at Dunedin the pedestal made of New Zealand marble, but less the two steps shown in the 'Anzac' design in the firm's catalogue. After some negotiation, the company agreed to inscribe the wording and Roll of Honour as part of the contract price of £600. The monument was to be delivered, if possible, within eight months, but not exceeding twelve months. The firm signed the contract on 3 September 1920.

Parkinson & Co. was an agent for the famous Carrara marble, so it was likely that the figure of the soldier would be carved from the white marble found near Carrara, a town on the west coast of northern Italy.[8]

Site Selected

Meanwhile the Memorial Committee and the Borough Council had decided, with a minimum of acrimony (perhaps an advantage of having the same chairman), on a site for the proposed monument. It would be built on the reserve at the intersection of Crookhaven (the present Centennial Avenue) and Tarbert Streets.

Most townspeople would not have known such a reserve existed, although it had been shown on maps since Connell's original 1863 plan of the town. He had laid out Dunorling Street from the bank of the Clutha River eastwards to Crookhaven Street, and then extended it further to join upper Tarbert Street. In so doing, a section of more than one acre in area was left isolated in the fork of the 'Y' between Tarbert and Crookhaven

Figure 19.5. The Kairuru quarry.
Upper: The quarry in operation.
Lower: The long-abandoned quarry as it is at present.

Streets. It was this isolated section that was marked as a reserve. However, the eastward extension of Dunorling Street, and the reserve, had been informally absorbed into the block designated as a 'Recreation Gound.'[9]

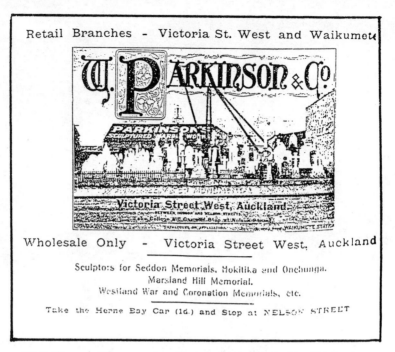

Figure 19.6. The sculpture and pedestal were supplied by W. Parkinson & Co, monumental masons of Auckland.

Poplars had been planted around the perimeter of the extended Ground and were now mature trees.

The first task was to fell a number of these trees which cut off the view of the reserve from the streets. Mr Hull, the local moving picture operator, offered to pay for the felling of the trees, but apparently no arrangement had been made about their subsequent removal. Remarks were passed in the Borough Council about the unsightliness of the fallen trees, and the desirability of cleaning up the site before Christmas. So it was decided to offer them for sale to the public for firewood but this brought in only £3 10s. In the end the Borough had to employ two men to help Mr Hull clear away the trees.[10]

While all this tree felling and general alteration to the corner of the Recreation Ground was taking place, the opportunity was taken to round off the corner of the park, leaving sufficient space between the new boundary and the proposed monument for a wide roadway. This left the monument site in the centre of a traffic roundabout.

Construction

Engineer J. R. Marks said that he would have detailed working drawings ready by 5 March. It is not too difficult to guess where these drawings were executed — there were advantages in having the boss of the local office of the Public Works Department on the committee! The blueprints, which still exist today, do not have any identification as to their source. It is very

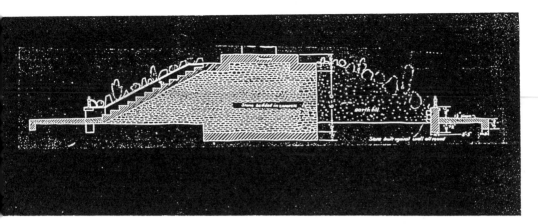

Figure 19.7. This copy of the original blue-print of the cross-section through the base shows the foundation of rocks set in concrete.

likely that they were drawn by Jack Lunn of the Department, who also acted as voluntary works supervisor of the monument project. George Hannay, who was the Borough dayman and also a skilled bricklayer and plasterer, was put in charge of concrete work.

Difficulties were met with immediately because of the stumps and roots of the felled trees. Digging them out, removing the disturbed ground and replacing it with rock proved a much longer and costlier job than estimated. The excavation was filled with slabs of schist rock and concrete, which were then built up to a height of six feet (1.8 m) above street level, and capped with an octagonal platform of poured concrete. A second, smaller octagonal terrace was formed on top of this bringing the height of the structure to eight feet (2.4 m).

At ground level a concrete wall nearly two feet (60 cm) high, surmounted by an ornamental iron railing 10 inches (25 cm) high, surrounded the structure. The iron railing and the numerous small, ornamental cast-iron posts for it were made by J. &. W. Faulkner, ironfounders of Dunedin. But when they arrived, there was difficulty in assembling the posts and rails and the firm had to be asked for instructions, which were duly sent. There is a marginal note from engineer Marks on the letter addressed to the Town Clerk, 'Hold payment till we try it' followed by another 'Now O.K.'

A set of steps six feet wide (1.8 m) leading from ground level to the upper octagonal platform completed the base of the monument.

The space between the outer wall and the upper platform was developed as a rock garden using 50 cart-loads of soil and selected rock.[11] An appeal was made to the Dunedin City Council Reserves Department for suitable rock plants but the Department went one better — with the plants they sent William Reid, a specialist in rock gardens, to supervise the construction and planting.

The completed foundations and base had cost £350, which was much more than estimated. After this was paid the committee had only another £500 on hand. This was of concern, as the marble figure and pedestal would cost £600 to land in Dunedin, and there was still the freight to Alexandra, the cost of inscribing extra names and the cost of erection — estimated to total about £200 — so the committee was still £300 short. It was decided to make one last effort to raise the extra money. A huge bazaar would be held in the Town Hall on 23 and 24 September 1921, with the RSA providing entertainment and running an Art Union in the Recreation Ground at the same time. The bazaar was a great success and raised £431.[12]

Figure 19.8. Details of the monument.
Left: The statue.
Right: The pedestal and wording.

The Names

In May 1921 word was received that the marble figure had been shipped from Italy and Parkinson's had finished the pedestal, so the committee began drawing up a list of names to appear on the monument. Immediately questions arose. Should the list include all those who served overseas or just those who were killed? The Roll of Honour recently installed at the District School listed all those pupils who served, so it was decided to list only those who had died. Should the list include the rank of the soldier, or should the principle that all were equal in the sacrifice they had made

Figure 19. 9. Monument + Area Office

prevail? In the end they were listed alphabetically without rank.

The committee published a list of 27 names in the newspaper and asked for comment and especially for omissions and mistakes. This brought a flood of suggestions and criticism, mainly to do with the omission of people from the outlying districts such as Earnscleugh, Fruitlands, Galloway and Moutere. As a result the committee decided to include the surrounding districts and published a new list of 42 names. These were sent to Auckland for engraving on the marble slabs.

Now that the monument was beginning to take shape, attention was turned to an eyesore that would detract from the location. The Committee secretary was instructed to write to the Minister of Defence pointing out that the Area Office, or Volunteers' Room which occupied a prominent position at the intersection, was shabby and had not been painted or done up in any way:

> Opposite the building we are erecting a handsome memorial to the soldiers from this district who fell in the late war, and, as the monument is nearing completion, my Committee feels that your Department should co-operate in improving the immediate environs.

We are not told of the outcome of this appeal.[13]

Meanwhile New Zealand Marble Ltd had supplied the marble slabs for the pedestal from its quarry in the bottom of a deep valley at Kairuru near Motueka. A block of marble had been broken out from the quarry face and cut into slabs by steam-driven saws. They were taken by horse-drawn trolley along an eight kilometre tramway to a wharf in Sandy Bay, where they were loaded on to a scow for Auckland. At the monumental works of

W. Parkinson & Company the slabs were cut to final size, polished, engraved and shipped to Dunedin by *SS Kanna* [14] on 10 September 1921.

When the ship from Italy arrived in Dunedin, Customs required a declaration that the sculpture was for public display, otherwise it would attract duty. A Dunedin forwarding firm was asked to open the cases, but found no damage so railed them on to Alexandra. Here the pedestal was assembled and erected by Robert Ross, an engineer and dredgemaster. Both the heavy central core of the pedestal and the figure of the soldier were lifted into place with the aid of a set of shearlegs.

Unveiling

The whole project was completed during the first week of November 1921. The Borough Council had co-operated by completing the erection of a substantial ornamental fence along the new Recreation Ground boundary. The unveiling ceremony was fixed for Armistice Day, 11 November. A procession of Returned Soldiers, Territorials and Cadets, headed by the Brass Band, marched up the main street from the Town Hall to the monument, where the assembly was addressed by the mayor, Mr Black. He paid special tribute to the work of the Women's Patriotic Association and the Gaiety Club in raising the money. Wreaths were laid, various other dignitaries spoke and the ceremony concluded with the Territorials firing three volleys, and the sounding of the 'Last Post.' [15]

Figure 19. 10 The unveiling

The proud Mayor, on a visit to Nelson over Christmas 1922, had at the Town Clerk's request, presented that city with a photograph of the finished monument and promised to send details and costs when he returned to Alexandra, A polite reminder from Nelson's Town Clerk at the end of March, suggesting that the matter must have slipped the Mayor's mind had to be followed by a telegram before the material was send. The letter of thanks stated that the Nelson Memorial Committee had decided to erect a memorial of the same design. It is sited near the Nelson Cathedral.

Even Parkinson & Co asked for a photograph, with 10 shillings enclosed to pay for it.

At the winding-up meeting in May 1922 the following summary of costs was given:[16]

Cost of foundations and base	£327
Cost of statue and pedestal erected	£663
Cost of rock garden and railings	£33
Total	£1043

As more than £1,300 had been raised, Alexandra had managed to complete its Fallen Soldiers' Monument debt free and still have money in hand. What was to be done with this money?

After many meetings and compromises it was decided to distribute the money as follows:[17]

1. £105 to be invested to provide prizes to four schools for essays on some subject related to the object and purpose of the Memorial.[18]

2. £50 to the early Pioneers' Memorial Committee towards cost of erecting Memorial Gates into Pioneer Park.

3. £50 to Alexandra Borough Council for a children's playground within the Recreation Ground.

4. Remaining money (about £100) to Alexandra Borough Council as a contribution towards the cost of the erection of the ornamental fence around the corner of the Park adjacent to the Monument.

NOTES

1. In Skird Street.
2. *The Pride and the Sorrow* 1990.
3. *Alexandra Herald* 14 April 1920.
4. Much of the detail in this chapter came from a file of correspondence, including the working drawings relating to the construction of the monument, kindly made available from the Alexandra Public Library by the former librarian Mrs Marie Waldron.
5. The firm, which was founded in 1886, still exists in the form of Parkinson & Bouskill Ltd, Monumental Masons with its head office in Onehunga Mall, Auckalnd and branches elsewhere.
6. *Alexandra Herald* 7 July 1920
7. S. Hurst Seager *War Graves and Memorials.*
8. The marble used for many famous sculptures including Michelangelo's 'David' came from Carrara's quarries.
9. Now known as 'Pioneer Park.'

Figure 19.11. The monument overlooks today's busy streets.

10. *Alexandra Herald* 8 December 1920.

11. After the garden was invaded by weeds which were difficult to eradicate, such as couch grass, the rocks were removed.

12. *Alexandra Herald* 21 September 1921.

13. This building was built about the turn of the Century as a headquarters for the Volunteers. It served for two years as a temporary high school. Later it became the practice room for the brass band and was moved back from the street frontage in 1931 when the fire station was built. It still exists, hidden behind the fire station building now used as a restaurant.

14. *SS Kanna* was a Union Steam Ship Co vessel of 1,049 tons. She was built in 1911 and used in the Trans-Tasman as well as coastal trade. She was sold in 1936 to Japanese interests and as the *Seian Maru* was sunk by an American submarine in the Northern Pacific in 1944.

15. *Alexandra Herald* 16 November 1921.

16. *Alexandra Herald* 10 May 1922.

17. *Alexandra Herald* 14 March 1923.

18. These prizes are still awarded although since 1973 the subject matter has been widened.

20.

FOREST IN THE DESERT

Living in the townships of Dunstan and Manuherikia in the early days was not very pleasant. Water was scarce, because every drop had to be carried from the river 30 metres or so up a very steep bank of loose gravel.. Perhaps it was as well that the inhabitants were not nearly so profligate in the use of water as are their modern counterparts. Then there was the wind.

The 1860s were the tail end of a long period of cold, stormy weather which had lasted for more than two centuries. Referred to as 'the Little Ice Age,' it is explained by climatologists as the result of prevalent El Nino weather patterns. Average temperatures dropped by more than a degree, with floods, heavy snowfalls, and gales more common than today.

Norwesters howled down the Dunstan Gorge to strike directly at the rickety Dunstan township built at the mouth. The calico and wooden framed buildings were regularly flattened, and even when more substantial buildings were erected their roofs were in constant danger of being lifted. By the time the wind had reached Manuherikia, 10 kilometres down the river, the funnelling effect of the gorge had lessened, but winds were still strong enough to cause difficulties to travellers. In late 1864, a newspaper correspondent who left Alexandra at 10 pm in the face of a north-west gale took three hours to reach Clyde:

> . . . being necessitated to beat about like a ship at sea; to face the wind was perfectly out of the question, and even with that precaution, I, when within a mile and a half of Clyde, was compelled to unsaddle my horse and let it go as I could neither ride, nor would the animal suffer to be led head to windward any longer.

A short time after settlement, a new ingredient was added to the townsfolk's misery — wind-borne dust and sand. Warmth and stability of houses had improved greatly as calico gave way to walls built from sods cut from the light sandy soils. These walls became a source of sand which was whipped up by the wind. To make things worse the surfaces of the crude streets were churned up by traffic and became ankle deep in loose dusty sand. Little wonder that it took only a breeze to send miniature sand storms swirling down the streets.

Figure 20.1 Alexandra in 1912. The lighter coloured streaks on Dunstan Flat in the background, are patches of loose sand.

Dust came off the river beaches also, and the *Otago Daily Times* correspondent described the situation:[1]

> . . .we have again experienced during the last two days a return to the Dunstan dust storms dreaded by everyone. . . they detract from all other advantages the district offers. The sandy beaches of the river afford a ready toy to the play of the wind. . . If these storms lasted long it would render the district uninhabitable for the effects of the fine micaceous dust on the lungs is most distressing. . . It is unbearable and disgustingly filthy.

Those crossing the river in the ferries suffered sore eyes and throats as fine sand from the river banks and beaches was driven in clouds along the surface of the water.[2]

Most early goldfields towns, of course, suffered from this dust nuisance but Alexandra and Cromwell were particularly unfortunate in that they both had large accumulations of loose sand, hidden by vegetation, lying on the up-wind side of the towns. No one appreciated the danger until gales began to blow sand and dust into the towns.

Settlers had quickly acquired domestic animals. They were mainly goats, but there were also many horses both for riding and for packing, and all of these were turned out to graze on the flat land immediately north of Alexandra township. As the tussock was eaten out and the surface broken by the animals' feet, sand was exposed and quickly began to move under the influence of strong winds. Only then was it realised that there was a large accumulation of deep sand lying along the town boundary.

It was a brave traveller who undertook the journey from Alexandra to Clyde at night because the winding track was frequently obliterated by drifting sand. It became so difficult to negotiate the sandy stretch on the track to Clyde, that in 1873 extraordinary measures were adopted in an attempt to build a road that would remain sand-free. The plan was to raise the road above the level of the surface so that the wind would blow any sand off the road.

During recent tree-felling, remnants of this raised roadway were found.[3] A causeway had been constructed by placing large slabs of schist rock on edge, giving the road surface the appearance of elongated cobble stones. Apparently only about 100 metres had been constructed. Perhaps the labour and expense involved in carting the huge amount of rock from the nearest source, nearly two kilometres distant, was too much. Or perhaps this length was sufficient to carry the road through the worst of the moving sand.

Figure 20.2. To form a road through the sand, schist slabs were placed on edge to make a raised causeway about four metres wide and 50 cm high.

Origin of the Sand

Where had this sand come from? It is clear that the bulk of the sand was derived from processes of natural erosion, and had accumulated long before the settlers arrived, but it was the activities of the settlers and their animals which exposed it to erosion by the wind.

The main source of sand was the flood plain, later destroyed during the early phase of the gold dredging era, which flanked both sides of the Clutha River above Alexandra. The flood plain became quite extensive above the junction of the Fraser River. Here the river valley widened into a basin several kilometres long, and more than a kilometre wide. The river broke into several channels as it made its way through this basin. During summer floods the flood plain was inundated, and sand was left behind as the water withdrew. Extensive sand deposits on this large area of flood plain and low terrace gave rise to the name 'Sandy Point' for a part of the

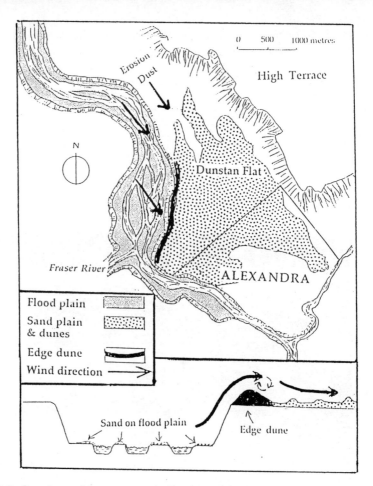

Figure 20.3. Sand was blown up on to the top of the terrace from the flood plain and formed a high dune along the edge (cross section below). It was then blown across Dunstan Flat towards Alexandra.

western side of the basin.

Dried sand from the flood plain was lifted by north-westerly gales which swept it up the terrace scarp along the eastern side of the river above Alexandra. As the wind eddied over the top of the scarp, the sand was dumped as an 'edge-dune,' which, judging from preserved remnants, was up to five metres high. Most of the sand was then redistributed by the wind in a south-easterly direction over Dunstan Flat towards Alexandra.

Later, during the dredging era of 1890-1912, more sand and dust was blown off the hundreds of hectares of dredge tailings.

The net result of all this activity was that an area of about 450 hectares had been covered by sand. Some was reworked by the wind into typical long dunes, and even some semi-circular 'barchan-type' dunes up to three metres high were recognised by the botanist, Cockayne, 90 years ago.[4]

Figure 20.4. Most of the edge dune has been destroyed by dredging and by sand quarrying. This remnant is about three metres thick.

Dust Storms

Accompanying the drifting sand were clouds of blinding dust that made life intolerable in Alexandra. Over-grazing of the thin vegetation on Dunstan Flat north of the town, and on the high terrace[5] on which the airport is now situated, exposed the sandy soils to the loosening action of frost. Gales lifted the fine components when the soil dried out in the spring. The correspondent for the *Otago Witness* described a bad day in 1898:

> Monday, the 21st, will long be remembered as the day of the great dust storm. It was the most terrible day I ever experienced — a real tornado. In many of the houses lamps had to be lit owing to the darkness. The town water race has been completely sanded up for a distance of five miles . . . Houses and straw stacks were carried off bodily and deposited some hundreds of yards away[6]

Alexandra, from all accounts, was just about uninhabitable because of drifting sand and airborne dust when a strong norwester gale was blowing. It is recorded that up to 100 mm of fine sand could be deposited over everything, indoors and out. It had to be shovelled out of the houses.[7]

An 1896 essay[8] entitled *The Flat*, written in a light-hearted way but obviously based on fact, described the perils of the journey from Alexandra to Clyde in a gig after nightfall. There was the constant searching with the aid of matches for already obliterated wheel tracks that marked the route through the sand dunes; the tangling with a fence; the fear of running over the edge of the terrace and the collision with abandoned dredging machinery. It was easier and safer to cross the Clutha River by punt and travel by way of Earnscleugh to Clyde, and when the bridges were built at Alexandra and Clyde this route was made even easier.

Twenty years later the sand and dust were as bad as ever. The newspaper noted that housewives had to be careful to choose a dust-free day to hang out their washing. The equinox gales were particularly trying:

> Tuesday of last week will be long remembered as one of the most wretched days experienced in Alexandra for some time. The wind blew with hurricane force and dust and pebbles were swept through the main street for several hours, making it very unpleasant for those who ventured out of doors. During the gale a large tree standing at the bottom of the street collapsed . . . [9]

The Borough Council was concerned with the constant problem of sand drift at the cemetery, and it wondered whether a corrugated iron fence or the planting of lupins might stop it. It was pointed out also that dust was blowing into shops and contaminating food. Council agreed that regular wetting down of the streets would be tried.

When Cockayne made his survey of the sand dunes of Central Otago in 1910, he noted that some small areas of marram grass had been planted, but no serious attempt to stabilise the drifting sand had been made. The track to Clyde via the Dunstan Flat was difficult enough for horse-drawn vehicles, but was well nigh impossible for motor vehicles. And it was not just the road that was in trouble. In November 1911 a gale deposited so much sand on to the railway line that the rails were completely covered,

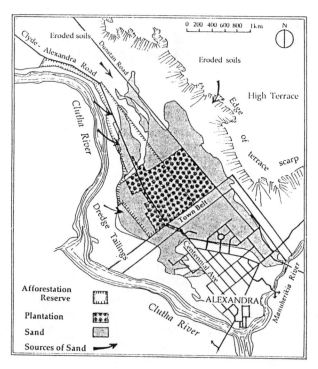

Figure 20.5. The sand covers a large area and extends into Alexandra. The designated Afforestation Reserve is outlined and the area in pine trees is shown. Included is the extensive area of self-sown trees.

254

and both the up and down trains were brought to a standstill, and held up until the line could be cleared by men with shovels.

Need for a Road

There were no doubt discussions between the Borough Council and the Vincent County Council, which was under pressure from the increasing number of motorists demanding that a proper road be constructed. Doubtless it was pointed out that the worst place was the Alexandra Town Belt where the sand was particularly deep and mobile. The answer seemed to be to revegetate the Town Belt.

Figure 20.6. Parts of the sand area in the mid-1950s, before they were planted with pine trees.

In response to a letter from the Alexandra Borough Council in 1923 seeking advice, the State Forestry Headquarters at Tapanui suggested that trees be planted on the waste ground, reminding the council at the same time that they were ready to receive any order for such trees. Trees were duly ordered and planted in the Town Belt by way of an experiment. Most survived, so in 1927 another 1,000 two year old *Pinus insignis* were ordered.

When the new mayor, William Bringans, took office on 4 May 1927, he mentioned in his inaugural address that he hoped, during his term of office, to see the road between Alexandra and Clyde completed. The reason a road had not been completed before was the problem of sand drift. It was realised by both the Vincent County and the Borough Council that the source of the loose sand would have to be stabilised if a road were to be constructed. Simply planting a belt of trees across the path of the drifting sand was futile.

It was Town Clerk Burgess who suggested that Council should approach the Lands Board to have all of the land between the Town Belt and Muttontown, and between the river and the Borough Endowment, vested in the Borough as an Afforestation Reserve. Only then could serious planting of trees and other vegetation be undertaken to protect the proposed road from sand drift. The Lands Board responded favourably, but warned the enthusiasts that the area had to be surveyed off and then vested in Council before Council could legally spend any money on the land.

In January 1929, a *Gazette* notice[10] announced that 335 acres (136 h) of Crown land on the outskirts of Alexandra had been vested in the Borough Council for the purposes of tree planting. The transfer came with conditions, however. In summary, these required the council to prepare a plan specifying the silviculture operations to be carried on over the next five years, and pointed out that it was unlawful to do anything before the plan was approved by the Commissioner of State Forests. Officers of the State Forestry Service were to have access to the forests at all times, and the council had to appoint a person to supervise and manage the tree planting operations. Finally the council had to prepare a yearly report for the Commissioner of State Forests, setting out in detail the technical, administrative and financial arrangements in place over the past year, and include a plan of operations and management for the coming year for the approval of the Commissioner.

Once the land was transferred, the Borough Council consulted the County engineer about the line of the proposed road, prepared plans of the proposed afforestation area, and appointed the required supervisor (the Town Clerk).

By mid-1929 the road was through. For its part, the Borough Council let tenders for forming and metalling the part that lay within the borough. Unfortunately the County was not able to line up its new road with the end of Crookhaven Street (Centennial Avenue). The Borough was forced to put a couple of bends into the short stretch of road connecting the end of Crookhaven Street with the new county road which had been brought to the borough boundary.[11] For immediate protection, marram grass was planted along the sides of the new road.

Tree Planting Begins

Two officers of the State Forest Service turned up in May 1929 to inspect the tree-planting project along the new Clyde road. It was pointed out to them that 2,000 trees had been planted during the 1928 planting season and 75% had survived. Plans for future plantings were discussed. They seemed pleased with what they saw and suggested belts of poplar trees should be planted to act as fire breaks.

It was at this time that a local was caught felling poplar trees in the Town Belt, apparently for use as fence posts.[12] A count of stumps showed he had just felled 72 trees and in fact had felled 109 trees over the last 10 years. Why no one had stopped him before was not explained. As a penalty he had to plant 1,000 two year old pine trees the following August, and maintain them for two years. This was later amended on the culprit's promise to put a kerosene tin around each tree. It had been found that one of these large tins, with top and bottom knocked out, placed over a tree, was effective in keeping rabbits and hares at bay during the crucial first two years of growth. Each year the council appealed for kerosene tins for which they were prepared to pay one penny each.[13]

A regular pattern developed of planting about 1,500 trees a year, concentrating at first on a narrow belt along both sides of the new road to Clyde. The council's annual report[14] for 1931 mentioned that the trees planted three years before were beginning to show up, and were already holding sand back from the road.

In 1932 during the Great Depression, the Unemployment Commissioner advised the council that State Forest Service had trees available under the No 5 Employment Scheme.[15] Taking advantage of this offer, 10,000 two-year-old trees were ordered for autumn planting and there was talk of ordering a further 50,000 for the spring.

When the Conservator of Forests visited in late 1932, he suggested that some *Pinus ponderosa* should be planted, as well as the usual *P. insignis (radiata)*. After the usual appeal for tins, 2,000 plants of this species were planted during the 1933 season and 5,000 of the same species the following season. Trees were planted in rows at 9ft (2.7m) intervals with a firebreak 20 metres wide after every 20 rows.

In 1939 there was an interesting development. The Clutha River Gold Dredging Co Ltd had completed converting their huge vessel from a river dredge to one capable of dredging into the river bank terraces. It now asked the council if it would approach the Minister of Mines to return a small part of the Town Belt and Afforestation area to the Mining District.[16] This meant that the land could then be dredged. The company offered Council £750 in cash. The only conditions were that Council plant no more trees on the affected land, and that Council would allow the big wire ropes which hold and control a dredge, to be anchored outside the boundaries of the mining land. Council didn't hesitate when such a golden egg was on offer and the deal was quickly completed.

It had been recommended in 1935 that the Borough Council establish its own nursery for pines and other trees. In a summary of the council's activities, it was reported in 1941[15] that trees grown in the council's nursery gave better results than those bought in from outside. This is the only reference to Council growing its own trees.[17]

Two Forestry Department men reported[18] on the plantation in August 1942, and were again quite satisfied with what they saw. They considered that the growth of the trees compared favourably with stands of similar age throughout Southland and Otago. The average height of the dominant trees was 34 ft (10.3 m) and they predicted that the trees would reach 100 ft (30 m) at 40 - 45 years of age. The two experts pointed out that the ground cover within the plantation was so sparse that it would not carry fire. If a fire did develop to the stage where it reached the tops of the trees (a 'crown' fire), the firebreaks would not stop it, so they could be dispensed with.

Figure 20.7. The plantation in 1949. Clutha River and tailings upper left. State Highway No. 8 passes through the plantation. Railway (since dismantled) on right. Light coloured ground on both sides of trees is sand-covered.

There was some excitement when it was rumoured that the Government was considering a large afforestation scheme for Central Otago to provide work for returning servicemen. The Borough Council wrote to W. A. Bodkin, the local Member of Parliament, asking him to press the case for the scheme to be initiated near Alexandra. The Commissioner of State Forests replied that the district was unsuitable for a big afforestation scheme, owing to the low annual rainfall, the summer heat, winter cold and prevalence of strong, drying winds.[19]

By the 1950s, some 36 hectares had been planted with a total of about 60,000 trees. To the casual observer they appeared to be, for the most part, rather scraggy, poorly grown specimens. This was not surprising because they had received little, if any, attention since they were planted. It says a lot for the tenacity of *Pinus radiata* that they survived at all, let alone grew. With only a 325 mm annual rainfall, searing summer heat, long periods of continuous hoar frost, and loose, infertile soils they still managed to achieve their sand-holding objective very successfully.

State Forestry officials who, as late as 1954, pointed out that only very few trees would ever produce good milling timber, did not regard the trees as a potential source of timber. For this reason the council regarded the trees simply as sand binders and, at best, potential firewood. It was made clear that, apart from the yearly planting allocation, little time or money had been, or would be, spent on them. After the State Forest Service officers had suggested in 1942 that some attempt should be made to thin and prune the trees, the Borough dayman did a little trimming along the roadside. But the bulk of the plantation had never been thinned or pruned, so the result was an almost impenetrable jungle of trunks and branches. Conditions on the floor of the forest had changed since the Forestry officers had stated in 1942 that there was insufficient ground cover to carry fire. Now the floor was thickly littered with needles and fallen branches — a first-class fire hazard. And the Alexandra Volunteer Fire Brigade became concerned.

Fire Hazard

The Fire Brigade was worried that one of the frequent grass fires, started from embers dropped by railway steam engines, could spread into the trees before it could be dealt with. If this happened, the fire fed by the untrimmed branches would immediately race up the trunks and become a 'crown' fire. Once a fire reached the tops of pine trees it would sweep through the plantation with a ferocity that was, at that time, beyond the power and ingenuity of fire fighters to control. There were no helicopters with monsoon buckets available at that time.

Apart from the loss of the trees, the main concern was that sparks and burning brands, borne aloft and carried over the town by wind, could set fire to the plentiful patches of tinder-dry grass throughout the town.

The Brigade suggested that a firebreak be cleared around the periphery of the plantation, to minimise the chances of fire spreading into the trees from outside; and that the trees be thinned and pruned to reduce the chances of a ground fire becoming a crown fire. But what was really

259

Figure 20.8. Stabilised sand dunes breached by sand quarrying.

needed was a supply of water. It was suggested a tank, to be filled from a small diameter pipe, could be built on the side of the main highway where it cut through the plantation.

Council, seeing little eventual profit from the plantation, was reluctant to spend money other than to continue planting trees, so the Fire Brigade did not get its water supply; but it did get the peripheral firebreak in a rather unusual way. The New Zealand State Electricity Department wanted to clear a narrow strip through the plantation for its new transmission line from the Roxburgh Dam. As compensation for the loss of the trees, the Department agreed to clear a firebreak round the plantation. This proved its worth on a number of occasions when grass fires started alongside the rails. Several times these fires were stopped only when they had reached the firebreak.

So far the plantation has not burned down but has continued its original function of holding the sand in place, so that with the help of sealed streets and irrigated lawns, Alexandra is now a pleasant dust-free town. The area under trees, which includes the plantations, together with an extensive area of self-sown pine, is about 100 hectares. And, contrary to State Forestry predictions, the trees are producing many thousands of dollars worth of timber logs as well as abundant firewood.

NOTES
1. *Otago Daily Times* 8 January 1863.
2. *Tuapeka Times* 10 October 1863.
3. *Tuapeka Times* 27 February 1875. The road took the form of a causeway built of schist stones placed on edge (like a horizontal stone wall) about four metres wide and about 50 cms above the general surface level. There is no record of the road being used or even completed.
4. *Report on the Dune Areas of New Zealand* 1911.

Figure 20.9. The pine plantation in 2000. Clutha River lower right, and golf course, on sand, left foreground. The marked kink in State Highway where it leaves the town and enters the plantation is clearly visible.

5. Park, J *Geology of the Alexandra Sheet* 1906. Park suggested that erosion of the soils on the high terrace was a major source of the extensive deposit of sand on Dunstan Flat. It is more likely that frost action on these vegetation-depleted soils followed by wind erosion, contributed dust rather than sand.

6 *Otago Witness* 30 March 1898.

7. McArthur 1992 p.102.

8. *Dunstan Times* 3 July 1896.

9. *Alexandra Herald* 1 November 1916.

10. *New Zealand Gazette* No. 7 1929 p.352.

11. It is very likely that the new road, including the new extension of Centennial Avenue, simply followed the old track which took the easiest route through the sand dunes. By 1929 trees were well established along both sides of the old track through the sand and this would almost automatically fix the line of the road.

12. Minutes Alexandra Borough Council meeting 7 October 1929.

13. *Alexandra Herald* 6 May 1931.

14. Minutes Alexandra Borough Council meeting 7 March 1932.

15. Minutes Alexandra Borough Council meeting 10 April 1939.

16. *Alexandra Herald* 7 May 1941.

17. In spite of extensive inquiries the site of this nursery has not been located.

18. Minutes Alexandra Borough Council meetings 7 September and 2 November 1942.

19. *Alexandra Herald* 9 September 1942.

REFERENCES
AND BIBLIOGRAPHY

Official Documents
Wardens' Court Records: Alexandra, Clyde, Roxburgh.
Company records
Otago Provincial Gazette
Votes and Proceedings Otago Provincial Council
Ordinances Otago Provincial Council
Appendices to the Journal of the House of Representatives (AJHR)
New Zealand Statutes
New Zealand Mines Record.

Newspapers:
Otago Daily Times
Otago Witness
Dunstan Times
Alexandra Herald
Cromwell Argus
Tuapeka Times

Books and Journals
Angus, J. H. *One Hundred Years of Vincent County* Dunedin 1977.
Bellamy, A. C. *Tauranga Fire Brigade: A Century of Service 1882-1982*
    Tauranga 1982.
Burton, A. H. *The Mining Investor's Guide to the Gold Dredging Companies*
    Dunedin February 1900.
Burke, B. A. *Genealogical and Heraldic Dictionary of the Landed Gentry of
    Great Britain and Ireland* Edition 4 London 1868.
Caygill, John *A. Chronology of Gold-dredging in Otago and Southland from
    1863 to1898* Unpublished report for Department of Lands and Survey,
    Dunedin 1984
Cockayne, L. *Report on the Dune-Areas of New Zealand* AJHR C —13 1911.
Cutten, W. H. 1899. *Dredging as a Profitable Means of Working Alluvial
    Auriferous Drifts.* A paper read to The New Zealand Institute of Mining
    Engineers and largely reproduced by P. Galvin in an article *The Gold-
    Dredging Industry* in New Zealand Official Year-Book 1899.

Cyclopedia of New Zealand Vol IV *Otago and Southland* Christchurch 1905.

Don, Alexander *Annual Inland Tour — Report* The Christian Outlook July 5 1897.

Gilkison, R. *Early Days in Central Otago* Dunedin 1930.

Hassing, G. M. *The Memory Log of G. M. Hassing* Dunedin 1911.

Hearn, T. J; Hargreaves, R. P. *The Speculators' Dream* Dunedin 1985.

Kitto, J. F. *The Practical Dredgeman's Manual* Dunedin 1900.

McArthur, Glad. *Lifetime of Gardening*, Alexandra 1992.

McCraw, John *Mine Fire!* Dunedin 1992.

———*Mountain Water and River Gold* Dunedin 2000.

Magnus, John, *Reminiscences of John Magnus of Alexandra or Early Central Otago 1887-1897* Handwritten manuscript.

———1926 *The Lost Chinaman* Alexandra 1928

McKellar, I. C.; Mutch, A. R; Wood, B. L. *National Resources Survey Part V Otago Region* Wellington 1967.

Mclean, Chris; Phillips, Jock *The Sorrow and the Pride* Wellington 1990.

Merryweather Ltd *Catalogue* London 1896.

Moore, C. W. S. *The Dunstan* Dunedin 1953.

Ng, James *Windows on a Chinese Past* Volume 3 Dunedin 1999.

Parcell, J.C. *Heart of the Desert* Dunedin 1951.

Park, J. *The Geology of the Area covered by the Alexandra Sheet, Central Otago Division* New Zealand Geological Survey Bulletin No. 2 1906.

Police force of New Zealand Report and Evidence of the Royal Commission H-2 1898

Pyke, Vincent *History of the Early Gold Discoveries in Otago* Dunedin 1887.

Ramage, G. A. *Place in the Sun* Alexandra 1990.

Robinson, K. A. *History of Gold Dredging in Central Otago, New Zealand* Unpublished report for Ministry of Energy Dunedin 1987.

Seager, S. Hurst *War Graves and Memorials* Wellington 1920.

Sinclair, R. S. M. *Kawarau Gold* Dunedin 1962.

Tyrrell, A. R. *River Punts and Ferries in Southern New Zealand* Dunedin 1996.

Williams, G. J. *Economic Geology of New Zealand* Melbourne 1974.

Wood, J. A. *Gold Trails of Otago* Reed Wellington 1970.

INDEX

Bold italics indicate Illustrations